AF593286

CIVIL AIRCRAFT OF THE WORLD

Gordon Swanborough

LONDON

IAN ALLAN LTD

Contents

Photo Credits

The author gratefully acknowledges the assistance of the public relations offices of manufacturers and operators throughout the world in providing photographs for publication in this edition, and of the following individuals for the use of their copyright photographs:

Eric E. Allen (p136T)
Aviation Photo News (p95T)
D. Balaguer (83T)
Alan Beaumont (p139C)
John Blake (p157B)
Austin Brown (pp69C, 137B)
Ray Brown (p139B)
P. Colwill (p56)
V. P. Cook (p147T)
Don Downie (p121TC)
James Gilbert (p134T)
J. M. Gradidge (pp71C, 153BC)
Peter H. T. Green (pp 27, 138B)
D. Heller (p69B)
M. J. Hooks (pp99T, 116C, 122T, 122B, 124B, 126C, 128TC, 129T, 132B, 135C, 147B, 149TC, 150T, 153T, 153B, 163TC, 169B)
A. J. Jackson (pp117B, 118T)
W. T. Larkins (pp113C, 154C)
Howard Levy (pp4, 36, 75B, 77T, 103T, 115C, 122C, 127T, 133B, 153TC, 154T, 162C, 164B, 165T)
I. Macfarlane (p29)
G. Mangion (pp43, 76B, 98T)
Andrew March (pp95B, 116B, 134B, 139T)
Peter March (pp28, 118TC, 126T, 128BC, 129C, 133C, 135T, 143B, 146B, 148B, 149B, 152T, 152C, 152B)
Harold G. Martin (p116T)
J. McNulty (p82B)
L. Mullins (p114B)
Steve Peltz (pp42, 60, 90, 128B, 130C, 132T, 151TC, 151BC, 166B)
J. W. Seele (p118B)
J. W. Underwood (p120T)
Mick West (pp62, 74B, 137BC)
Gordon S. Williams (p89B)
Mano Ziegler (p156C)
I. Zopp (p47)

B=Bottom, C=Centre, T=Top

First published 1968
This edition 1980

ISBN 0 7110 1018 8

Published by Ian Allan Ltd, Shepperton, Surrey; and printed by Ian Allan Printing Ltd at their works at Coombelands in Runnymede, England

Introduction

In the two years since publication of the previous edition of *Civil Aircraft of the World*, there have been a number of significant developments, all of which have a bearing on the contents of this completely revised edition. Notably, a number of important new types of airliner have moved from the project stage into full scale development, including the A310 version of the Airbus, the Boeing 757 and Boeing 767, and the British Aerospace BAe146.

In the business aircraft field, several new types have entered the flight test phase, such as the Cessna Citation III, Canadair Challenger, Mitsubishi Diamond, Learjet Longhorn 50 series and Rockwell Sabreliner 65, while still other projects have emerged, such as the Foxjet and the Learfan. The development and production of helicopters has continued apace and the output of smaller general-aviation aircraft, intended primarily for club and private ownership, has been maintained, although this is one field in which brand-new designs are slow to appear.

All the new types, in production or under development, find their place in the pages of this edition. To make room for them, however, without increasing the number of pages and thus adding substantially to the price, it has been necessary to delete the entries for a number of the older types of aircraft and those that are almost out of service. It is one of the features of the civil aviation business that the many different types of aircraft built over the years tend to linger on in ones or twos in odd corners of the world, serving perhaps as a freighter here, a water-bomber there, a crop-duster maybe or just the proudly-owned antique of an aviation 'buff'. All this makes it virtually impossible for the compiler of a volume such as the present one to avoid making arbitrary decisions as to what to include and what to leave out.

This edition includes every type of civil aircraft in production or under development in mid-1979; other types, no longer in production, are included on the basis of numerical importance, technical interest and other factors to present, overall, a balanced picture of the civil aircraft produced and used throughout the world.

The presentation of photos, silhouettes and data generally follows the pattern established in previous editions, but the contents are now arranged in five, rather than four, parts. A new Part Two groups together the freighter and specialised types previously included under the Part One heading of 'Major Airliners' — which they are not. This has made space to include in Part One a number of the smaller types now used in increasing numbers by the third level/commuter airlines.

Another change with this volume concerns its authorship. John Taylor, joint originator and editor of *Civil Aircraft of the World* and its predecessor volumes, has reluctantly found it necessary to relinquish this chore, in order to devote all his energies to editing *Jane's All the World's Aircraft*, for which he enjoys a well-deserved international reputation. This edition — and, no doubt, many more to come — nevertheless bears the clear imprint of John Taylor's contribution over many years, as the present editor is happy to acknowledge.

GS

Addenda

Piper PA-32 Saratoga. For 1980, Piper dropped the Cherokee Six 300 (page 142) and the T-tailed Lance 2 variants (page 143) and introduced instead four models of the Saratoga, featuring a new wing of increased span with tapered outer panels, and a low-mounted tailplane. The Saratoga variants are the PA-32R-301 and PA-32R-301T with retractable landing gear and the fixed-undercarriage PA-32-301 and PA-32-301T, the 'T' variants having turbosupercharged engines.

Cessna Clipper. From the experimental Model 303 (first flown on 14 February 1978) Cessna has developed the six-seat Clipper light twin, powered by 250hp Continental TSIO-520AE engines. First flown on 17 October 1979, the Clipper is expected to be available for delivery from end-1981.

British Aerospace Jetstream. First flight of the prototype Jetstream 31 (page 81) was made at Prestwick on 28 March 1980. The aircraft is an original HP-built example, repurchased from an American operator and modified to have Garrett AiResearch TPE-331-10 engines.

De Havilland Canada Dash-8. Late in 1979, de Havilland of Canada launched development and prototype construction of the 32-seat DHC-8, a STOL commuterliner based on DHC-7 experience. Powered by two 1,500shp Pratt & Whitney PT7A-1 turboprops, the prototype is expected to fly in 1982.

Boeing 767. Latest customers for the new Boeing transport (page 17) are Ansett Airlines of Australia (five), Western Airlines (six plus six on option), China Airlines (two) and Britannia Airways (two).

Learavia Learfan 2100. The UK government decided early in 1980 to join with Learavia in forming a joint company, Lear Fan Ltd, to initiate production of the Learfan 2100 (page 99) in a factory at Aldergrove, NI. Four prototypes are being built by Learavia at Reno, Nevada, and first production deliveries are scheduled for 1982.

Saab/Swearingen. An agreement between these two companies signed on 25 January 1980 provides for joint development, production and marketing of a 30-seat commuterliner powered by two turboprops. Prototype first flight is expected in late 1982.

Dornier Do 28E Skyservant. Dornier is developing, for 1981 delivery, new versions of the Skyservant with a TNT wing, as first flown on a Do 28D test-bed on 14 June 1979 (page 92). The Do 28E-1 will have 15 seats and the Do 28E-2 will have a lengthened fuselage for 19 passengers; the engines will be Pratt & Whitney or Garrett AiResearch turboprops.

Part One

Aérospatiale N262, Frégate and Mohawk 298 France

Short-range airliner, in service
Photo and data: Mohawk 298
Silhouette: N262

Accommodation: Flight crew of 2 and up to 29 passengers
Powered by: Two 1,120shp Pratt & Whitney PT6A-45 turboprops
Span: 74ft 1.75in (22.60m)
Length: 63ft 3in (19.28m)
Gross weight: 23,370lb (10,610kg)
Max cruising speed: 246mph (396km/h)
Range: 633 miles (1,020km) with max payload (FAA reserves) at 254mph (408km/h)

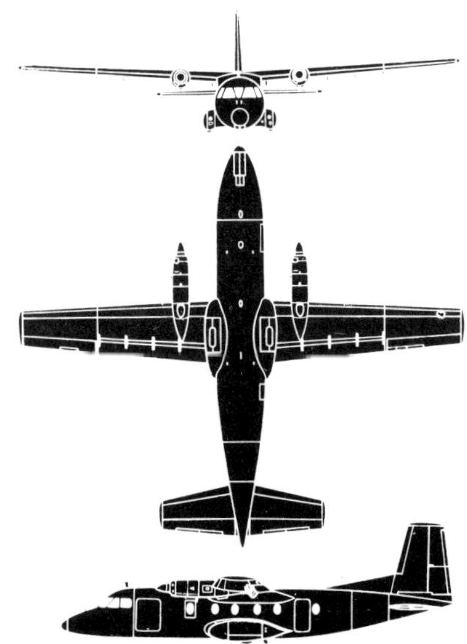

The original prototype MH-250 Super Broussard, developed by Max Holste, had an unpressurised square-section fuselage and was powered by two Wasp piston engines. It flew on 20 May 1959 and was followed on 29 July 1960 by a second prototype, designated MH-260, with 986ehp Bastan IV turboprops and a longer fuselage. Ten pre-production 260s were built by Nord-Aviation and some of these were operated temporarily by Air Inter and Wideroe's Flyveselskap. Nord developed the 262 with a new circular-section pressurised fuselage and flew the prototype on 24 December 1962. The first four production aircraft (Srs B) went into service with Air Inter in July 1964. These were followed by the generally similar Srs A with 1,080ehp Bastan VIC engines. Principal users of this version, of which 67 were built, include, in 1979, Air Algerie, Allegheny, Altair, Cimber Air, Ransome Airlines, Rousseau, Swift Air, TAT, and the French armed forces. During 1970, Aérospatiale introduced the Srs C, with uprated Bastan VIIA engines and increased wing span. This version, and the military Srs D, were named Frégate. Deliveries of the Frégate included one for the East African Community, two for Gabon Government and one for the French SFA, as well as 24 military Srs Ds for the French Air Force. Production of the type ended in France early in 1975 with 110 built; but Allegheny in the USA inaugurated, with Aérospatiale help, a conversion programme to fit PT6A-45 engines, five-bladed propellers, air conditioning and new interiors. Known as the Mohawk 298, the first of these conversions flew on 7 January 1975, and FAA certification was obtained in October 1976; Allegheny put the first of a fleet of nine into service in early 1977.

Aérospatiale SE210 Caravelle

France

Medium-range airliner, in service
Photo: Super Caravelle 12
Silhouette and data: Caravelle VIR

Accommodation: Flight crew of 2-4 and up to 99 passengers, single class
Powered by: Two 12,600lb (5,725kg) st Rolls-Royce Avon 532R or 533R turbojets
Span: 112ft 6in (34.30m)
Length: 105ft 0in (32.01m)
Gross weight: 110,230lb (50.000kg)
Max payload: 18,080lb (8,200kg)
Max cruising speed: 525mph (845km/h) at 25,000ft (7,620m)
Typical range: 1,430 miles (2,300km) with max payload (with reserves)

The prototype Caravelle flew for the first time on 27 May 1955 and the first production aircraft three years later, on 18 May 1958. The Caravelle I went into service with Air France and SAS in mid-May 1959. Caravelle Is (19 built) were delivered with Avon 522s and a gross weight of 95,900lb, but during 1961 they were converted (together with 13 Caravelle IAs with Avon 523s) to Caravelle III standard with Avon 527s and 101,400lb gross weight. Another 78 Caravelle IIIs were built as new aircraft. The Caravelle VIN (53 built) has Avon 531s and noise suppressors, but is otherwise similar to the III; the Caravelle VIR (56 built) has Avon 533s and thrust-reversers. The first major modification of the design produced the Caravelle Super B (also known as the Caravelle 10B or Super Caravelle). This had a 3ft 4in (1m) fuselage 'stretch', new wing leading-edge, improved flaps and other refinements, plus JT8D-1 turbofans. The first flight was made on 3 March 1964 and 22 were built. A version known as the Caravelle 10R (first of 20 flown on 18 January 1965) was similar to the VIR but has JT8D-7 turbofans. A further development of the 10R was the Caravelle 11R (six built with longer fuselage and forward freight loading door, first flown on 21 April 1967). Biggest stretch of the basic design is represented by the final version, the Caravelle 12, first flown on 29 October 1970. This has JT8D-9 engines and 10ft (3.05m) longer fuselage than any previous version. Only customers were Sterling Airways, which ordered seven and received the first on 12 March 1971, and Air Inter, which leased five. Production of the Caravelle was completed at the end of 1972, a total of 282 being built, including three unsold prototypes. About half the Caravelles were still serving with regular airlines in 1979, principal users including Aerotal Colombia, Aerovias del Cesar, Air Afrique, Air Charter International, Air France, Air Gabon, Air Inter, Aviaco, Catair, China Airlines, Euralair, Europe Air Service, FEAT, Finnair, Indian Airlines, Libyan Arab Airlines, LTU, Minerve, Sabena, SAETA, SAN, SATA, Sobelair, Sterling, Syrian Arab, TAE and Trans Europa.

Airbus A300

International

Large-capacity short/medium haul transport in production and service
Photo: A300B4
Silhouette: A300B2/B4
Data: A300B4-200

Accommodation: Flight crew of 3 and up to 336 passengers (high-density layout)
Powered by: Two 52,500lb (23,835kg) st General Electric CF6-50C1 or C2 turbofans
Span: 147ft 1.25in (44.84m)
Length: 175ft 11in (53.62m)
Gross weight: 363,800lb (165,000kg)
Max payload: 77,600lb (35,200kg)
Max cruising speed: 567mph (911km/h) at 25,000ft (7,620m)
Range: 3,400 miles (5,463km) with max payload and typical reserves

Development of an 'airbus' transport as a collaborative venture was first discussed by British and French companies in June 1965. Subsequently, Germany joined a three-nation consortium and a Memorandum of Understanding covering joint design studies was signed on 26 September 1967. Britain withdrew in March 1969 and the A300B continued subsequently as a Franco-German project, the principal partners being Aérospatiale in France and Deutsche Airbus in Germany (representing the German airframe companies MBB and VFW-Fokker) with Hawker Siddeley participating in the programme on a private commercial basis, responsible for design and production of the wing and general design and marketing assistance. Participation by the Dutch government was confirmed during 1970 and resulted in Fokker-VFW being responsible for the wing moving surfaces. Spain joined the project in 1971 and CASA builds portions of the tailplane. Britain rejoined the consortium as a full partner with a 20% share on 1 January 1979, with British Aerospace continuing to produce the wing for the A300 and the A310 (qv). Two prototypes of the A300, flown on 28 October 1972 and 5 February 1973, were B-1s with fuselage length of 167ft 2.25in (50.97m). First production models were B-2s with dimensions as shown above; the first flew on 28 June 1973 and entered service in May 1974 with Air France. This version is now known as the A300B2-100 and is also used by Air Inter, Indian Airlines and TDA. South African Airways ordered four A300B-2Ks (now A300B2-200) which have improved Krueger leading-edge flaps and SAS adopted the A300B2-121 with JT9D-59A engine (first flown 28 April 1979), all other B2s having CF6-50C engines. The B4 version has a gross weight of 330,700lb (150,000kg) and more fuel. First flown on 26 December 1974, it is now designated A300B4-100, with gross weight increased to 347,200lb (157,500kg) while the A300B4-200 has a still higher weight and provision for more fuel. Customers for the A300B4, some with JT90-59A engines but most with the CF6-50C1 or C2, include Aero Condor, Air Afrique, Air France, Alitalia, Bavaria-Germanair, Cruzeiro do Sul, Eastern Airlines, Egyptair, Garuda, Hapay Lloyd, Iberia, Korean, Laker, Lufthansa, Malaysiair, Olympic, Philippine Airlines, PIA, Singapore, Thai and Trans European. Hapay Lloyd was also the first to order the A300C4 variant with side-loading freight doors. Sales of the A300 totalled 167 by mid-1979, with 78 more on option.

Airbus A310

International

Medium capacity short/medium-haul transport, under development
Silhouette: A310-200
Data: A310-202

Accommodation: Flight crew of 3 and up to 255 passengers (high density); typical mixed class, 214
Powered by: Two 48,000lb (21,792kg) st General Electric CF6-80A turbofans
Span: 144ft 0in (43.9m)
Length: 153ft 1in (46.7m)
Gross weight: 291,010lb (132,000kg)
Max payload: 71,500lb (32,400kg)
Max cruising speed: 518mph (833km/h) at 35,000ft (10,668m)
Range: 1,725 miles (2,776km) with max payload and typical reserves

The A310 was launched in July 1978 as the second member of the Airbus family, with the backing of several European airlines, of which Swissair was the first to confirm a definite order. Originally projected as the A300B10, the A310 has the same fuselage as the A300, but with 13 standard frame sections removed to reduce the seating capacity. The wing is all-new, designed by British Aerospace and featuring double-slotted Fowler flaps on the trailing edge and full-span leading-edge slats, with a combination of inboard ailerons and spoilers for roll control. The tailplane is smaller than on the A300, the main undercarriage is revised and engine pylons are redesigned. A version designated A310-100 was initially planned with a gross weight of 266,755lb (121,000kg) but the basic model is now the A310-200 at a weight of 291,010lb (132,000kg), with the A310-300 projected for future development at a weight of 309,750lb (140,500kg). The higher gross weight version will have the same dimensions and fuel capacity but bigger payload and will be able to carry an equivalent payload some 650 miles (1,050km) farther. First flight of the A310 was scheduled for late 1981, with airline service starting in 1983. Swissair placed the first order for A310s on 14 March 1979 with a contract for 10 (plus 10 on option) to be powered by 46,900lb (21,293kg) st Pratt Whitney JT9D-7R4C turbofans. Subsequent orders by Lufthansa (25 plus 25 on option), KLM (10 plus on option) and Air France (5 plus 10 on option) were for the version with CF6-80A engines. Air Afrique has ordered two, Martinair has ordered three (including two A310-200C convertibles), B.Cal ordered three and Sabena ordered three.

Antonov An-12

USSR

Medium-range transport, in service

Accommodation: Flight crew of 5 and 100-130 passengers or freight
Powered by: Four 4,000ehp Ivchenko AI-20K turboprops
Span: 124ft 8in (38.0m)
Length: 108ft 7.25in (33.1m)
Gross weight: 134,480lb (61,000kg)
Max payload: 44,090lb (20,000kg)
Max cruising speed: 373mph (600km/h)
Range: 2,110 miles (3,400km) at 342mph (550km/h) with 22,050lb (10,000kg) payload

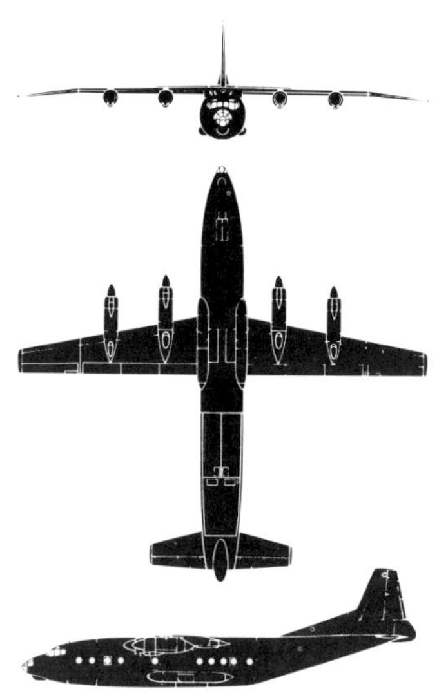

This efficient but ageing freighter was closely related to the An-10 airliner, which first flew in March 1957 with 4,000hp Kuznetsov NK-4 engines. Production An-10s, with AI-20K engines, entered service with Aeroflot in July 1959 in an 84-seat version and were followed in February 1960 by the An-10A, which had some modifications to the arrangement and shape of the ventral fins, and was built in 100-, 120- and 130-passenger versions. No examples of the An-10 or An-10A were exported, and the type was withdrawn from Aeroflot service in 1973. The An-12 was evolved from the same basic design, primarily as a military transport with rear-loading doors and a tail turret. Some examples, with the rear turret crudely faired in, were operated in civil markings by Aeroflot and one or two foreign airlines including Ghana and Cubana. They were followed by a definitive civil version, the An-12V, with the rear turret removed and a complete fairing in its place. The main cargo compartment is unpressurised, but there is a small pressurised compartment for 14 passengers just aft of the flight deck. Examples of the An-12 have been operated by LOT, Air Guinée, Bulair, Cubana and Aeroflot, and are seen frequently in Egyptian and Algerian civil markings, in addition to being operated by several air forces outside the Soviet Union. The An-10 was known by the NATO code-name 'Cat'; the An-12 is 'Cub'.

Antonov An-24, An-26, An-30 and An-32 USSR

Short-range airliner, in service
Photo: An-24PB
Silhouette: An-24
Data: An-24V Srs II

Accommodation: Flight crew of 3-5 and up to 50 passengers
Powered by: Two 2,550ehp Ivchenko AI-24A turboprops
Span: 95ft 9.5in (29.20m)
Length: 77ft 2.5in (23.53m)
Gross weight: 46,300lb (21,000kg)
Max payload: 12,125lb (5,500kg)
Cruising speed: 280mph (450km/h) at 19,700ft (6,000m)
Range: 341-1,490 miles (550-2,400km) at 280mph (450km/h)

Details of the An-24 feeder-liner (NATO code-name 'Coke') were first given by Russian sources in mid-1960 and it entered service on Aeroflot's routes from Moscow to Saratov and Voronezh in September 1963. The production versions have longer engine nacelles than the prototypes, ventral fins and other changes. Refinements in the An-24V increased the number of seats to 50 and allowed operation at higher weights; the first production batch, Srs I, had 2,550hp AI-24 engines while the later Srs IIs have AI-24As with water injection. Two more versions announced in 1967 were the An-24RV, with a 1,985lb (900kg) st auxiliary turbojet in the rear of the starboard nacelle; and An-24T for mixed passenger/freight services, with ventral loading door and twin ventral fins. The An-24P is a version with special modifications for use in the fire-fighting role. A further variant, revealed in 1969, is the An-26 (NATO code-name 'Curl'), a more extensively modified, rear-loading transport, for military as well as civil use. This has a widened rear fuselage and 2,820ehp AI-24T engines. Another version in use since 1974 is the An-30 (NATO code-name 'Clank'), which differs from the An-24 primarily in having special equipment in the forward fuselage for aerial survey duties. Nearly 1,000 examples of the An-24/26 family are believed to have been built by the time production ended in 1978, and there have been numerous foreign users, including Air Guinée (4), Air Mali (2), Air Mongol (5), Balkan Bulgarian Airlines (9), Cubana (10), Egyptair (9), Interflug (7), Iraqi Airways (2), LOT (17) and Tarom (20). In 1977, details became available of the An-32 (NATO code-name 'Cline'), which is basically an An-26 airframe fitted with 5,100eph AI-20M turboprops to improve the performance from 'hot and high' airfields. The An-32 is primarily intended for military use.

Antonov An-28

USSR

General-purpose light transport, in production and service

Accommodation: Flight crew of 1-2 and up to 15 passengers
Powered by: Two 960hp Glushenkov TVD-10A turboprops
Span: 72ft 2in (21.99m)
Length: 42ft 7in (12.98m)
Max payload: 3,750lb (1,700kg)
Max take-off weight: 13,450lb (6,100kg)
Max cruising speed: 217mph (350km/h)
Range: 620 miles (1,000km)

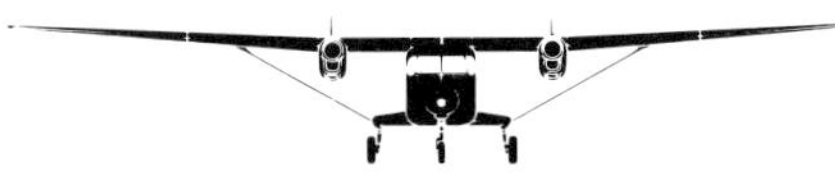

First flown in September 1969, but revealed outside Russia only in 1972, this light transport was initially designated as the An-14M and was a derivative of the earlier An-14, from which it differed in having 810shp Isotov TVD-850 turboprops and a new, larger fuselage. In the course of prototype flight trials, various changes were made: the undercarriage, retractable on the first An-14M, is now fixed, and the size and shape of the vertical tail surfaces has been varied. A pre-production example with these changes, redesignated as the An-28, first flew with the same TVD-850 engines but was re-engined in April 1975 with 960shp Glushenkov TVD-10 engines. These have now been confirmed as the choice for production models of the An-28 which are being built exclusively in Poland at the PZL-Mielec factory. Deliveries were expected to begin during 1980 with Aeroflot needs to be given first priority before the An-28 was made available for export to other nations. Within the Soviet Union, the An-28 is expected to replace the many hundreds of elderly An-2 biplanes that are still in service.

Beechcraft 99

USA

Light transport and third-level airliner, in production and service
Data: B99

Accommodation: Pilot and 15 passengers
Powered by: Two 680shp Pratt & Whitney PT6A-27 turboprops
Span: 45ft 10.5in (14.00m)
Length: 44ft 6.75in (13.58m)
Gross weight: 10,900lb (4,944kg)
Max cruising speed: 283mph (445km/h)
Max range: 838 miles (1,348km)

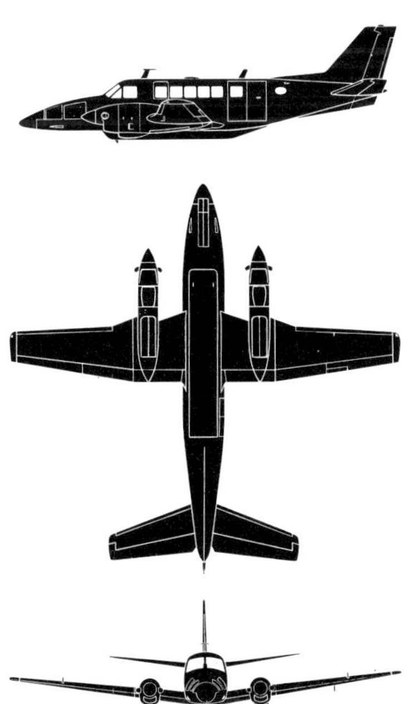

Beech Aircraft developed the Model 99, primarily for use by the third-level airlines and air taxi operators, from the original Queen Air by lengthening the fuselage and fitting turboprop engines. A long-fuselage prototype first flew, with piston-engines, in December 1965 and with the new engines (PT6A-20s) in July 1966. A production prototype flew early in 1968 and deliveries began on 2 May of that year, still with 550hp PT6A-20 engines. The Model 99A and A99A introduced the PT6A-27 engines derated to 550shp, and the B99 followed, with the same engines full rated. Production of the Beech 99, in the final B99 Airliner version, ended in 1975 with 164 delivered, most of which had been acquired by US operations. During 1979, however, Beech announced it was re-entering the commuter airliner market, and was putting into production the C99 version with the same overall dimensions as the B99 but with 783shp PT6A-34 engines giving improved performance, and some structural improvements. Deliveries of the C99, which may be known as the Beech 1500 when introduced into service, were to begin in the second half of 1981. Beech also said it would develop a 13-passenger version of the Super King Air 200 for commuter airline use as the Beech 1300 Airliner, to be followed by a stretched-fuselage 19-seat version, the Beech 1900 Airliner (qv).

Boeing 707 and Boeing 720

USA

Long-range airliner, in production and service
Photo, silhouette and data: 707-320C

Accommodation: Flight crew of 3-5 and up to 202 passengers or 13 freight pallets
Powered by: Four 18,000lb (8,165kg) st Pratt & Whitney JT3D-3B turbofans
Span: 145ft 9in (44.42m)
Length: 152ft 11in (45.6m)
Gross weight: 333,600lb (151,454kg)
Max payload: 83,447lb (37,885kg)
Max cruising speed: 600mph (965km/h) at 25,000ft (7,620m)
Range: 3,925 miles (6,320km) with max payload at 532mph (856km/h) (typical reserves)

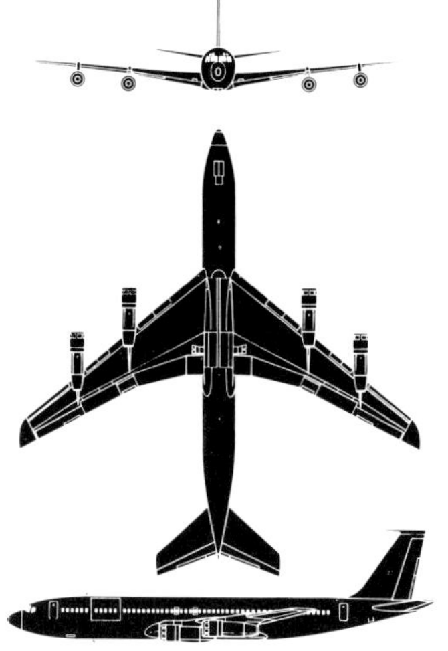

First flown on 20 December 1957, the initial model of the Boeing 707, the 707-120 (13,500lb P&W JT3C-6 engines), was tailored to the needs of US domestic operators, but it was used for a short time on the North Atlantic route by Pan American, starting on 26 October 1958. The standard 707-120 is 144ft 6in (44.04m) long and has a gross weight of 257,000lb (116,575kg); a version with a shorter fuselage was purchased only by Qantas, and a version with JT4A-3 engines, the 707-220, was sold only to Braniff. With aerodynamic refinements, the 707-120B differed from the -120 primarily in having JT3D-1 turbofan engines. In addition to new-production -120Bs, several airlines had their -120 fleets converted to the new standard. Smallest member of this Boeing family was the 720, with the same span of 130ft 10in (39.88m) but length of 136ft 2in (41.50m) and maximum weight of 229,000lb (103,875kg) with JT3C-7 or JT3C-12 engines. First flown on 25 November 1959, it was later offered with JT3D-1 or -3 turbofans and the same aerodynamic improvements as the 707-120B, then being known as the 720B.

The Intercontinental Boeing 707-320 has a longer fuselage, larger wing and more power, plus longer range. The first was flown on 11 January 1959, with 15,800lb st JT4A-3 engines; later versions had uprated -5, -11 or -12 engines. A contemporary was the 707-420, first flown on 19 May 1959, with Rolls-Royce Conway 508 engines rated at 17,500lb (7,938kg) st. Following development of the 707-120B and the 720B with turbofan engines and aerodynamic improvements Boeing introduced the 707-320B with similar modifications. The first flight was made on 31 January 1962, and this version eventually succeeded the 707-320 in production. Similar to the -320B in most respects was the -320C, with a large freight-loading door in the forward fuselage side and able to carry mixed loads of freight and passengers. By mid-1979, Boeing had sold 787 Model 707s and 154 Model 720s (including military and non-airline variants) and production was continuing. A prototype 707 fitted with 22,000lb (9,980kg) st CFM-56 engines was first flown on 27 November 1979.

Boeing 727

USA

Short/medium-range airliner, in production and service
Photo and silhouette: Srs 200
Data: Advanced 727-200

Accommodation: Flight crew of 3 and 134-189 passengers
Powered by: Three 16,000lb (7,257kg) st Pratt & Whitney JT8D-17 turbofans
Span: 108ft 0in (32.92m)
Length: 153ft 2in (46.69m)
Max ramp weight: 209,500lb (95,026kg)
Max payload: 41,750lb (18,935kg)
Max cruising speed: 699mph (964km/h) at 24,700ft (7,530m)
Range: Up to 2,940 miles (4,846km) with full passenger payload (typical reserves) at 570mph (917km/h) at 30,000ft (9,145m)

Production of the Boeing 727 began at the end of 1960. The first basic 727-100 series aircraft flew on 9 February 1963. Deliveries to United Air Lines began on 29 October that year and the first passenger service was flown by Eastern on 1 February 1964. Boeing also developed two variants with side-loading freight doors and fuselage fittings for mixed passenger-freight loads; these are the 727C convertible and 727QC 'quick-change' versions, the latter having passenger seats mounted on pallets for rapid installation. On 27 July 1967, Boeing flew the first 727-200, with a 10ft (3.05m) longer fuselage, 14,000lb (6,350kg) st JT8D-7 or 14,500lb (6,577kg) st JT8D-9 engines and other improvements. Subsequently, the uprated engines also became applicable to the 727-100 series, which have a maximum take-off weight of 169,000lb (76,657kg). The advanced 727-200 appeared in 1972 with higher gross weights, quieter engines and other improvements. In 1977, the Advanced 727-200 was available with 14,500lb (6,577kg) st JT8D-9A or 15,500lb (7,030kg) st JT8D-15 or 16,000lb (7,257kg) st JT8D-17 or 17,400lb (7,892kg) st JT8D-17R engines (the last-mentioned with Boeing-developed automatic thrust reserve), and was certificated at taxi weights up to 209,500lb (95,026kg) depending on configuration and fuel capacity. As the world's best selling jet airliner, the Boeing 727 had amassed 1,715 orders from 96 operators by late-1979 and was still selling steadily. Deliveries by that time totalled 1,533. The production total included 407 Boeing 727-100s (no longer in production) and 164 727C/QC variants with the large freight door.

Boeing 737

USA

Short-haul jet airliner, in production and service
Photo, silhouette and data: Srs 200

Accommodation: Flight crew of 2 and up to 130 passengers
Powered by: Two 16,000lb (7,257kg) st Pratt & Whitney JT8D-17 turbofans
Span: 93ft 0in (28.35m)
Length: 100ft 0in (30.48m)
Max gross weight: 117,000lb (53,070kg)
Max payload: 35,100lb (15,920kg)
Max cruising speed: 576mph (927km/h) at 22,000ft (6,890m)
Max range: 1,580 miles (2,540km) with max payload (typical reserves) at Mach 0.78 at 30,000ft (9,145m)

Deliveries of the basic Boeing 737 Srs 100 began in December 1967, less than four years after design work was started. This was made possible by utilising many components and assemblies already in production for the Boeing 727. In particular, the basic body structure of the two types is similar, with identical doors, side panels, ceilings, seats and certain systems. The engines are basically the same, with some commonality of cowlings despite its switch from fuselage to wing mounting. The Boeing 737 is in production at the company's complex of factories in the Seattle area, with final assembly in Plant No 2 at Boeing Field, where the first flight was made on 9 April 1967. The initial production version, for which Lufthansa was the first customer was the Srs 100, with 14,000lb (6,350kg) st JT8D-7 engines and up to 115 seats. Also in production are 'C' passenger/cargo convertible and 'QC' quick-change versions, the latter with palletised seats, and the Srs 200 with a 6ft 4in (1.93m) longer fuselage, more seats and JT8D-9 or JT8D-15 engines. The first Srs 200 flew on 8 August 1967, followed by the first passenger/cargo convertible model on 18 September 1968. Production of the -100 soon gave way to the longer-fuselage versions, only 30 of the initial model being built (for Avianca and MAS in addition to Lufthansa). The -200 has been further developed, with deliveries since May 1971 being of the Advanced -200 type. There have been progressive increases in engine thrust and in certificated weight, with the JT8D-9A, -15, -17 and -17R available for installation (see details under Boeing 727 entry), and Boeing plans a further increase in gross weight to 129,500lb (58,740kg). Sales by late-1979 totalled 740, including the 30 -100s and the 19 -200s delivered to the USAF as T-43 navigation trainers. Deliveries totalled 608 at that time.

Boeing 747

USA

Long-range transport, in production and service
Photo, silhouette and data: Srs 200

Accommodation: Flight crew of 3-4 and 363-500 passengers
Powered by: Four 53,000lb (24,040kg) st Pratt & Whitney JT9D-70A turbofans
Span: 195ft 8in (59.64m)
Length: 231ft 4in (70.51m)
Gross weight: 820,000lb (372,280kg)
Max payload: 155,429lb (70,500kg)
Max speed: 608mph (978km/h) at 30,000ft (9,150m)
Range: 4,600 miles (7,400km) with max payload

The Boeing Co announced details of the Boeing 747 in April 1966, with a preliminary commitment from Pan American for 25. Largest passenger transport yet put into production, the aircraft quickly became known as the 'Jumbo Jet'. It has one main cabin level with capacity for a maximum of 500 seats arranged ten-abreast across the 20ft (6.10m) width. A typical layout provides for 306 economy class passengers and 57 first class, with a lounge on an upper level behind the flight deck seating eight or, in later models, up to 32 economy class passengers.

The first 747 (a company-owned prototype) flew for the first time on 9 February 1969 and Pan American inaugurated Boeing 747 services on the New York-London route on 22 January 1970. Early aircraft had 43,500lb (19,730kg) st JT9D-3D turbofans, and a gross weight of 710,000lb (322,050kg); but late in 1970 Boeing certificated the 747A at 733,000lb (332,480kg), with JT9D-3AW engines and the 46,950lb (21,296kg) st JT9D-7A or 48,570lb (22,030kg) st JT9D-7AW are also now available. On 11 October 1970, the Boeing 747B made its first flight, this being a further development with an inital gross weight of 775,000lb (351,535kg) and JT9D-7 or JT9D-7A engines; subsequent development of this -200 model (now the basic variant) has made available the 48,000lb (21,772kg) st JT9D-7F, the 50,000lb (22,679kg) st JT9D-7FW or JT9D-7J and the 53,000lb (24,040kg) st JT9D-7Q or JT9D-70A, with gross weights eventually going up to 820,000lb (371,946kg). In addition, Boeing has certificated versions of the 747 powered by the General Electric CF6-50E, -50E1 and -50E2 of 52,500lb (23,814kg) st (first flown on 26 June 1973) and the Rolls-Royce RB211-524B at 50,100lb (22,725kg) st (First flown 3 September 1976). In September 1973 Boeing began delivery to Japan Air Lines of the 747SR, a special short-range, reduced-weight version; and in the same month announced an order from Pan American for the 747SP, which has a 48ft (14.6m) shorter fuselage and greater range. First flights of these versions were made on 4 September 1973, and 4 July 1975 respectively. In 1977, the 747-100B was announced, having the structural improvements of the 747SR and the same range of engines as quoted above for the 747-200B, with weights of 710,000lb (322,050kg) to 750,000lb (340,500kg). For cargo-carrying, Boeing developed the 747F (first flown 30 November 1971), with upward-hinged nose for straight-in loading, and more recently the 747 Combi, with a side-loading cargo door for more flexible mixed passenger/cargo loads. A few operators specified both nose-loading and side-loading freight doors. By late-1979, sales totalled 507, including some 30 747Fs and about 70 Combis with side-loading freight door. Deliveries totalled 403 at that time.

Boeing 757 USA

Medium-range transport, in production

Accommodation: Flight crew of 2-3 and 196 passengers (high density); typical mixed class, 177
Powered by: Two 37,400lb (16,980kg) st Rolls-Royce RB211-535C turbofans
Span: 124ft 6in (37.95m)
Length: 155ft 3in (47.32m)
Gross weight: 220,000lb (99,880km)
Max payload: 53,000lb (24,062kg)
Max cruising speed: 540mph (869km/h) at 35,000ft (10,670m)
Range: About 1,250 miles (2,000km) with max payload

The 757 was launched in August 1978 as the second new Boeing jetliner for the 1980s, following a few months after the launch of the 767 (qv) and after several years of intensive project and market studies. The concept of the 757 was based on a high degree of commonality with the Boeing 727, which it is designed to replace, but as the design definition neared completion, more and more new features were adopted until the only portion of the 727 retained is the basic body cylinder. The 757 features an all-new wing, with podded engines, a new low tail unit and a new front fuselage and flight deck which has more in common with the 767 than the 727. The launching customers, who announced their intention of ordering the 757 in August 1978 but did not sign definitive contracts until March 1979, were British Airways and Eastern Air Lines. The former ordered 19 with options on 18 more, and the latter ordered 21 with options on 24. Both companies selected the Rolls-Royce RB211-535 to power their 757s, although the General Electric CF6-32C is quoted as an alternative by Boeing. An increased gross weight of 230,000lb (104,420kg) has also been offered by Boeing for later aircraft. The development programme provides for a first flight in February 1982 and first deliveries in January 1983.

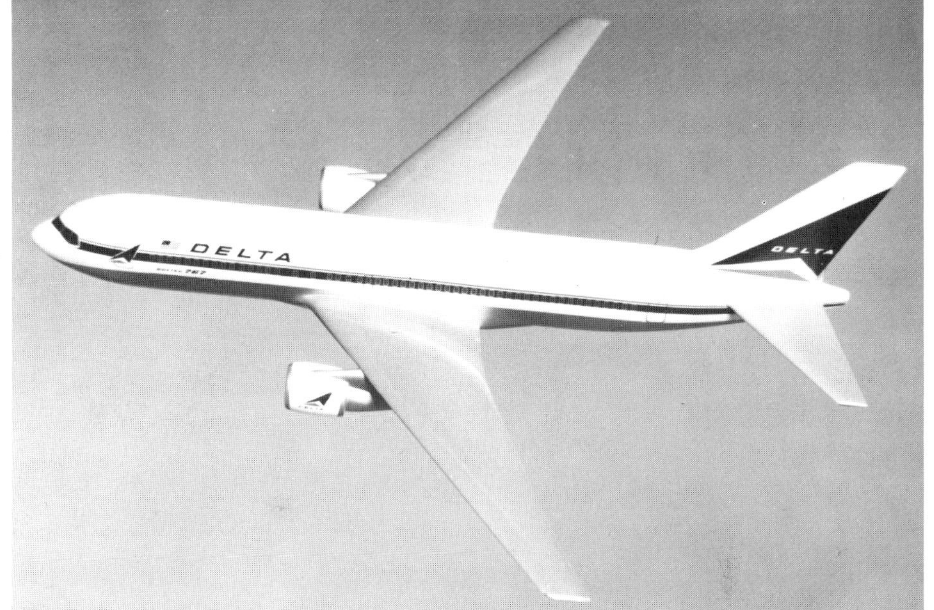

Boeing 767

USA

Medium/long-range transport, in production
Data: 767-200 (United Air Lines)

Accommodation: Flight crew of 3 and up to 289 passengers (high density); typical mixed class, 211
Powered by: Two 44,300lb (20,112kg) st Pratt & Whitney JT9D-7R4A turbofans
Span: 155ft 0in (47.24m)
Length: 159ft 0in (48.53m)
Gross weight: 282,000lb (128,030kg)
Max payload: 61,000lb (27,694kg)
Max cruising speed: 528mph (850km/h) at 39,000ft (11,887m)
Range: About 2,300 miles (3,700km) with max passenger load

After many years of design activity around a new transport, referred to as the Boeing 7X7, Boeing was able to launch this aircraft as its first completely new civil aircraft since the 747 in July 1978, backed by a launching order from United Air Lines, which contracted for 30 and subsequently took an option on 37 more. The 767 was a wholly new design, featuring an advanced-technology wing and extensive use of modern construction methods and materials. In the Boeing tradition, a range of options was offered in terms of fuselage length, fuel capacity, gross weight and power plant, and the variant ordered by United had originally been the longer-fuselage Srs 200. After the 767 had been launched, this became the standard model and the shorter-fuselage Srs 100 was de-emphasised; versions of the Srs 200 with weights up to 310,000lb (140,740kg) are currently planned, however. Subsequent to the launch, orders were placed by American Airlines (30 plus 20 on option), Delta (20 plus 22) and Pacific Western (four plus two), these airlines specifying 48,000lb (21,800kg) st CF6-80A engines and a 300,000lb (136,200kg) gross weight; and by Air Canada (12 plus 18) for the 310,000lb (140,740kg) version, with JT9D-7R4 engines. By the end of 1979, orders from All Nippon (25 plus 15 options), CP Air (four plus four options) and TWA (10 plus 10 on option) brought the overall total to 263. Final assembly of the 767 is at a new facility at Everett alongside the Boeing 747 production line, with component manufacture widely sub-contract; Aeritalia in Italy has a 15% share in the programme (and of the risk) and a group of Japanese manufacturers, CTDC, shares similarly. First flight of the Boeing 767 was scheduled to be made in September 1981 with five aircraft used in the flight test and certification programme to allow deliveries to begin in August 1982.

British Aerospace/Aérospatiale Concorde International

Medium/long-range supersonic transport, in service
Photo: Concorde 206

Accommodation: Flight crew of 3-4 and up to 128 passengers
Powered by: Four 38,050lb (17,260kg) st (with 17% afterburning) Rolls-Royce Olympus 593 Mk 610 turbojets
Span: 83ft 10in (25.56m)
Length: 203ft 9in (62.10m)
Gross weight: 408,000lb (185,070kg)
Max cruising speed: Mach 2.02 (1,354mph/ 2,179km/h) at 50,000ft (15,250m)
Range: 3,870 miles (6,230km) at Mach 2.02 with max payload

Culminating several years of design effort in Britain, a joint design for a supersonic transport was evolved in 1962; on 29 November in that year the British and French Governments signed an agreement to initiate work as a joint venture. Aérospatiale had design responsibility for the airframe, sharing its manufacture with BAC, and Rolls-Royce had design authority for the Olympus engines, with SNECMA contributing the exhuast system and afterburners. The first of two prototypes, known as Concorde 001 (F-WTSS) made its first flight at Toulouse on 2 March 1969 followed by 002 (G-BSST) at Bristol on 9 April. Both prototypes reached Mach 2 for the first time during November 1970. First flown on 17 December 1971, was Concorde 01, the first of two pre-production models, with a longer fuselage, smaller windows, a revised windscreen with fixed step and a gross weight of 385,000lb. Concorde 02 first flew on 10 January 1973, and was externally similar to the production aircraft, with an extended rear fuselage fairing and revised wing leading edge. The first two production Concordes, identified now as Concorde 201 and 202, flew on 6 December 1973 and 13 February 1974, respectively in France and Britain, followed by Nos 203 and 204 on 31 January and 27 February 1975. Following certification (in France on 2 October and Britain on 5 December 1975) Concorde entered commercial service with Air France and British Airways on 21 January 1976, and both airlines inaugurated the first supersonic transatlantic services (to and from Washington) on 24 May 1976. Services to New York began on 22 November 1977 and, on 12 January 1979, Braniff began operating Concordes (leased from Air France and BA) between New York and Dallas/Fort Worth. The last two production Concordes flew on 26 December 1978 (No 215 in France) and 20 April 1979 (No 216 in Britain).

British Aerospace (BAC) One-Eleven UK

Short-haul jet airliner, in production and service
Photo, silhouette and data: Srs 500

Accommodation: Flight crew of 2 and up to 119 passengers
Powered by: Two 12,550lb (5,692kg) st Rolls-Royce Spey 512DW turbofans
Span: 93ft 6in (28.50m)
Length: 107ft 0in (32.61m)
Gross weight: 99,650-104,500lb (45,200-47,400kg)
Max payload: 27,089lb (12,286kg)
Max cruising speed: 541mph (871km/h) at 21,000ft (6,400m)
Max range: 1,705 miles (2,744km) at 461mph (742km/h) with capacity payload and typical reserves

First flown on 20 August 1963, the One-Eleven was evolved by BAC from an earlier project by Hunting Aircraft. The first production model flew on 19 December 1963 and airline services started in April 1965 by BUA and later the same year by Braniff, Mohawk and Aer Lingus. The Srs 200 aircraft for these customers had 10,330lb (4,686kg) st Spey 506 engines. On 13 July 1965, BAC flew a prototype of the Srs 300/400, with 11,400lb (5,171kg) st Spey 511s and higher operating weights. The Srs 400 was intended specifically for the US market, with American equipment. The same prototype was later modified to Srs 500 standard, with longer fuselage, and first flew in this form on 30 June 1967. The Srs 500 also has uprated Spey 512DWs, increased span and gross weight of up to 104,500lb (47,700kg); it entered airline service in 1968. During 1970, the Srs 500 prototype was again modified, to Srs 475 standard with the short fuselage of the original One-Eleven combined with the long-span wing and uprated engines. In this guise, it first flew on 27 August 1970. By mid-1979, orders for the One-Eleven totalled 225, and production of a further batch had been authorised, against expected future orders. In June 1979, the Romanian Government concluded an agreement with BAe under which it will put the One-Eleven into production in Romania to meet domestic needs and for export. The deal includes delivery of three complete One-Elevens and 22 in sets of components for assembly in Romania, after which it is planned to produce 60 at the rate of six a year up to 1995. Principal users of the One-Eleven in 1979 are Aer Lingus, Allegheny, Austral, Aviateca, Bahamasair, Bavaria-Germanair, British Airways, British Caledonian, British Island Airways, British Midland Airways, Cyprus Airways, Dan-Air, LACSA, Laker, Monarch, PAL, Quebecair, TACA and Tarom. The Series 475 has been purchased only by Air Malawi, Air Pacific, Faucett and the Oman Air Force, plus one as part of the deal between Romania and BAe.

British Aerospace (HS) 146

UK

Feeder-jet transport, under development
Silhouette and data: Srs 100

Accommodation: Flight crew of 2 and up to 93 passengers (high density); typical mixed class 71-88
Powered by: Four Avco-Lycoming ALF 502-11 turbofans rated at 6,700lb (3,040kg) st each
Span: 86ft 6in (26.36m)
Length: 85ft 10in (26.16m)
Gross weight: 73,850lb (35,500kg)
Max cruising speed: 491mph (790km/h)
Range: 650 miles (1,050km) with max payload,. 1,200 miles (1,930km) with 71 passengers

The British Aerospace 146 was launched on 29 August 1973, as the HS146, at that time a joint venture between the British government and the privately-owned Hawker Siddeley Group. It was the outcome of a long period of gestation and many project designs, starting with the de Havilland DH123. Little more than a year after launch, the HS146 was suspended, however, because of rapidly inflating development costs and the recession in the airline market. After the nationalisation of Hawker Siddeley and its merger into British Aerospace, the original design of the 146 was resurrected and in the light of a newly-favourable market forecast, it was re-launched as the BAe146 on 10 July 1978, becoming the first new project of the state-owned industry. Initial aircraft are to Srs 100 configuration and the first flight was expected to be made in November 1980, with six more in 1981 and certification in February 1982. In the same month, the first Srs 200 was scheduled to fly, this being a stretched version with seats for up to 109 (typically, 82-96) and higher operating weights. A military version, the BAe146M, with a new rear fuselage incorporating rear loading doors and a ramp, is the responsibilty of the Manchester Division of British Aerospace, the civil variants being handled by Hatfield-Brough Division with manufacture spread round the entire group.

British Aerospace (HS) 748

UK

Short-range airliner, in production and service
Photo: Srs 2
Data: Srs 2B

Accommodation: Flight crew of 2-3 and 40-58 passengers
Powered by: Two 2,280ehp Rolls-Royce Dart 536 turboprops
Span: 102ft 6in (31.24m)
Length: 67ft 0in (20.42m)
Gross weight: 46,500lb (21,092kg)
Max payload: 12,500lb (5,670kg)
Economical cruising speed: 278mph (488km/h) at 17,000ft (5,180m)
Range: 530 miles (852km) with max payload at 259mph (417km/h), with reserves

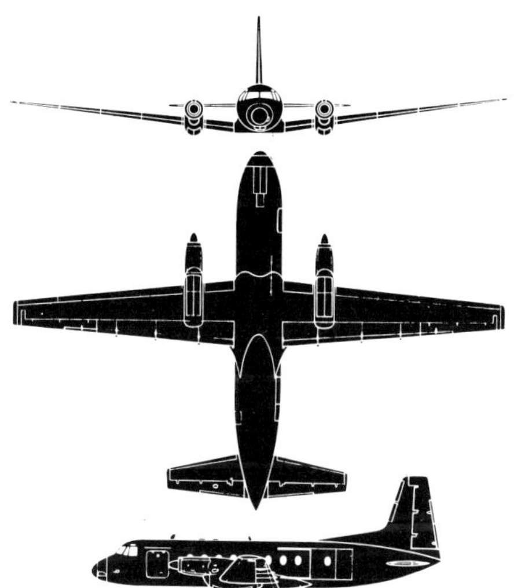

The Hawker Siddeley Group — now part of British Aerospace — decided to go ahead with the design and development of this twin-Dart feeder-liner in January 1959. The first prototype (G-APZV) flew for the first time on 24 June 1960, followed by the second (G-ARAY) on 10 April 1961, and the first Srs 1 production aircraft (G-ARMV), with 1,880ehp Dart 514 engines, on 30 August 1961. Later in 1961, G-ARAY was fitted with 2,105ehp Dart RDa7 engines as the prototype Srs 2. Skyways Coach Air (now part of Dan-Air) ordered three Srs 1s and became the first company to operate the 748 in the spring of 1962. Other orders for the Srs 1 came from Aerolineas Argentinas, BKS Air Transport (now Northeast) and Smiths Aviation Division. Airline users of the Srs 2 and more powerful Srs 2A include Air Ceylon, Air Gabon, Air Illinois, Air Malawi, Air Pacific, Air Polynesie, Avianca, Botswana Airways, Bouraq Indonesian, British Airways, COPA (Panama), Dan-Air, Gateway Aviation, Ghana Airways, Korean Airlines, LAN-Chile, LAV, LIAT, Merpati, Nusantara, Midwest, Mount Cook Airlines, PAL, Quebecair, Reunion Air Service, Royal Nepal Airlines, SAA, SAESA, SATA, SATENA, TAME, Thai Airways, Trinidad & Tobago Air Services, Varig and Zambia Airways, in addition to several air forces and military agencies. Indian Airlines Corporation received 18 Srs 2s from a production line set up in India by the Kanpur Division of Hindustan Aeronautics Ltd. After developing a maritime reconnaissance version of the design known as the Coastguarder, in 1977, British Aerospace announced a new production standard as the Srs 2B in 1978. This features uprated engines, a 4ft (1.22m) span increase, modified tail unit and other changes; the first production example flew on 22 June 1979. Total sales of the 748 stood at 345 in late-1979 including military versions and a total of 89 assembled in India.

Convair-Liner 240, 340 and 440, and Convair 580 and 600/640

USA

Medium-range airliner, in service
Photo: Convair 600
Silhouette: Convair 580
Data: Convair 640

Accommodation: Flight crew of 3-4 and 44-56 passengers
Powered by: Two 3,025ehp Rolls-Royce Dart 542-4 (RDa10) turboprops
Span: 105ft 4in (32.12m)
Length: 81ft 6in (24.84m)
Gross weight: 55,000lb (24,950kg)
Max payload: 15,800lb (7,167kg)
Range: 1,900 miles (3,060km)

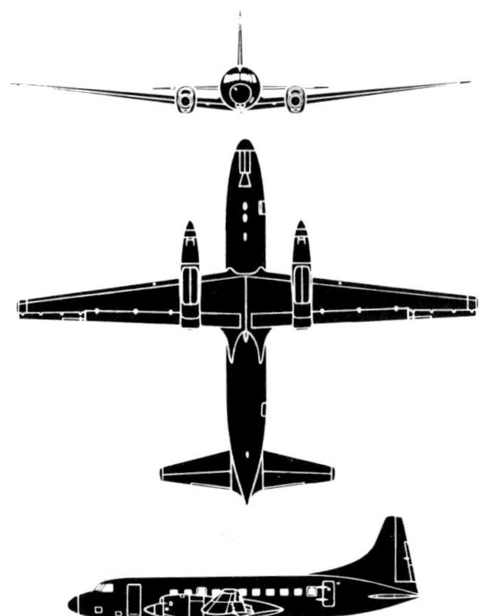

The original Model 240 (first flight 16 March 1947) was built as a DC-3 replacement, with 2,400hp R-2800-CA18 engines, span of 91ft 9in (27.98m), gross weight of 42,500lb (22,544kg), and accommodation for 40 passengers. Very few remain in airline service, alongside larger numbers of improved 340s and 440 Metropolitans. The first 340 flew on 5 October 1951, featuring increased span, longer fuselage accommodationg 44 passengers, new engines (R-2800-CB16 or CB17s) and increased loaded weight of 47,000lb (21,318kg). The prototype Model 440 Metropolitan flew on 6 October 1955, with redesigned engine nacelles and other detail changes to improve performance and reduce cabin noise. Turboprop versions were developed with Allision 501-D13 (CV-580) and Rolls-Royce Dart (CV-600 and 640) engines. The first CV-580 with Allison engines (a 340 conversion) flew on 19 January 1960 and airline service (with Frontier) began in June 1964. A total of 130 Convairs was converted to 580s and users in 1979 included Aspen, Avensa, Commuter Airlines, Evergreen, Frontier, Gem State Airlines, Great Lakes, Mountainwest Aviation, Quebecair, Republic Airlines, and Summit. The first Convair 600 (240 conversion) flew on 20 May 1965 and the first 640 (340/440 conversion) on 20 August 1965. Central Airlines was the first to take delivery of the Dart-engined version, on 20 September 1965. Principal users of the Dart-powered version in 1979 were Aerolineas Colonia of Uruguay, Air Algerie, SMB Stage Line, Texas International and — an all-cargo version — Zantop.

Convair 880 (Airlifter) and 990 Coronado — USA

Medium-to-long-range passenger transport, in service
Photo, silhouette and data: CV-990A

Accommodation: Flight crew of 3-5 and up to 106 passengers
Powered by: Four 16,000lb (7,280kg) st General Electric CJ805-23B turbofans
Span: 120ft 0in (36.58m)
Length: 139ft 2.5in (42.43m)
Gross weight: 253,000lb (114,760kg)
Max payload: 26,440lb (11,992kg)
Max cruising speed: 615mph (990km/h) at 20,000ft (6,100m)
Range: 3,800 miles (6,115km)

The Convair family of high-speed jet transports was first announted in April 1956, when TWA and Delta ordered 30 and 10 respectively, under the projected names of Skylark 600 and Golden Arrow. The original version, which became known as the Convair 880, first flew on 27 January 1959, with 11,200lb (5,080kg) st CJ805-3 engines. Additional fuel capacity was offered in the Convair 880-M, which also introduced uprated engines and higher operating weights. This version flew on 3 October 1960, and was specified by various foreign airlines ordering the type. Most operators had phased-out their Convair 880s by 1973, the last of the original users being Cathay Pacific, which had replaced its 880s by Boeing 707s by 1975. In 1979, Gulfstream American was developing a freight conversion of the CV-880 known as the Airlifter, with a side-loading freight door in the forward fuselage and a 51,000lb (23,150kg) freight payload. Gulfstream American owned or held options on 22 CV-880s for conversion. Two former Cathay Pacific CV-880Ms were being operated in 1979 by Singapore Aircraft Leasing.

Developed from the Convair 880 to meet the needs of American Airlines for a transcontinental trunk transport, the Convair 990 Coronado (known until the end of 1960 as the Convair 600) had a 10ft (3.05m) longer fuselage and turbofan engines. It was also distinguished by four 'area-rule' conical fairings aft of the wing trailing-edges. The first flight was made at San Diego on 24 January 1961. The 990 was certificated in December 1961 and during 1962 American Airlines began putting 20 CV-990As into service, the 'A' in the designation indicating a series of modifications, especially to the engine pod and pylon shape, to reduce drag. Only 37 were built and by 1977 none of the original operators of the Convair 990 still had the type in service. The principal operator in 1979 was Spantax, using 12 for (principally) IT flights. A few others were used by private transport groups in the USA.

Dassault-Breguet Mercure

France

Short/medium-range large-capacity transport, in service
Data: Mercure 100

Accommodation: Flight crew of 2-4 and up to 162 passengers
Powered by: Two 15,500lb (7,030kg) st Pratt & Whitney JT8D-15 turbofans
Span: 100ft 3in (30.55m)
Length: 114ft 3.5in (34.84m)
Gross weight: 124,560lb (56,500kg)
Max payload: 35,715lb (16,200kg)
Max cruising speed: 575mph (926km/h) at 20,000ft (6,100m)
Range: 690 miles (1,110km) with 150 passengers (with reserves)

The Mercure programme was launched by Dassault as a private venture in 1968, in an attempt to provide a European alternative to established US short-haul 'twins'. The French Government agreed subsequently to provide 56% of the launching costs, and Dassault concluded agreements with companies outside France in respect of a further 30% shared between Italy, Belgium, Spain, Switzerland and Canada. The first prototype had 15,000lb (6,800kg) st JT8D-11 engines, with which it made its first flight on 28 May 1971. It was re-engined subsequently with JT8D-15s, in which form it flew again in September. A further series of modifications made in November included the introduction of dihedral on the tailplane. A second prototype, also with JT8D-15 engines, made its first flight on 7 September 1972,followed by the first production example on 19 July 1973. Air Inter, the French domestic airline, placed an order for 10 Mercures, of which the first was delivered on 15 May 1974 and entered service later that summer. Subsequently, additional equipment was installed to give the Mercure the ability to operate in ICAO Cat III meteorological conditions. Delivery of the fleet of 10 was completed in 1975, when Mercure production came to an end. Under the name of Super Mercure and more recently as Mercure 200, Dassault-Breguet projected an improved development of the basic design, and in 1976 this formed the basis of the ASMR (advanced short-to-medium range) transport proposal that was studied jointly by Dassault-Breguet and McDonnell Douglas Corporation, with CFM-56 turbofans and a stretched fuselage to seat about 180 passengers. This study had ended by 1978 and no further development of the Mercure was then planned.

De Havilland DHC-6 Twin Otter

Canada

General-purpose light STOL transport, in production and service
Photo and data: Srs 300

Accommodation: 1-2 pilots and up to 20 passengers
Powered by: Two 652ehp Pratt & Whitney PT6A-27 turboprops
Span: 65ft 0in (19.81m)
Length: 51ft 9in (15.77m)
Gross weight: 12,500lb (5,670kg)
Max payload: 4,430lb (2,010kg)
Max cruising speed: 210mph (338km/h) at 10,000ft (3,050m)
Range: 115 miles (160km) with max payload

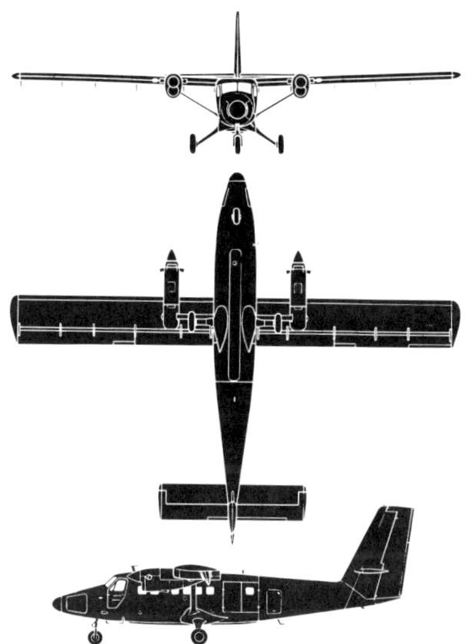

As suggested by its name, the Twin Otter was derived from the single-engined Otter retaining much of the latter's fuselage and wing structure but having two turboprop engines. Developed as a private venture, the first Twin Otter flew on 20 May 1965, and deliveries began in July 1966. The initial Srs 100 production version (115 built), with 579ehp PT6A-20 engines, was superseded by the Srs 200 (115 built), with a lengthened nose and higher operating weights, followed in turn by the Srs 300 described alongside. Most Twin Otters operate with land undercarriage but float and ski versions are also in service. Six special Twin Otters delivered in 1974 were Srs 300S, and had modifications to permit their use on an experimental inter-urban STOL service between Montreal and Ottawa. But late-1979, overall sales of the Twin Otter were approaching 700, with 600 delivered, and de Havilland was studying a Srs 400 for the US commuter airline market. This was expected to have higher operating weights, up to a maximum of 14,000lb (6,350kg), probably with a lengthened fuselage and 750shp PT6A-34 engines.

De Havilland DHC-7 Dash-7

Canada

Short-range STOL third-level and commuter airliner, in production and service

Accommodation: Flight crew of 2 and 50 passengers
Powered by: Four 1,120shp Pratt & Whitney (Canada) PT6A-50 turboprops
Span: 93ft 0in (28.35m)
Length: 80ft 7.5in (24.58m)
Gross weight: 43,500lb (19,731kg)
Max payload: 12,150lb (5,511kg)
Max cruising speed: 271mph (436km/h) at 8,000ft (2,440m)
Range: 810 miles (1,303km) with full passenger payload

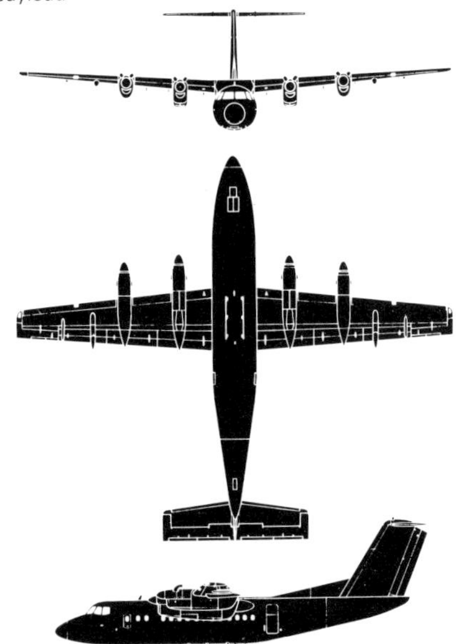

Latest in the de Havilland Canada range of specialised STOL aircraft, the Dash-7 is also the largest aircraft built by the Ontario company to date. Earlier aircraft in the series were the Beaver, Otter, Twin Otter, Caribou and Buffalo. The Dash-7, which is designed and built with the financial backing of the Canadian Government, is a completely new design, utilising de Havilland's accumulated expertise in achieving short take-off and landing characteristics through aerodynamic lift systems — that is, the use of large double-slotted flaps operating in the slipstream from the four large-diameter, slow-turning propellers. The Dash-7 prototype first flew on 27 March 1975, and a second, pre-production model flew on 26 June 1975. Production of an initial series of 50 had been authorised by the end of 1976 and the first production Dash-7 made its first flight on 30 May 1977. After certification, the Dash-7 entered service with the Rocky Mountain Airways in February 1978 and Spantax became the first European operator of the type a few weeks later. Other customers up to the middle of 1979 included Air Innsbruck, Air Pacific, Air Wisconsin, Alidair, Alyemda, Brymon Airways, the CAF, Emirate Air Services, Greenlandair, Ransome Airlines, SAHSA, Time Air, Wardair, Westcoast Air and Wideroes. The Canadian Coast Guard acquired two Dash-7R Ranger patrol variants and projected future civil versions are the Srs 200 with 1,230shp PT6A-55 turboprops and 46,000lb (20,866kg) gross weight, and the Srs 300 with stretched fuselage to seat up to 60.

Douglas DC-3 (and Dakota, C-47, Tri Turbo-3) USA

Medium-range passenger or freight transport, in service
Photo: DC-3
Data: Dakota 4

Accommodation: Flight crew of 3 and up to 36 passengers
Powered by: Two 1,200hp Pratt & Whitney R-1830-90C or -90D piston-engines
Span: 95ft 0in (28.96m)
Length: 64ft 5in (19.66m)
Gross weight: 28,000lb (12,701kg)
Max payload: 6,620lb (3,000kg)
Normal cruising speed: 170mph (274km/h) at 6,000ft (1,828m)
Max range: 1,510 miles (2,420km)

Most widely-used air transport in history, this aircraft began life as the 14-passenger Douglas DST (Douglas sleeper transport) and 21-passenger DC-3 of 1936. These, in turn, had been developed, by way of the DC-2, from the DC-1, which made its first flight on 1 July 1933. The DST was first flown at Santa Monica on 22 December 1935 and entered service in May 1936, with American Airlines. During the war, it became America's standard medium-range military transport, under such designations as C-47, C-53 and C-117, and many of the 10,225 then built were converted subsequently for civil use. In addition, 430 new DC-3s were produced, mostly before the war, with a few after 1945. In civil use, these aircraft are usually known as DC-3s or Dakotas, the latter being the RAF name for the military transport version during the war. Although the use of the DC-3s on scheduled passenger services is now dwindling, there are parts of the world where this aircraft's performance and low cost have for many years made it indispensable, and it is still quite widely used for charter, cargo and other flights. ICAO statistics indicated that 871 DC-3s were still in service as commercial transports in 1969, representing just over 12% of the total number of transport aircraft then operating in the ICAO contracting states. This figure has subsequently declined, but several hundred remain in commercial use, some of which have only recently been offered for civil ownership after many years of military service. On 2 November 1977, Specialized Aircraft Inc flew the first Tri Turbo-3, a DC-3 conversion with three 1,175shp PT6A-45 turboprops.

Douglas DC-4 (and Carvair)

USA

Medium-range passenger and freight transport, in service
Photo: DC-4 water bomber
Silhouette and data: DC-4

Accommodation: Flight crew of 2-3 and up to 85 passengers
Powered by: Four 1,450hp Pratt & Whitney R-2000 piston-engines
Span: 117ft 6in (35.82m)
Length: 93ft 5in (28.47m)
Gross weight: 73,000lb (33,112kg)
Max cruising speed: 207mph (333km/h)
Typical range: 1,150 miles (1,850km) with max payload

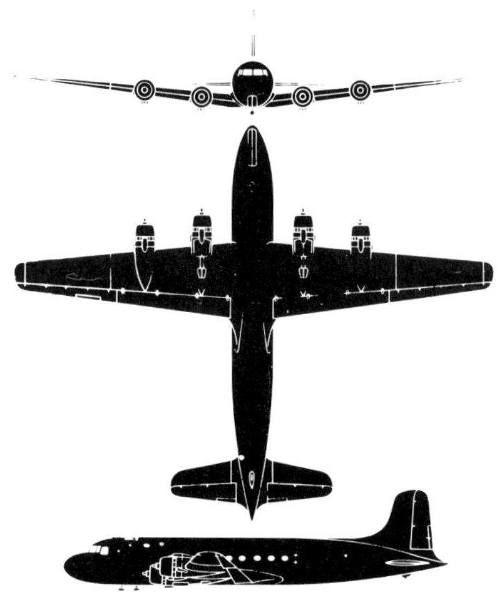

The prototype DC-4, which received its American C of A as a civil airliner in May 1939, was a triple-finned design with four 1,450hp P&W R-2180 Twin-Hornet engines and seats for 52 passengers; it was first flown on 7 June 1938. After service trials, the design was scaled down, refined and put into production. Before it could enter airline service, US wartime requirements led to its further modification into a military transport, and most of the aircraft of this type remaining in service today are ex-military C-54 Skymasters, although 79 commercial DC-4s were built postwar. The C-54 was first flown on 14 February 1942, and entered service during 1943; airline service began early in 1946. Few major airlines still use the DC-4, but scores remain in service with independent operators and charter companies throughout the world, principally for freighting with large loading doors and special floors. Based on the Douglas DC-4 airframe, the Carvair is a specialised freighter, the design of which was originated by Aviation Traders Ltd. The primary requirement was the carriage of vehicles on cross-channel services to and from Britain, and for this purpose the front end of the DC-4 was extensively redesigned to permit straight-in loading of cars or freight. This called for relocation of the flight deck in a 'hump' high above the normal fuselage top line; associated with this modification was an increase in vertical tail area, and internal changes included the re-routing of control runs. The prototype Carvair conversion (G-ANYB) made its first flight on 21 June 1961, and 21 were eventually converted, a few of which were still serving in 1979.

Douglas DC-6 and DC-7 Series

USA

Long-range airliner, in service
Photo, silhouette and data: DC-7C

Accommodation: Flight crew of 3-5 and 69-105 passengers
Powered by: Four 3,400hp Wright R-3350-18EA-4 Turbo-Compound piston-engines
Span: 127ft 6in (38.8m)
Length: 112ft 3in (34.23m)
Gross weight: 143,000lb (64,865kg)
Max payload: 21,500lb (8,752kg)
Cruising speed: 310mph (499km/h) at 20,000ft (6,100m)
Typical range: 4,100 miles (6,600km) at 274mph (440km/h) with 15,000lb (6,804kg) payload

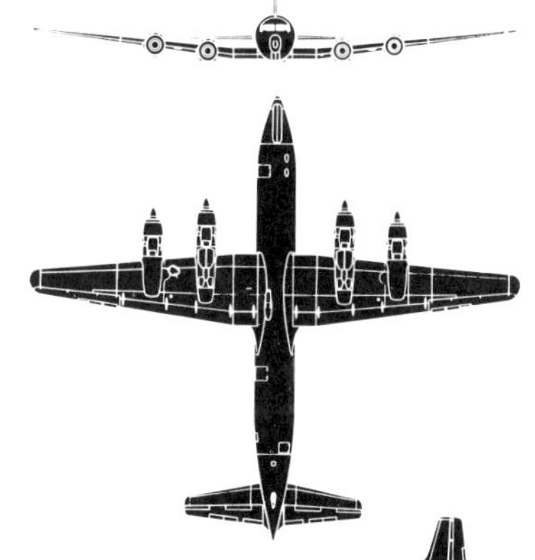

The DC-6 was developed after the war as a larger, more powerful and pressurised successor to the DC-4, the prototype being built to a military order with the designation XC-112. The first flight was made on 15 February 1946. The initial airline version had 2,400hp R-2800-CA-15 engines and was 100ft 7in (30.66m) long. It was followed by the longer DC-6A Liftmaster freighter and the DC-6B passenger-carrying version. The DC-6A, built initially for Slick Airways, had a length of 105ft 7in (32.2m), while the DC-6B was further lengthened to 106ft 8in (32.51m) by installation of an optional nose radar. First flights were made, respectively, on 29 September 1949 and 10 February 1951. Including 167 military models of the DC-6A (USAF C-118A, USN R6D-1), Douglas built 704 aircraft of the DC-6 series, of which 175 were DC-6s, 77 DC-6As and 286 DC-6Bs. More than 100 DC-6s and DC-6Bs continue in use in various parts of the world, principally as freighters and for low-cost charter flights, including one or two modified to have swing-tail straight-in loading. A further development of the DC-4/DC-6 line, the basic DC-7 differed mainly in having four 3,250hp R-3350-18DA1 engines, a length of 108ft 11in (33.24m), and a loaded weight of 123,200lb (55,429kg). The DC-7B was an intercontinental version with 3,350hp R-3350-18DA4 engines, increased fuel tankage and a loaded weight of 126,000lb (57,153kg). Final development was the very-long-range DC-7C Seven Seas. These three variants made their first flights on 18 May 1953 (DC-7), 25 April 1955 (DC-7B) and 20 December 1955 (DC-7C), and production totalled 336. The advent of jet transports rendered the DC-7s obsolete for service on the international trunk routes for which they had been designed, but many operators converted their aircraft to DC-7F standard as freighters and several dozen of these remain in service in 1979 in various parts of the world.

EMBRAER EMB-110 Bandeirante

Brazil

Short-haul feeder-line transport, in production and service
Photo and data: EMB-110P2

Accommodation: Flight crew of 2 and up to 21 passengers
Powered by: Two 750hp Pratt & Whitney PT6A-34 turboprops
Span: 50ft 2.5in (15.30m)
Length: 49ft 6.5in (15.10m)
Gross weight: 12,500lb (5,670kg)
Max payload: 3,706lb (1,681kg)
Max cruising speed: 259mph (417km/h)
Range: 309-1,180 miles (497-1,900km) according to payload

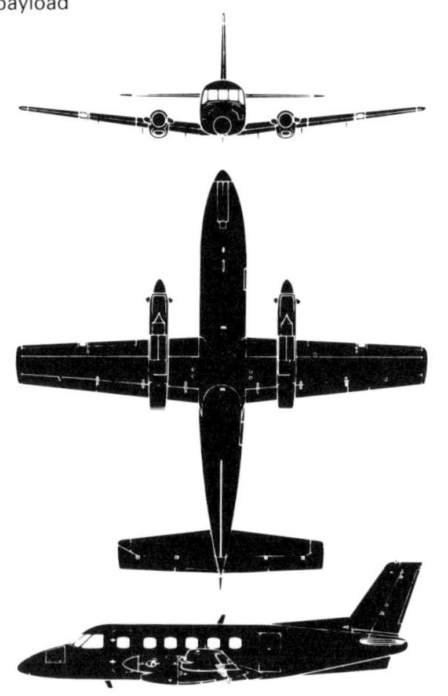

The EMB-110 was developed to meet a Brazilian Air Force requirement for a general-purpose light transport, and the prototype first flew on 26 October 1968, followed by the first production C-95 on 9 August 1972. After initial military requirements had been met, EMBRAER offered a civil version of the Bandeirante, at first for use by Brazilian airlines and private companies, and subsequently for export, in which field it has enjoyed considerable success. The original passenger transport was the EMB-110C with 15 seats; to meet the needs of the Brazilian commuter airlines, the EMB-110P was produced with 18 seats and PT6A-34 engines as an optional alternative to the PT6A-34s. The EMB-110P1 and P2 were the principal versions in 1979, featuring a 2ft 9.5in (0.85m) fuselage 'stretch'; the P1 also has an enlarged rear door for cargo loading and a convertible interior. Other civil versions include the EMB-110B1 for aerial survey, the EMB-110E with executive interior and the EMB-110S1 for geophysical survey duties. More than 200 Bandeirantes had been sold by mid-1979, of which over half were for civil use. Also under development was the EMB-120 Brasilia, a 30-seat commuterliner powered by two 1,500shp PT7A-1 turboprops.

Fokker F27 Friendship and Fairchild Hiller F-27/FH-227

Netherlands/USA

Short/medium-range airliner, in production and service
Photo, silhouette and data: Mk 500

Accommodation: Flight crew of 2-4 and 36-56 passengers
Powered by: Two 2,255ehp Rolls-Royce Dart 532-7R turboprops
Span: 95ft 2in (29.00m)
Length: 82ft 2.5in (25.04m)
Gross weight: 45,000lb (20,410kg)
Max payload: 13,585lb (6,162kg)
Normal cruising speed: 298mph (480km/h) at 20,000ft (6,100m)
Typical range: 1,082 miles (1,741km) with 52 passengers

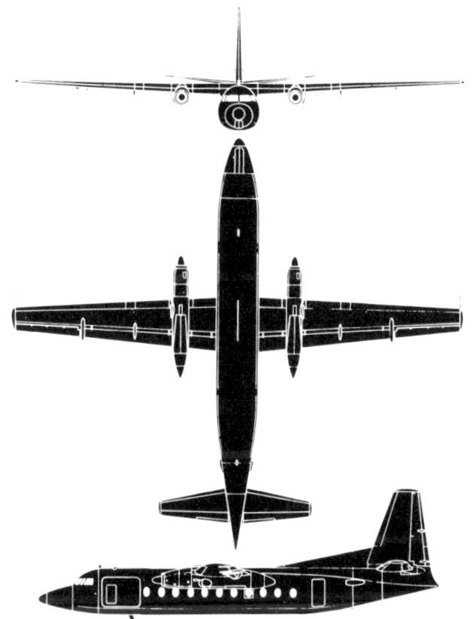

The first prototype of the Friendship (PH-NIV), which flew on 24 November 1955, was powered originally by Dart 507 turboprops and had seats for 28 passengers. The second prototype (PH-NVF), flown on 31 January 1957, was representative of production aircraft, which are still being built by Fokker in the Netherlands. The first Fokker-built production Friendship flew on 23 March 1958 and the first built under licence by Fairchild in the USA flew on 15 April 1958. Deliveries of the latter began in August of that year, and West Coast Airlines was the first to operate the F-27, on 28 September 1958. Deliveries of the Fokker-built F27 also began in 1958, to Aer Lingus, which started operating this type in December. Fokker variants are identified as Mk 100 with Dart 514 engines; Mk 200 with more powerful Dart 532-7s; Mk 300, as 100 but with large cargo loading door and freight floor; Mk 400, as 300 but with Dart 532-7s; Mk 500 with 4ft 11in (1.5m) fuselage 'stretch' (first flown 15 November 1967); and Mk 600, as Mk 200 with added cargo door and quick-change features for passenger or cargo use, but without the Mk 400 freight floor. In 1976, Fokker flew a prototype of the F27 Maritime, a radar-equipped variant for off-shore patrol, based on the Mk 600 airframe, and deliveries of this version began in 1978. As a development of the F27, Fairchild introduced two longer-fuselage versions in 1965, the FH-227 with 6ft (1.83m) stretch and FH-227B with further refinements to permit operation at higher weights. The FH-227C/D/E were modernised versions. Total orders by mid-1979 were for 690 aircraft, for some 150 customers in 60 countries. The total includes 128 F-27s and 77 FH-227s by Fairchild, and more than 160 delivered for military or executive use; the remainder were for airlines.

Fokker F28 Fellowship

Netherlands

Short-range jet airliner, in production and service
Photo, silhouette and data: Mk 4000

Accommodation: Flight crew of 2 and up to 85 passengers
Powered by: Two 9,900lb (4,495kg) st Rolls-Royce Spey 555-15H turbofans
Span: 82ft 3.75in (25.09m)
Length: 97ft 1.75in (29.61m)
Gross weight: 71,000lb (32,200kg)
Max cruising speed: 523mph (843km/h) at 21,000ft (6,400m)
Range: 1,150 miles (1,852km) with max payload

Fokker announced first details of the F28 in April 1962. Two German companies, MBB and VFW-Fokker, participate in the programme to the extent of some 35% (with the German Government contributing 60% of the German share); Shorts have a 19% share in the Fellowship programme, and are responsible for the detail design and construction of the outer wings and other, smaller components. First flight of the F28 (with Spey 550 engines) was made on 9 May 1967, with the second and third aircraft following later in that year. The first order was placed by LTU of Germany; other orders brought total sales to 152 by late-1979, the customers including Aerolineas Argentinas, Aero Peru, Air Anglia, Air Gabon, Air Ivoire, Air Nauru, Air Niugini, Ansett Airlines of Australia, Aviaction, Braathens, Burma Airways, Cimber Air, Garuda, Germanair, Ghana Airways, Iberia, Itavia, KLM/NLM ('City Hopper') Linjeflyg, Martinair, Nigeria Airways, Perlita/Pertamina, Royal Swazi Air, and THY and the governments of Argentina, Colombia, Congo, Ivory Coast, Malaysia, Netherlands, Nigeria, Peru and Togo. The Fellowship Mk 2000 had its fuselage lengthened by 7ft 3in (2.2m) to accommodate up to 79 passengers. The prototype F28 converted to Mk 2000 standard was flown for the first time on 28 April 1971 and the sales total includes 97 Mk 1000 and 10 Mk 2000. A further development programme was initiated in 1972 to provide the F28 with leading-edge slats, permitting an increase in weight without penalising airfield performance. Other modifications included quietened and uprated Spey engines and extended wingtips. The new models were designated Mk 5000 (short fuselage) and Mk 6000 (long fuselage); the prototype Mk 2000 was converted to a Mk 6000 and flew in this form on 27 September 1973. These variants were superseded, however, by the Mk 3000 and Mk 4000, with the extended-span wing and engine improvements but no slats; these, respectively, have Mk 1000 and Mk 2000 fuselage lengths. The Mk 1000C and Mk 3000C have a forward freight door and convertible interiors.

Government Aircraft Factories N22, N24 Nomad

Australia

Twin-turboprop STOL utility transport, in production and service
Photo and data: N24A

Accommodation: Crew of 1-2 and 15 passengers or freight
Powered by: Two 400shp Allison 250-B17B turboprops
Span: 54ft 0in (16.46m)
Length: 47ft 1.25in (14.36m)
Gross weight: 9,400lb (4,263kg)
Normal cruising speed: 193mph (310km/h)
Max range: 840 miles (1,352km), with reserves

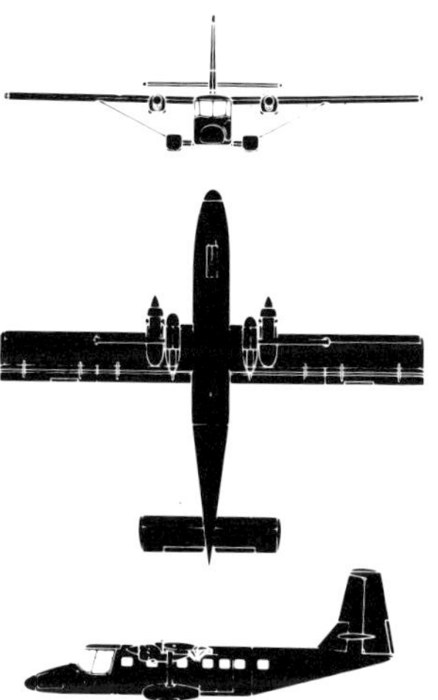

This light STOL transport originated in 1965, when the Fishermen's Bend headquarters of the GAF began design studies for a turboprop utility transport aircraft with both military and civil applications. The first of the two N2 prototypes, produced with government funds, flew on 23 July 1971 and the second on 5 December. The basic N22 production version was similar to the prototypes, although the military version had provision for armour protection, self-sealing fuel tanks and external weapons. After certification on 11 August 1972, the N22 eventually entered commercial service on 18 December 1975. The N22B was the production standard in 1979, with increased gross weight. A higher capacity commercial model was also produced as the N24 and the first six of these were delivered to the Northern Territory Aeromedical Service in 1977. The N24A is the current production version, the fuselage being 3ft 9in (1.14m) longer than that of the N22. About 100 Nomads of all versions had been sold by mid-1979.

Handley Page HPR7 Herald

UK

Short-range airliner, in service
Photo and data: Srs 200

Accommodation: Flight crew of 3 and 38-56 passengers
Powered by: Two 2,105ehp Rolls-Royce Dart 527 turboprops
Span: 94ft 9.5in (28.89m)
Length: 75ft 6in (23.01m)
Gross weight: 43,000lb (19,500kg)
Max payload: 11,700lb (5,307kg)
Max cruising speed: 275mph (442km/h) at 15,000ft (4,575m)
Typical range: 700 miles (1,125km) with max payload at 275mph (442km/h) with reserves

Design of the original HPR3 Herald, by the Reading subsidiary of Handley Page Ltd, was based on an extensive market survey conducted from 1950 onwards. As originally projected, the Herald had four Leonides Major piston-engines and two prototypes were flown in this form, but changing market conditions led to a reappraisal of the design and the substitution of two Darts for the four piston-engines. Both prototypes (G-AODE and G-AODF) were re-engined to this standard, the first flight with Darts being made on 11 March 1958. The first Srs 100 production aircraft (G-APWA) flew in October 1959, and three went into service with BEA on Scottish routes. These aircraft were sold to Autair in 1966 and then to Lineas Aereas La Urraca in 1970. A Herald Srs 200 version, with 42in longer fuselage, was announced in 1960 and British Island Airways had a fleet of 12 of this version operational in 1977. Other users of the Herald 200 at that time were Air Manila (1), Arkia (4), British Air Ferries (8) and Europe Aero Service (2). Also during 1977, eight military Herald Srs 400s originally supplied to the Royal Malaysian Air Force were re-acquired for civil use by UK operators.

By mid-1979, the principal users were British Island Airways with 13 and British Air Ferries with 14, of which six were leased to BIA in 1979 when the latter, as one of the airlines owned by British and Commonwealth Shipping Group, took over the international services flown by BAF, subsequently merging BIA and Air Anglia as Air UK. In addition Air-Bridge Carriers had three Heralds, Europe Air Service in France had two and Lineas Aereas La Urraca still used one.

Hawker Siddeley (DH 106) Comet 4 UK

Medium-range airliner, in service
Photo, silhouette and data: Comet 4B

Accommodation: Flight crew of 2 and 71-101 passengers
Powered by: Four 10,500lb (4,760kg) st Rolls-Royce Avon 525 turbojets
Span: 107ft 10in (32.87m)
Length: 118ft 0in (35.97m)
Gross weight: 158,000lb (71,665kg)
Max payload: 23,900lb (10,840kg)
Max cruising speed: 526mph (846km/h) at 23,500ft (7,160m)
Typical range: 3,120 miles (5,020km) with max payload at 462mph (743km/h)

The first Comet 4 (G-APDA), one of a batch of 19 ordered by BOAC, made its first flight at Hatfield on 27 April 1958, and the next two ('PDB and 'PDC) flew the first-ever jet services across the Atlantic on 4 October 1958. This was the initial version of a new family of Comets evolved from the world's first commercial jet transport. Its predecessors were the Comet 1 and 1A, with four de Havilland Ghost engines, used by BOAC and other operators; the Comet 2 with slightly longer fuselage and Avon 504 engines delivered to RAF Transport Command; and the Comet 3 with much longer fuselage and many other changes. The first production Comet 4B, with shorter wing and no tanks on the wings, flew on 27 June 1959, and this type entered service with BEA in April 1960. The Comet 4C combined the long fuselage of the 4B and the long span of the Comet 4; the first flew in October 1959. By the late 1970s, the only commercial operator of the Comet was Dan-Air which had built up a fleet of nine 4Bs and 11 4Cs by the beginning of 1977, having acquired the last three 4Cs from EgyptAir, the only other recent user of the type. The Comets are being gradually replaced by newer jet types as their airframes become time-expired and the operational fleet in 1979 included only three Comet 4Bs and the six Comet 4Cs that the company had acquired from the RAF and which were, in fact, the last Comets produced. The last of the Dan-Air Comets was expected to be retired at the end of 1980.

Hawker Siddeley (DH 114) Heron (and Saunders ST-27)

UK

Short-range transport, in service
Photo: Lycoming-Heron
Data: Heron 2

Accommodation: Flight crew of 2 and 14-17 passengers
Powered by: Four 250hp Gipsy Queen 30 Mk 2 piston-engines
Span: 71ft 6in (21.79m)
Length: 48ft 6in (14.78m)
Gross weight: 13,500lb (6,123kg)
Cruising speed: 183-191mph (295-307km/h)
Range: 1,180 miles (1,900km) with 2,100lb (925kg) payload

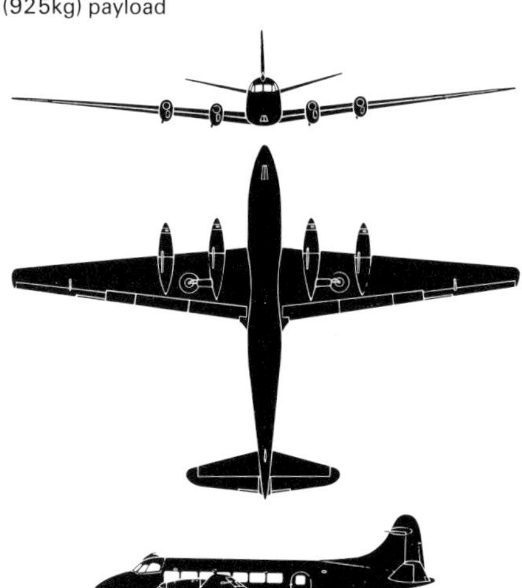

The Heron was developed as a larger-capacity four-engined partner to the Dove; more than 140 were built eventually for feeder-line, local service and executive duties. The Heron 1, of which the prototype (G-ALZL) flew on 10 May 1950, had a fixed tricycle undercarriage. The Heron 2 (prototype G-AMTS flown on 14 December 1952) had a retractable undercarriage and could be fitted optionally with feathering airscrews. Final production versions of both series carried the suffix 'B', while the 'C' and 'D' suffixes indicated specially furnished executive models. In the USA, the Riley company developed a conversion programme to fit 290hp supercharged Lycomings, giving a max speed of 285mph (459km/h), and in 1979 the Puerto Rican local service airline Prinair was using a fleet of 26 of these Riley-Herons, being the largest airline user of the type. A stretched and re-manufactured version of the Heron was developed in Canada by Saunders Aircraft Corporation as the ST-27, with two 783hp PT6A-34 turboprops. A prototype version was flown in England on 28 May 1969, and Saunders produced 12 ST-27s in Canada, most of these being acquired by Air Atonabee after the demise of Saunders in 1976. A single ST-28, which had an all-new airframe, flew on 12 December 1975.

Hawker Siddeley (DH121) Trident — UK

Short/medium-range airliner, in service
Photo: Trident Super 3B
Silhouette: Trident Three
Data: Trident 2E

Accommodation: Flight crew of 3-4 and 128-180 passengers
Powered by: Three 11,960lb (5,425kg) st Rolls-Royce Spey Mk 512-5W turbofans
Span: 98ft 0in (29.87m)
Length: 114ft 9in (35.0m)
Gross weight: 144,000lb (65.500kg)
Max payload: 29,600lb (13,426kg)
Max cruising speed: 596mph (960km/h) at 30,000ft (9,150m)
Typical range: 2,464 miles (3,965km) with 21,378lb (9,679kg) payload and typical reserves

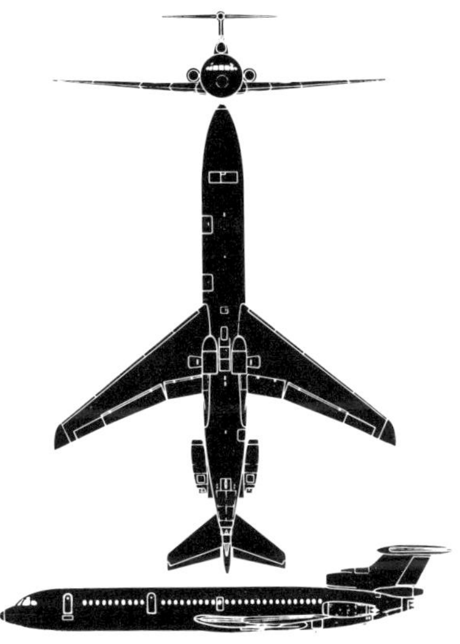

British European Airways (now British Airways) set down its general requirements for a short-haul jet transport in July 1956. To this specification, the DH121, Bristol 200 and Avro 740 were eventually offered and the DH121 was selected in 1958. A contract for 24 was confirmed on 12 August 1959. The first of the BEA Trident 1s (G-ARPA) made its first flight on 9 January 1962, with 9,850lb (4,468kg) st Spey 505 engines, up to 103 seats, and span of 89ft 10in (27.38m). The basic model was followed by 15 Trident 1Es with 11,400lb (5,170kg) st Spey 511-5 engines, up to 115 seats, 95ft (28.96m) wing span and improved high-lift devices, principally for other customers but some eventually serving with BEA/British Airways. By the beginning of 1977, few Trident 1s remained in service. In 1965, BEA ordered 15 Trident Twos (2Es) with higher operating weights and longer range. The first flight of this version was made on 27 July 1967, and it entered service in April 1968. Two were bought subsequently by Cyprus Airways, and China ordered 33 for CAAC.This variant was followed by the Trident Three, which has a longer fuselage, more seats and a Rolls-Royce RB162-86 jet in the rear fuselage to boost take-off performance. The first flight was made on 11 December 1969; and the first take-off using the RB162 was made on 22 March 1970. BEA ordered 26 Trident Threes and put the type into service in April 1971. China placed an order for two Super Trident 3Bs, with 152 seats, increased fuel and gross weight of 158,000lb (71,667kg), delivery of these aircraft in 1975 completing production of the Trident Three series. The last Trident Two for CAAC was delivered in June 1978, ending production with a total of 117 built. Following the discovery of fatigue cracks in several Tridents, the British Airways fleet of Srs Twos and Threes was being modified to have 3ft (91cm) less span and other changes to reduce in-flight bending moments.

Ilyushin Il-14 and Avia 14

USSR

Short-range airliner, in service
Photo: Il-14

Accommodation: Flight crew of 3 and 18-28 passengers
Powered by: Two 1,900hp ASh-82T piston-engines
Span: 103ft 11in (31.67m)
Length: 69ft 9in (21.26m)
Gross weight: 38,000lb (17,235kg)
Max payload: 5,400lb (2,450kg)
Max cruising speed: 198mph (318km/h) at 9,500ft (2,900m)
Typical range: 920 miles (1,480km) with full payload at 161mph (260km/h)

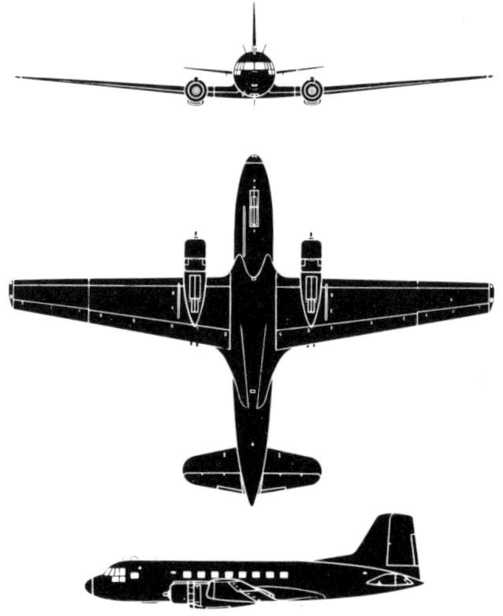

Ilyushin's Il-14, developed from the similar but lower-powered Il-12, was one of the most-produced postwar transports, having been built by the thousand for use by the Soviet Air Force, Aeroflot and the airlines of China and countries in eastern Europe. Two versions were built for civil use: the Il-14P, seating 18-26 passengers, and the Il-14M with a longer cabin to seat 24-28. The East German State Aircraft Factory (VEB) built 80 examples of the Il-14P, and many more were produced at the Avia factory in Czechoslovakia. The Czech-built Avia-14 could be fitted with tip-tanks; the passenger version was known as the Avia-14 Salon, and a version with large loading doors and strengthened floor was built as a freighter. Many Il-14P and Il-14M airliners were later converted to Il-14T freighters; well over 50 are still in service with Aeroflot in Russia, some in the Polar region. A few others can be seen in service with airlines such as Cubana (about 10) and Mongolian (three). CAAC of China is believed to have more than 50 still operational, including Il-14M and Il-14P versions. In East Germany, Interflug uses a single VEB-built Il-14P for calibration flights and crew training.

Ilyushin Il-18

USSR

Medium-range airliner, in service
Data: Il-18D

Accommodation: Flight crew of 4-5 and up to 122 passengers
Powered by: Four 4,250ehp Ivchenko AI-20M turboprops
Span: 122ft 8.5in (37.40m)
Length: 117ft 9in (35.90m)
Gross weight: 141,100lb (64,000kg)
Max payload: 29,750lb (13,500kg)
Max cruising speed: 419mph (675km/h) at 30,000ft (9,150m)
Range: 2,300 miles (3,700km) with max payload (1-hour reserve) at 388mph (625km/h)

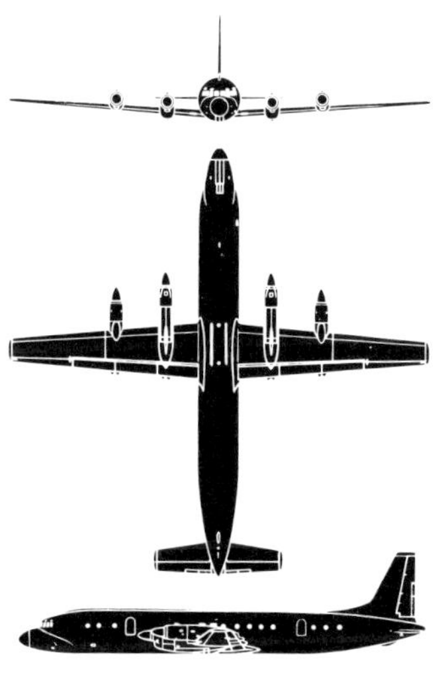

The Il-18 is a contemporary of the American Electra, and is comparable in performance with the Electra and Vanguard. It was first flown in July 1957, and a batch of 20 was quickly produced for service trials and proving and development flights. Scheduled freight services were operated by Il-18s in the early months of 1959, followed by the first passenger services, on routes from Moscow to Alma Ata and Adler, on 20 April. The Il-18 was introduced on many new domestic and international routes by Aeroflot from 1960. It proved to be among the most successful Soviet airliners for export, deliveries being made to Air Guinee (3), Air Mali (3), Air Mauritanie (1), Balkan Bulgarian Airlines (12), CAAC in China (at least 15), CSA (11), Cubana (5), EgyptAir (5), Ghana Airways (8, later returned to Russia), the East German Interflug (16), LOT (8), Malev (9), Royal Afghan Airlines (1), Tarom (14) and Yemen Arab Airlines (1), as well as to several foreign governments and air forces. The standard Aeroflot version was the 90/110-seat Il-18V, with 4,000ehp AI-20K engines. The Il-18E (more accurately rendered from the Soviet form as Il-18Ye) had more powerful AI-20M engines and revised internal layout, and the Il-18D was similar with increased fuel capacity, higher weights and other improvements. More than 800 Il-18s are believed to have been built, mostly for Aeroflot, and about half this number were still serving in 1979.

Ilyushin Il-62 and Il-62M

USSR

Long-range jet airliner, in production and service
Photo: Il-62
Silhouette and data: Il-62M

Accommodation: Flight crew of 5 and up to 198 passengers
Powered by: Four 25,350lb (11,500kg) st Soloviev D-30K turbofans
Span: 141ft 9in (43.20m)
Length: 174ft 3.5in (53.12m)
Gross weight: 363,435lb (165,000kg)
Max payload: 50,700lb (23,000kg)
Normal cruising speed: 528-560mph (850-900km/h)
Range: 4,970 miles (8,000km) with max payload (1-hour fuel reserve)

First details of the Il-62 were given in the Soviet press in September 1962, followed in January 1963 by the first flight of the prototype. In September 1963, it was reported that three Il-62s were being flight tested, with 16,535lb (7,500kg) st Lyulka AL-7 engines fitted temporarily. When the intended 20,150lb (10,500kg) st Kuznetsov NK-8-4 engines became available, considerable flight development was undertaken, including work necessary to overcome low-speed handling problems associated with the wing design. The Il-62 entered scheduled service with Aeroflot during 1967, replacing Tu-114s and Tu-104s on selected internal routes. In September 1967, Il-62s took over from Tu-114s on the service to Montreal, this being the first transatlantic jet service by Aeroflot. It was followed by inauguration of a Moscow-New York service in July 1968; and the Il-62 first appeared at London Airport on 11 May 1968, operated on lease by CSA. CSA has seven Il-62s in service in 1979, Cubana has four, the East German Interflug five, LOT seven, Tarom four, CAAC five. The re-engined Il-62M appeared in 1971 and entered service with Aeroflot on the Moscow-Havana route in 1974. In addition to the more powerful and more economic engines, it has an extra fuel tank in the fin; normal seating capacity is 186. A further development, the Il-62MK, had D-30KU engines derated to 24,250lb (11,000kg) st each and higher take-off and landing weights. With up to 195 seats, this version has a range of 5,965 miles (9,600km).

Ilyushin Il-86

USSR

Large-capacity medium-range tranport, in production

Accommodation: Flight crew of 3-4 and up to 350 passengers, nine-abreast in a single class layout; typical mixed class layout for 206 eight-abreast and 28 six-abreast
Powered by: Four 28,635lb (13,000kg) st Kuz-Kuznetsov NK-86 turbofans
Span: 157ft 8.5in (48.06m)
Length: 195ft 4in (59.54m)
Gross weight: 454,150lb (206,000kg)
Max payload: 92,500lb (42,000kg)
Cruising speed: 560-590mph (900-950km/h) at 30,000ft (9,000m)
Range: 2,235 miles (3,600km) with full passenger payload

Evolution of an 'airbus' type of aircraft to operate on Aeroflot trunk routes within the Soviet Union, where air traffic has been growing at a rapid pace in recent years, began in the late 1960s, when design proposals were made by the Antonov, Ilyushin and Tupolev design bureaux. Of these proposals, that by Ilyushin (known as the Il-86) was selected for further development in 1972. The favoured configuration was then rear-engined, similar to that of the Il-62, with a much enlarged fuselage. Further design study, however, showed that the weight penalty of the rear-engined arrangement was unacceptable in an aircraft of this size, and by the end of 1972 work was concentrated on an aircraft with four wing pods, using for the first time in a Soviet airliner, the classic configuration favoured on the US West Coast. A unique feature of the Il-86, from the earliest design stage, is the provision of vestibules at lower-deck level, beneath the main passenger floor, allowing passengers to board by way of air-stairs in the vestibule doors, stow their carry-on baggage and then proceed to internal stairways to the main deck. Also beneath this deck are two cargo holds designed to accommodate standard LD3 containers. When first announced, it was expected that the Il-86 would fly in 1975, powered by Soloviev D-30KP turbofans; a delay of one year ensued when it was decided to make use of a more powerful and new Kuznetsov engine that is reported to have undergone initial flight testing beneath the wing of an Il-62. The Il-86 made its first flight on 22 December 1976, and the first aircraft from the production line at Voronezh flew on 24 October 1977.

Let L-410 Turbolet

Czechoslovakia

Twin-turboprop light passenger/freight transport, in production and service
Photo and data: L-410UVP

Accommodation: Flight crew of 1-2 and 15-19 passengers
Powered by: Two 730ehp Walter M601B turboprops
Span: 63ft 9.5in (19.49m)
Length: 47ft 5in (14.47m)
Gross weight: 12,566lb (5,700kg)
Max payload: 2,885lb (1,310kg)
Max cruising speed: 227mph (365km/h) at 9,850ft (3,000m)
Max range: 646 miles (1,040km), with reserves

This twin-turboprop light transport is a product of the Let National Corporation at Kunovice. Design began in 1966, with the object of producing an aircraft suitable for operation from grass airfields. The L-410 prototype flew for the first time on 16 April 1969, with 715ehp Pratt & Whitney PT6A-27 turboprops, which became standard on production L-410As, intended primarily for export to Western nations. Deliveries began in September 1971, initially to Slov-Air, a newly-formed Czechoslovakian internal airline, and five L-410As were supplied to Aeroflot for evaluation. The L-410M with Czechoslovakian M601 engines first flew in 1974 and deliveries began in 1976, this version being intended primarily for Eastern nations. The L-410AF is a special photo-survey version with enlarged and extensively glazed nose. Recommendations made by Aeroflot after its evaluation of the L-410As led to the development of the L-410UVP, which has a longer fuselage to improve passenger comfort, increased wing span, spoilers on the wing, a taller fin and rudder and dihedral on the tailplane. A prototype with a longer fuselage flew in 1977 but was lost during flight testing and the first L-410UVP appeared in 1979.

Lockheed L-188 Electra

USA

Medium-range airliner, in service
Data: L-188C

Accommodation: Flight crew of 3-4 and 66-99 passengers
Powered by: Four 3,750ehp Allison 501-D13 turboprops
Span: 99ft 0in (30.17m)
Length: 104ft 8in (31.90m)
Gross weight: 116,000lb (52,615kg)
Max payload: 26,400lb (11,975kg)
Max cruising speed: 405mph (652km/h) at 22,000ft (6,700m)
Typical range: 2,500 miles (4,020km) with 22,000lb (9,980kg) payload at 380mph (611km/h)

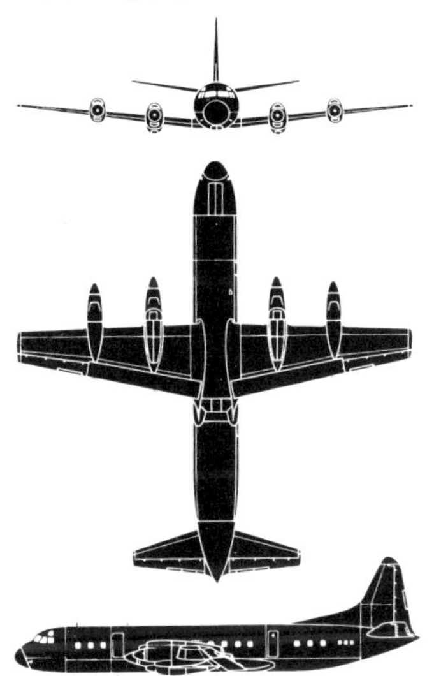

Development of the Electra was begun to meet the specific needs of US domestic operators in 1956, and the first flight was made on 6 December 1957. Fourteen airlines ordered 165 Electras, and the last of these were delivered in May 1962. Eastern Air Lines was first to put the Electra into service on 12 January 1959, followed by American Airlines on 23 January and other US operators during 1959. First overseas airlines to use the Electra were Cathay Pacific, Ansett-ANA, TAA and Qantas, all in 1959. The first Electra operator in Europe (and the only European airline to order the Electra) was KLM, which operated the type from 1959 to 1968. Major US airlines which operated large fleets of Electras have replaced them with jet aircraft, but the type has seen service with many smaller airlines, mainly in North, Central and South America and Australasia, on passenger and freight services, and some of these operators still use it. Considerable numbers of Electras have been modified for freighting, by Lockheed Aircraft Services, with a large freight-loading door in the forward fuselage. More recently, American Jet Industries (now Gulfstream American Inc) produced a similar conversion scheme for the Electra to suit it to the cargo role, with a hydraulically-operated outward/upward opening door, pressurised cargo cabin, strengthened floor and provision for a pallet loading system. Thus modified, the Electra can carry a load of 35,000lb (15,875kg) for nearly 2,000 miles (3,220km) cruising at 403mph (649km/h). Nearly 100 Electras were flying in regular airline service at the beginning of 1979.

Lockheed L-1011-1, -100, -200 TriStar

USA

Large-capacity medium range transport in production and service
Photo: L-1011-1
Data: L-1011-200

Accommodation: Flight crew of 3 and up to 400 passengers
Powered by: Three 48,000lb (21,772kg) st Rolls-Royce RB211-524 turbofans
Span: 155ft 4in (47.34m)
Length: 177ft 8.5in (54.2m)
Gross weight: 466,000lb (211,374kg)
Max payload: 72,800lb (33,022kg)
Cruising speed: 560mph (901km/h) at 35,000ft (10,670m)
Range: 4,450 miles (7,160km) with 273 passengers

The Lockheed company re-entered the commercial aircraft scene in June 1968 when it decided to go ahead with production of the Model 385 TriStar — its first airliner since the turboprop Electra. After early studies of a twin-engined design to meet an American Airlines outline specification of 1965, Lockheed elected to use a three-engined layout, with two underwing pods and the third engine in the rear fuselage. A broadly similar layout was chosen independently for the competitive DC-10. Initial orders for the TriStar came from Eastern Air Lines and Delta Air Lines. First flight was made at Palmdale on 16 November 1970, and four more TriStars had flown by December 1971; airline deliveries began in April 1972. The first Tri-Star passenger service was operated by Eastern on 15 April and scheduled services began 11 days later. The customer airlines for TriStars of the original type (see also TriStar 500) comprise Air Canada, All Nippon, British Airways, Cathay Pacific, Delta, Eastern, Gulf Air, LTU, Saudia, Trans Carib Air and TWA. Most are TriStars of the original L-1011-1 type, with 42,000lb (19,050kg) st RB211-22B engines and 430,000lb (195,045kg) gross weight; some later aircraft have 43,500lb (19,730kg) st RB211-22F engines. Also in service are a few L-1011-100s with the -22 engines, either 450,000lb (204,120kg) or 466,000lb (211,374kg) weight and extra fuel for increased range. With this same increased fuel capacity and alternative higher weights, the L-1011-200 has 48,000lb (21,772kg) st RB211-524 engines. A prototype with these engines first flew on 12 August 1976 and the -200 has been specified by Saudia, British Airways and Trans Carib Air.

Lockheed L-1011-500 TriStar

USA

Large capacity long-range transport, in production and service

Accommodation: Flight crew of 2-3 and up to 300 passengers
Powered by: Three 50,000lb (26,680kg) st Rolls-Royce RB211-524B turbofans
Span: 164ft 4in (50.08m)
Length: 164ft 2.5in (50.05m)
Gross weight: 496,000lb (224,980kg)
Max payload: 97,037lb (44,015kg)
Cruising speed: 558-605mph (899-973km/h) at 30,000ft (9,145m)
Range: 6,000 miles (9,683km) with max payload

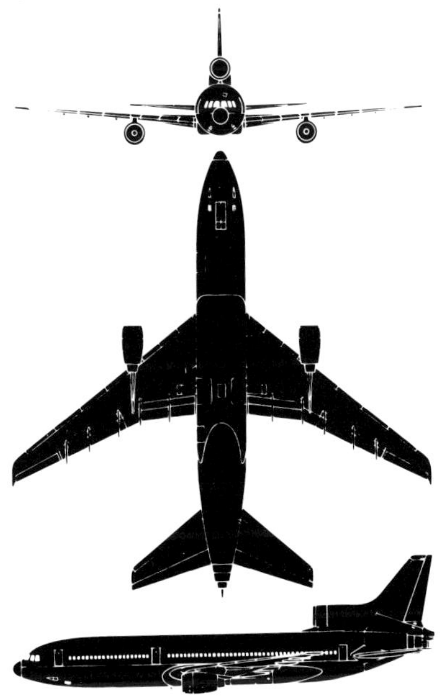

The L-1011-500 version of the Lockheed TriStar was launched in August 1977 when British Airways placed an initial order for six to add to its previously ordered fleet of L-1011-1s. The -500 differed in having the fuselage shortened by 13ft 6in (4.11m), reducing the accommodation to 246 in typical mixed class layouts; increased fuel capacity for greater range; higher operating weights and uprated engines. In addition, Lockheed developed 'active controls' for the TriStar while the -500 was being produced and these have become a standard feature of the production version; active controls involve a 9ft (2.74m) increase in wing span, modifications to the ailerons and other changes to improve efficiency in cruising flight and thereby reduce fuel consumption. The first -500 TriStar (without active controls) flew on 16 October 1978 and entered service with British Airways in May 1979. Other customers for this variant include Delta, Pan American, Air Canada, Aero Peru and LTU. A projected variant combining the original fuselage with the increased fuel capacity and higher weights of the -500 has been designated the L-1011-250. Other projected variants are the L-1011-300 with a lengthened fuselage and the -400 with a shorter fuselage and an advanced-technology wing. By end-1979, total firm sales of all TriStar variants stood at 237, with another 70 on option.

McDonnell Douglas DC-8 Srs 10 to 50 USA

Long-range airliner, in service
Silhouette and data: DC-8 Srs 50

Accommodation: Flight crew of 3-5 and 116-179 passengers
Powered by: Four 18,000lb (8,172kg) st Pratt & Whitney JT3D-3B turbofans
Span: 142ft 5in (43.41m)
Length: 150ft 6in (45.87m)
Gross weight: 325,000lb (147,415kg)
Max payload: 34,360lb (15,585kg)
Max cruising speed: 580mph (933km/h) at 30,000ft (9,150m)
Range: 5,720 miles (9,205km) with max payload

The DC-8 was developed by the Douglas Aircraft Co (prior to its merging with McDonnell) during the early 1950s, to maintain the company's competitive position vis-a-vis Boeing, which flew the prototype of its first jet transport in July 1954. A year later, in June 1955, Douglas decided to proceed with construction and certification of its own comparable jetliner, the DC-8, and in October 1955 Pan American became the first customer with an order for 20. Several versions of the DC-8 were offered from the start and these eventually became designated as the Srs 10, with 13,500lb (6.124kg) st P&W JT3C-6 turbojets and 273,000lb (123,830kg) gross weight, principally for US domestic airlines; the similar Srs 20 with 15,800lb (7,167kg) st JT4A-3 engines; the intercontinental Srs 30 with 16,800lb (7,620kg) st JT4A-9 or 17,500lb (7,945kg) st JT4A-11 engines and weights up to 315,000lb (142,880kg); and the similar Srs 40 with 17,500lb (7,945kg) st Rolls-Royce Conway 509 turbofans. The first DC-8 (a Srs 10) flew on 30 May 1958; the first Srs 20 was the second example to fly, on 29 November 1958, and the first Srs 30 flew on 21 February 1959. Production of these versions totalled (in addition to one company-owned prototype demonstrator), 28 Srs 10s, 34 Srs 20s, 57 Srs 30s and 32 Srs 40s. Still with the same overall dimensions, the DC-8 Srs 50 introduced JT3D turbofan engines and was first flown on 20 December 1960. The Srs 50 Jet Trader introduced a side-loading freight door and convertible passenger/cargo interior. A total of 87 Srs 50s and 54 Srs 50 Jet Traders was built, bringing the total for all these early versions to 293; a number of Srs 10s, 20s and 30s was later converted to Srs 50 standard.

McDonnell Douglas DC-8 Srs 60 and 70 USA

Long/very-long range airliner, in service
Photo: DC-8 Srs 61
Silhouette and data: DC-8 Super 63

Accommodation: Flight crew of 3-5 and up to 259 passengers
Powered by: Four 19,000lb (8,618kg) st Pratt & Whitney JT3D-7 turbofans
Span: 148ft 5in (45.23m)
Length: 187ft 5in (57.12m)
Gross weight: 350,000lb (158,760kg)
Max payload: 67,735lb (30,719kg)
Max cruising speed: 600mph (965km/h) at 30,000ft (9,150m)
Range: 4,500 miles (7,240km) with max payload (normal reserves)

For 10 years after starting work on the DC-8 programme, Douglas maintained the same overall dimensions for all variants of the design (see previous page). In 1965, however, three new versions emerged, offering two alternative fuselage lengths and other changes to meet specific airline requirements. The three new models were known collectively as the Super Sixty series. All had turbofan engines — either 18,000lb (8,172kg) st JT3D-3Bs or 19,000lb (8,618kg) st JT3D-7s — and comprised the Srs 61, similar to the Srs 50 with fuselage lengthened by 36ft 8in (11.18m) to accommodate up to 259 passengers; the Srs 62 with fuselage lengthened only by 6ft 8in (2.03m) but with other modifications for maximum range including extended wingtips, more fuel and low-drag nacelles and pylons; and the Srs 63 combining the long fuselage of the Srs 61 with the aerodynamic refinements of the Srs 62. All three models were available in all-passenger, convertible or all-cargo configuration. The first Srs 61 flew on 14 March 1966, the first Srs 62 on 29 August 1966, and the first Srs 63 on 10 April 1967. A total of 263 Super Sixty series DC-8s were built, made up of 78 Srs 61, 10 Srs 61CF, 52 Srs 62; 16 Srs 62C/AF, 41 Srs 63 and 66 Srs 63CF/AF/PF. To extend the useful life of the Sixty-series DC-8s, as well as improving their operating economics and maximum range, a retrofit programme was launched in mid-1979 to introduce 22,000lb (9,988kg) st GE/SNECMA CFM-56 turbofans. Converted Srs 61, 62 and 63 are redesig-Srs 63, two Srs 61) and United (30 Srs 61). Spantax, Capitol International, Cargolux and Transamerica later contracted for a total of 15 more Srs 70s. The first Srs 71 was to fly in 1981.

McDonnell Douglas DC-9 Srs 10 to 30 USA

Short/medium-range jet airliner, in production and service
Photo: Srs 30
Silhouette and data: Srs 10

Accommodation: Flight crew of 2 and up to 115 passengers
Powered by: Two 75,500lb (7,030kg) st Pratt & Whitney JT8D-15 turbofans
Span: 93ft 5in (28.5m)
Length: 119ft 4in (36.37m)
Gross weight: 108,000lb (49,000kg)
Max payload: 29,860lb (13,550kg)
Max cruising speed: 572mph (918km/h)
Range: 1,100 miles (1,770km) with max payload

Design studies for the DC-9 were started by Douglas soon after the DC-8 had been launched. After several configurations had been considered, the now-familiar rear-engined short/medium-range airliner was announced in April 1963. First flight of the prototype was made on 25 February 1965, followed by four more DC-9s in the initial Series 10 form by the middle of that year. Certification was completed in record time, to permit Delta Air Lines to fly the first commercial service only nine months after the DC-9's first flight, on 29 November 1965. Altogether, 113 DC-9 Srs 10s were sold, plus 24 DC-9 Srs 10F/CFs incorporating a side-loading freight door in the forward fuselage; these variants are no longer in production. As a first step towards evolving a complete family of short-haul transports from the basic DC-9, Douglas developed the Srs 30 with more powerful engines, increased span, a 14ft 11in (4.6m) longer fuselage, full-span wing leading-edge slats and double-slotted flaps. The first flight of a Srs 30 was made on 1 August 1956, and Eastern Air Lines began scheduled services with this version on 1 February 1967. Successive Srs 30 variants have offered 14,000lb (6,350kg) st JT8D-7, 14,500lb (6,575kg) st JT8D-9, 15,000lb (6,804kg) st JT8D-11 and 15,500lb (7,031kg) st JT8D-15 engines; and an extended-range version became available in 1976 with extra fuel, increased gross weights and JT8D-17 engines. A Srs 30CF convertible version was also produced. After the Srs 30 had been developed the company produced 10 Srs 20s to a special SAS requirement, featuring the Srs 10 fuselage with Srs 30 wings for 'hot and high' airfield operation. The first Srs 20 flew on 18 September 1968, with JT8D-9 engines.

McDonnell Douglas DC-9 Srs 40, 50 and 80 USA

Short/medium range airliner, in production and service
Photo and silhouette: Srs 50
Data: Srs 80

Accommodation: Flight crew of 2 and up to 139 passengers
Powered by: Two 18,500lb (8,392kg) st Pratt & Whitney JT8D-209 turbofans
Span: 107ft 10in (32.87m)
Length: 147ft 10in (45.06m)
Gross weight: 140,000lb (63,502kg)
Max payload: 40,203lb (18,236kg)
Max cruising speed: 558mph (898km/h) at 25,000ft (7,620m)
Range: 2,372 miles (3,817m) with typical payload

Continuing the policy of offering a wide range of DC-9 variants to match the needs of particular airlines, McDonnell Douglas followed up the Srs 30 with the Srs 40. First flown on 28 November 1967, this variant had JT8D-9 or JT8D-15 engines, more fuel and an increased length of 125ft 7.25in (38.28m), providing accommodation for 125 passengers; gross weight of this version, which has only been ordered by SAS and Toa Domestic, was set at 114,000lb (51,710kg). The DC-9 Srs 50 which was announced in July 1973, is lengthened by a further 12ft 7.25in (3.84m) compared with the Srs 30, to seat up to 139 passengers, and has JT8D-17 engines. The first Srs 50 flew on 17 December 1974 and this variant entered service with Swissair on 24 August 1975. In 1975, a DC-9 was test-flown with refanned JT8D-109 engines, providing a basis for the development of the DC-9 Super 80, which was given a go-ahead in October 1977 and features 18,500lb (8,400kg) st JT8D-207 refanned engines, a still longer fuselage (14ft 3in (4.23m) more than the Srs 50), increased span and numerous other improvements. Swissair was the first customer and by the time the first example flew on 18 October 1979, 11 customers had ordered 70 Super 80s and taken options on 22. Total DC-9 orders had then passed the 1,050 mark, with over 900 delivered.

McDonnell Douglas DC-10 USA

Large-capacity medium/long-range transport, in production and service
Photo, silhouette and data: Srs 30

Accommodation: Flight crew of 5 and up to 345 passengers
Powered by: Three 49,000lb (22,226kg) st General Electric CF6-50A or 51,000lb (23,133kg) st CF6-50C or 52,500lb (23,814kg) st CF6-50C2 turbofans
Span: 165ft 4in (50.39m)
Length: 182ft 1in (55.50m)
Gross weight: 572,000lb (259,450kg)
Max payload: 106,550lb (48,330kg)
Max cruising speed: 564mph (908km/h) at 31,000ft (9,450m)
Range: 4,606 miles (7,413km) with max payload (with reserves)

Design of the DC-10 was crystallised during 1966, after American Airlines had circulated an outline requirement for a large-capacity transport capable of operating from smaller airports on its US domestic network and over short-to-medium ranges. Following initial studies of a twin-engined aeroplane, the company selected a three-engine layout and orders from American Airlines and United Air Lines early in 1968 signalled a go-ahead. The initial variant was the Srs 10, intended primarily for US domestic service, powered by 41,000lb (18,597kg) st CF6-6D1 engines and with a gross weight of 440,000lb (199,580kg). The first Srs 10 flew for the first time on 29 August 1970, and first airline services were flown in August 1971. For operation over longer (intercontinental) ranges, the Srs 30 had greater fuel capacity, higher operating weights, uprated CF6 engines, a 10ft (3.05m) increase in span and an additional, central main undercarriage leg. The Srs 40 was similar to the 30 but introduced 48,500lb (22,000kg) st Pratt & Whitney JT9D-20 or (later) 53,000lb (24,040kg) st JT9D-59A engines, the gross weight with the former being 555,000lb (251,744kg), as it was for the earlier Srs 30s. The Srs 40 was the first of the intercontinental models to be ordered (by Northwest) was therefore the first to fly, on 28 February 1972; deliveries began on 10 November 1972. The first Srs 30 flew on 21 June 1972 and entered service at the end of the year. A passenger/cargo convertible version of the DC-10 was also developed, with side-loading cargo doors, and the first such Srs 30CF flew on 28 February 1973. By mid-1979, DC-10 sales totalled 342 with 51 more on option. A number of possible 'stretched' variants had been offered to the airlines as the Srs 61, 62 and 63.

NAMC YS-11

Japan

Short/medium-range airliner, in service
Silhouette: YS-11A-300
Data: YS-11A-200

Accommodation: Flight crew of 2 and 52-60 passengers
Powered by: Two 3,060ehp Rolls-Royce Dart 542-10K turboprops
Span: 105ft 0in (32.00m)
Length: 86ft 3.5in (26.30m)
Gross weight: 54,010lb (24,500kg)
Max payload: 14,508lb (6,581kg)
Max cruising speed: 291mph (469km/h) at 15,000ft (4,575m)
Range: 680-2,000 miles (1,090-3,215km) at 281mph (452km/h) at 20,000ft (6,100m)

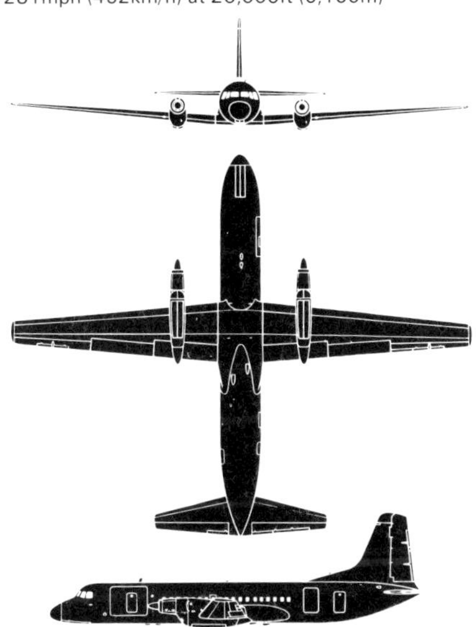

First postwar Japanese transport of original design, the YS-11 was developed by a consortium of the nation's manufacturers, primarily to meet the requirements of Japanese civil and military operators. The first of two prototypes flew on 30 August 1962, and the first production model in the autumn of 1964. Toa Airways (later merged with JDA to become Toa Domestic) operated the first airline service with the YS-11 on 1 April 1965, and All Nippon also began using the type during that year. In 1966, NAMC announced a new series of YS-11s with higher operating weights, permitting an increase of up to 2,970lb (1,347kg) in payload for a given range. These new versions were the YS-11A-200 passenger model (first flown on 27 November 1967), YS-11A-300 mixed passenger/cargo type (flown in 1968) and YS-11A-400 freighter (first flown on 17 September 1969); the -300 and -400 have enlarged doors for freight loading, the latter having been built only for military use. During 1970, certification was obtained for the YS-11A-500 and -600, similar respectively to the -200 and -300 with 1,100lb (500kg) increase in gross weights, but only a few examples of these variants were sold by the time YS-11 production came to an end, in 1972. A total of 182 YS-11s had been built; operators in 1979 included Air Ivoire, All Nippon, Austral, China Airlines, Merpati Nusantara, Olympic, PT Pelita Air Service, Philippine Airlines, Piedmont, Pinehurst Airlines, Reeve Aleutian, SGA (Zaire), Southwest Air Lines (Japan), Toa Domestic and Transair (Canada).

Pilatus Britten-Norman BN-2A Mk III Trislander UK

Light feeder-line transport, in production and service
Data: BN-2A Mk III-2

Accommodation: Flight crew of 1-2 and 16-17 passengers
Powered by: Three 260hp Lycoming O-540-E4C5 piston-engines
Span: 53ft 0in (16.15m)
Length: 47ft 6.25in (14.48m)
Gross weight: 10,000lb (4,536kg)
Max payload: 3,550lb (1,610kg)
Max cruising speed: 166mph (267km/h)
Max range: 1,000 miles (1,610km)

The original Britten-Norman company developed the unconventional Trislander by extending the fuselage of the Islander and adding a third engine. The extra length was provided by inserting a 7ft 6in (2.29m) portion of standard parallel-section fuselage and the third engine was located in a nacelle on the fin. Apart from some structural strengthening, the remainder of the airframe remained substantially unchanged. After a long-fuselage version of the Islander had been tested in 1968, the second prototype Islander was converted to the full three-engined configuration and flew as the Islander III prototype (now named Trislander) on 11 September 1970. A production prototype Trislander flew on 6 March 1971, and deliveries began in June of that year. Production was transferred to Belgium in 1973 after the Fairey Group acquired Britten-Norman but was restored to the original Isle of Wight site after Pilatus had acquired the company from the Fairy Group receiver. in 1979. First production Trislanders had a gross weight of 9,350lb (4,245kg) but this was increased to 10,000lb (4,540kg) in the BN-2A Mk III-1. On 18 August 1974, the first flight was made of the BN-2A Mk III-2 version, which features a lengthened nose incorporating baggage stowage space. About 50 Trislanders had been delivered by the middle of 1979.

Shorts 330

UK

Commuter and local-service passenger and freight transport in production and service

Accommodation: Flight crew of 2 and 30 passengers, 7,500lb (3,400kg) of freight, or mixed passenger/cargo loads
Powered by: Two 1,156shp Pratt & Whitney (Canada) PT6A-45A turboprops
Span: 74ft 8in (22.76m)
Length: 58ft 0.5in (17.69m)
Gross weight: 22,400lb (10,160kg)
Max payload: 5,850lb (2,655kg) in passenger configuration
Max cruising speed: 227mph (365km/h) at 10,000ft (3,050m)
Range: 506 miles (814km) at 227mph (365km/h) with 30 passengers and baggage, no reserves

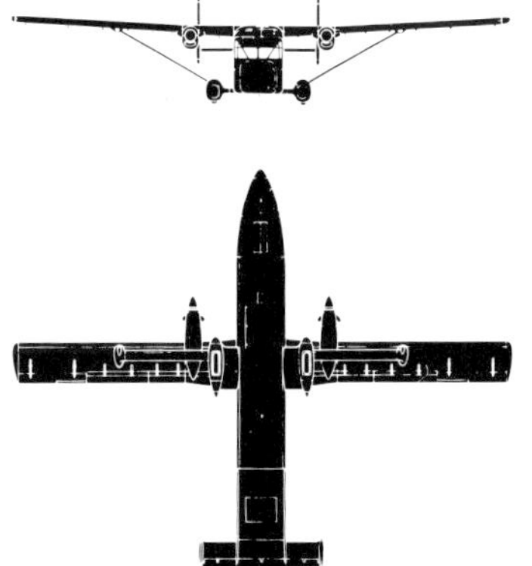

Derived from the Skyvan, the SD3-30 embodies the same outer wings, tail unit and large cabin cross-section. By lengthening the cabin 12ft 5in (3.78m), Shorts have produced a suitable replacement for the current generation of 18/20-seat commuter transports on routes where traffic is expanding rapidly. Passengers enter through a rear door on the port side. This is supplemented on freight-carrying versions by a door at the front large enough to admit standard D size containers. Seven containers of this size can be packed into the cabin, with ample room around them for other freight. The floor is only 3ft (0.91m) above the ground, for easy loading, and the aircraft can be supplied with a large Skyvan-type ramp-door under the rear fuselage if required. Two prototypes of the SD3-30 were built initially; the first of these flew on 22 August 1974 and the second on 8 July 1975. The first production aircraft flew on 15 December 1975, and British certification was obtained on 18 February 1976. Initial orders for three aircraft each, had been placed by Time Air of Canada and Command Airways of the USA, and the first commercial service was flown by the SD3-30 (now known as the Shorts 330) on 24 August 1976, in the Time Air colours. By mid-1979 the sales total had passed the 50 mark, customers including Air North, ALM in the Netherlands Antilles, DLT in Germany, Loganair in the UK and Golden West Airlines, Hawaiian Air, Henson Aviation, Mississippi Valley Airlines, Suburban Airlines, Chautauqua Airlines, and Metro Airlines in the USA.

Shorts SC7 Skyvan and Skyliner UK

General-purpose light STOL transport, in production and service
Photo and data: Skyvan Srs 3

Accommodation: Flight crew of 1-2 and up to 19 passengers, 12 stretchers or 4,600lb (2,085kg) of freight
Powered by: Two 715shp AiResearch TPE 331-201 turboprops
Span: 64ft 11in (19.79m)
Length: 40ft 1in (12.21m)
Max payload: 4,600lb (2,086kg)
Gross weight: 12,500lb (5,670kg)
Cruising speed: 173-203mph (278-327km/h) at 10,000ft (3,050m)
Range: 187-694 miles (300-1,115km), with reserves according to payload

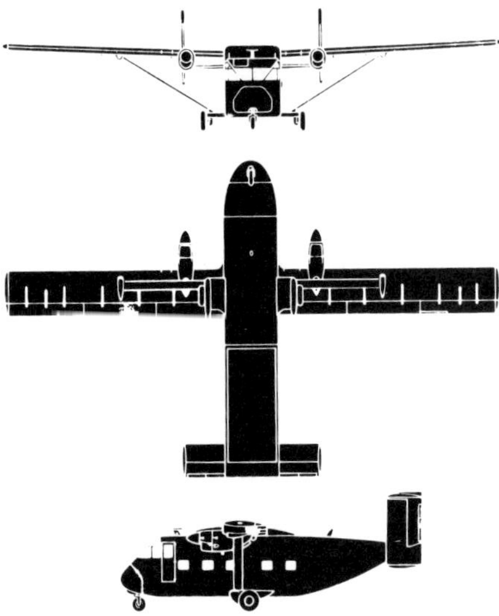

The Skyvan was designed as a simple, capacious utility transport able to lift a two-ton payload from any half-mile airstrip. The prototype flew originally, on 17 January 1963, with 390hp Continental GTSIO-520 piston-engines. Following the decision to switch to turboprop power, it was re-engined with Astazou IIs, flying again on 2 October 1963. Three development aircraft and 16 initial production Srs 2 Skyvans were next produced with 730ehp Astazou XIIs, before TPE 331 engines were standardised for the Srs 3, first flown on 15 December 1967. Deliveries began in the following Summer, with a few converted Srs 2 airframes preceding genuine Srs 3s. Civil and military orders for about 130 TPE 331-engined aircraft had been received by mid-1979, including one Srs 3A Skyvan with a gross weight of 13,700lb (6,215kg) and nine all-passenger Skyliners able to carry 19 or 22 passengers in de luxe accommodation. Many of the 60 or so Skyvan 3s included in the overall total were also in airline use. Customers for the VIP Skyliner Executive model have included the King of Nepal.

Swearingen Metro and Merlin IV

USA

Twin turboprop commuter airliner and corporate transport, in production and service
Photo and data: Metro II

Accommodation: Flight crew of 2 and up to 20 passengers or varied passenger/cargo payloads
Powered by: Two 940shp AiResearch TPE 331-3UW-303G turboprops
Span: 46ft 3in (14.10m)
Length: 59ft 4.75in (18.10m)
Gross weight: 12,500lb (5,670kg)
Max payload: 3,920lb (1,778kg)
Cruising speed: 279-294mph (449-473km/h) at 10,000ft (3,050m)
Range: 100 miles (160km) with max payload and reserves

The Swearingen company, which became a wholly-owned subsidiary of Fairchild Industries in 1971, had previously developed and started production of the Metro as the largest in its range of twin-turboprop aircraft. These had originated as developments of the Beech Queen Air, for which the company first developed a new pressurised fuselage, and then a turboprop installation in the original wing structure. With these types established in production as the Merlin II series, Swearingen then developed new wings and tail units, so that the Merlin III business transport and the larger Metro commuter-liner were entirely original designs. A prototype of the Metro first flew on 26 August 1969, and the type was certificated on 11 June 1970, but none had been delivered for airline use up to the time the company was forced to close down in mid-1971 through financial difficulties. Only after production was resumed under Fairchild management did sales of the Metro begin to pick up, with six delivered in 1973, eight in 1974, six in 1975 and considerably increased annual quantities since then. In 1975, a number of improvements were introduced, including larger windows, and the designation Metro II was adopted; versions of the same airframe for business use are designated Merlin IVA. At least 12 US commuter airliners were operating Metros in 1979, and several export sales had been recorded, to companies in Europe, the Middle East and South America.

Tupolev Tu-124 (and Tu-104) USSR

Medium-range airliner, in service
Photo: Tu-104
Silhouette and data: Tu-124V

Accommodation: Flight crew of 4 and 56 passengers
Powered by: Two 11,905lb (5,400kg) st Soloviev D-20P turbofans
Span: 83ft 9.5in (25.55m)
Length: 100ft 4in (30.58m)
Gross weight: 83,775lb (38,000kg)
Normal payload: 13,225lb (6,000kg)
Max cruising speed: 540mph (870km/h)
Range: 760 miles (1,220km) with max payload at 497mph (800km/h) at 33,000ft (10,000m), with reserves

Andrei Tupolev's design bureau developed the Tu-124 from the earlier Tu-104 design for service on the more important short-range routes in Russia. First flown in 44-seat prototype form in June 1960, the design was developed into the 56-seat production model Tu-124V which entered service in October 1962 and became one of Aeroflot's standard short-range airliners during 1965-66. Three were delivered to CSA in 1964, and two to Interflug of East Germany, these being the only examples exported for airline use. Two other versions of the Tu-124 were reported to have entered service with Aeroflot, with a higher standard of cabin furnishing and fewer seats. These were the Tu-124K, with a 24-seat main cabin and two other compartments for four and eight passengers respectively; and the Tu-124K2, with individual cabins for four and two, and a 16-seat rear compartment. Aeroflot continued to operate a handful of Tu-124s in 1979. The Soviet airline also still employed considerable numbers of veteran Tu-104s on domestic services, mostly equipped to Tu-104V standard, with 100 seats, 21,385lb (9,700kg) st Mikulin AM-3M-500 turbojets and range of 1,305 miles (2,100km) at 497mph (800km/h) with max payload. The Tu-104A had only 70 seats and a slightly shorter cabin. The Tu-104 was the Soviet Union's first jet transport, and only the second in the world to enter commerical service, after the Comet. The design was based on that of the Tu-16 bomber, using the same wings and power plant, with a new fuselage and modified tail unit. Over 200 were built, all for service with Aeroflot with the exception of six supplied to the Czech airline CSA.

Tupolev Tu-134

USSR

Short/medium-range airliner, in production and service
Photo and Data: Tu-134A

Accommodation: Flight crew of 3 and up to 80 passengers
Powered by: Two 14,990lb (6,800kg) st Soloviev D-30-2 turbofans
Span: 95ft 2in (29.00m)
Length: 122ft 0in (37.10m)
Gross weight: 103,600lb (47,000kg)
Max payload: 18,000lb (8,200kg)
Cruising speed: 466-559mph (750-900km/h)
Typical range: 1,243 miles (2,000km) with 18,108lb (8,215kg) payload at 466mph (750km/h) at 32,800ft (10,000m), with reserves

Operationally in the same class as the BAC One-Eleven and Douglas DC-9, the Tu-134 was a development of the Tu-124 and was referred to at first as the Tu-124A. The principal difference lay in the relocation of the engines on the aft fuselage and the use of a 'T'-tail; many other detail changes and improvements were also made. First flight of the Tu-134 is believed to have been made towards the end of 1962 and Aeroflot put 72-seat production aircraft into service in 1967 on domestic and international routes in Europe. During 1969, a developed version designated the Tu-134A was publicly demonstrated; this has a fuselage lengthened by 6ft 11in (2.10m), up to 80 seats, increased baggage space, thrust reversers on improved models of the D-30 engine, APU and improved electronics. Originally, both the Tu-134 and Tu-134A had the distinctive Tupolev nose with a navigator's station, but later examples — particularly those for export — have radar in a conical nose fairing. Users of the Tu-134 and Tu-134A, apart from Aeroflot, include Aviogenex with six Tu-134A, Balkan Bulgarian (five Tu-134 and six Tu-134A), CSA (13 Tu-134A), Interflug (six Tu-134 and 23 Tu-134A), LOT (five Tu-134 and seven Tu-134A) and Malev (four Tu-134 and two Tu-134A). Aeroflot is believed to have at least 250 in service.

Tupolev Tu-144

USSR

Medium/long-range supersonic airliner, in service

Accommodation: Flight crew of 3-4 and up to 140 passengers
Powered by : Four 44,090lb (20,000kg) st (with afterburning) Kuznetsov NK-144 turbofans
Span: 94ft 6.5in (28.80m)
Length: 215ft 6in (65.70m)
Gross weight: 396,830lb (180,000kg)
Normal cruising speed: Mach 2.2 (1,452mph; 2,336km/h) at 52,500-59,000ft (16,000-18,000m)
Max range: 4,030 miles (6,500km) with 140 passengers at Mach 1.9 (1,243mph; 2,000km/h)

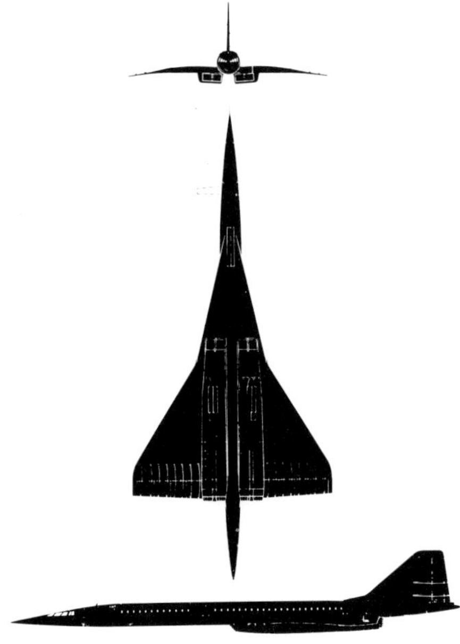

In general conception, size and performance, the Tu-144 resembles the Concorde, although Russia chose to use turbofan rather than turbojet engines, with afterburners for continuous operation in flight, and designed the Tu-144 for a higher cruising speed. The development programme for the Tu-144 included flight testing of a scale model of the ogival wing on a modified MiG-21. The first flight of the Tu-144 was made on 31 December 1968, to make it the world's first SST in the air. The first supersonic flight was made on 5 June 1969 and Mach 2 was achieved for the first time in May 1970. This aircraft was followed by a second, similar, prototype. The design then underwent a radical revision. The wings were increased in span by nearly 4ft (1.15m) and cambered over the full area, giving a curved trailing-edge. The fuselage was lengthened by nearly 19ft (5.7m), and the engines were moved outboard into paired ducts. The undercarriage was redesigned, and 'moustache' retractable foreplanes were added to improve take-off and landing characteristics. On 26 December 1975, Aeroflot inaugurated a regular scheduled operation between Moscow and Alma Ata. Following Soviet custom with brand-new commercial aircraft, however, this operation was intended primarily as a proving trial and only freight was carried. The first regular passenger service, on the same route and at a frequency of two flights a week, was inaugurated on 1 November 1977, but this was suspended on 1 June 1978 after 51 round trips had been completed, following the loss of a Tu-144 on a non-commercial flight. Regular services were resumed during the summer of 1979.

Tupolev Tu-154

USSR

Medium/long-range jet airliner, in production and service
Photo and data: Tu-154B
Silhouette: Tu-154A

Accommodation: Flight crew of 3-4 and up to 167 passengers
Powered by: Three 23,150lb (10,500kg) st Kuznetsov NK-8-2 turbofans
Span: 123ft 2.5in (37.55m)
Length: 157ft 1.75in (47.90m)
Gross weight: 211,650lb (96,000kg)
Max payload: 39,680lb (18,000kg)
Cruising speed: 560mph (900km/h) at 36,000ft (11,000m)
Range: 1,710 miles (2,750km) with max payload

The Tu-154 is a second-generation aircraft that was designed to replace the Tu-104 from the same design bureau, and the Il-18 and An-10 on those routes where traffic growth required a larger aeroplane. Whilst retaining several features of the Tupolev family of jet transports, the Tu-154 also broke with Tupolev tradition in some aspects of fuselage design, such as the nose, which no longer contains a navigation station, and the small close-pitched windows replacing the former generously-sized transparencies at each seat row. Location of the three engines at the rear of the fuselage matched Western practice, and the Tu-154 was in the same general bracket as the HS Trident Three and the Boeing 727-200, although having a much better field performance to meet Soviet requirements. The prototype made its first flight on 4 October 1968 and a pre-production model was under test by 1970. Aeroflot proving flights, carrying freight and mail, began in August 1971, and scheduled services started in February 1972. A version designated Tu-154A, with uprated NK-8-2U engines, increased fuel capacity and higher operating weights, entered service with Aeroflot in 1974, and this was followed in 1975 by the Tu-154B, with changes in the navigation equipment, modified cabin layout to seat up to 169 compared with the previous 144-152, and a further increase in max operating weight. Aeroflot was reported to have more than 200 Tu-154 variants in service by mid-1979 and exports have been made to Balkan Bulgarian (13, including one with VIP interior for government use), Malev (7) and Tarom (8).

VFW-Fokker 614

Germany

Short-range airliner, in service

Accommodation: Flight crew of 2 and 36-44 passengers
Powered by: Two 7,760lb (3,520kg) st Rolls-Royce M.45H Mk 501 turbofans
Span: 70ft 6.5in (21.50m)
Length: 67ft 6in (20.60m)
Gross weight: 44,000lb (19,950kg)
Max payload: 17,547lb (7,976kg)
Max cruising speed: 457mph (735km/h) at 25,000ft (7,620m)
Range: 978 miles (1,574km) with max payload, no reserves

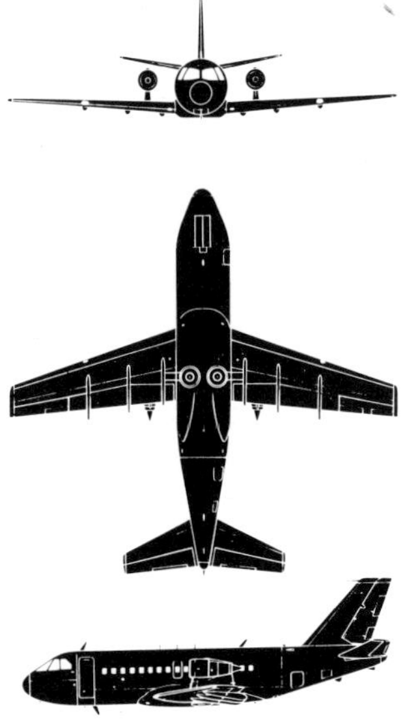

The VFW-614, distinguished by its novel engine arrangement with over-wing nacelles, had been under development for several years when construction began in August 1968, following German government backing. Risk-sharing partners in the programme included Fokker-VFW in the Netherlands, SABCA and Fairey in Belgium and MBB in Germany. The first of three prototypes made its first flight at Bremen on 14 July 1971. It was lost in the following February, but two more prototypes flew on 1 February and 10 October 1972 respectively, and VFW-Fokker received a full production go-ahead from the Federal German government on 13 December 1972. A number of options for VFW-614s were announced, but few of these were, in the event, taken up and the first firm order proved to be that from Cimber Air of Denmark. German certification of the VFW-614 was obtained on 23 August 1974 and the first production aircraft flew on 28 April 1975, entering service with Cimber Air towards the end of the year. Other operators by mid-1977 were Air Alsace (with three) and Touraine Air Transport, which had ordered eight. Lack of further firm sales forced VFW-Fokker to abandon production of the VFW 614 at the end of 1977, although at that time a licence for its production in Romania was at an advanced stage of negotiation. In 1979, Cimber Air decided to withdraw its VFW 614s from service but Air Alsace was continuing to operate the VFW-614. The possibility of putting into production in the USA a stretched 60-seat derivative, designated GAC-616, was investigated by Gulfstream American Corporation in 1979 but did not proceed.

Vickers (BAC) VC10 and Super VC10

UK

Medium/long-range airliner, in service

Photo: VC10
Silhouette and data: Super VC10

Accommodation: Flight crew of 3-5 and up to 174 passengers
Powered by: Four 22,500lb (10,205kg) st Rolls-Royce Conway 550 turbofans
Span: 146ft 2in (44.55m)
Length: 171ft 8in (52.32m)
Gross weight: 335,000lb (151,950kg)
Max cruising speed: 568mph (914km/h) at 38,000ft (12,460m)
Typical range: 4,630 miles (7,450km) with max payload at 550mph (885km/h)

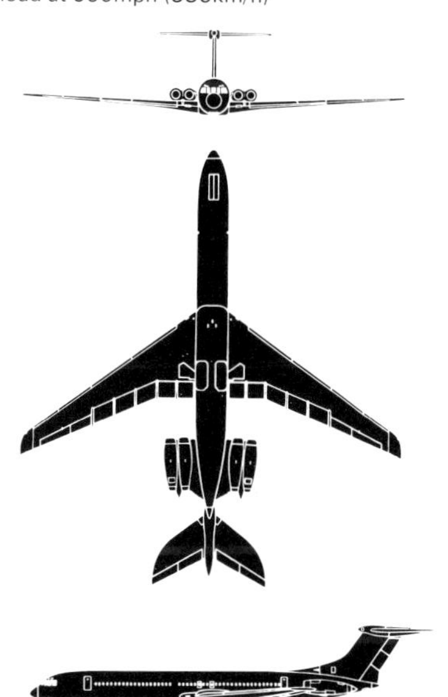

Vickers' development of this 'second-generation' jet transport was begun to meet a BOAC requirement for an aeroplane to operate over the Empire routes, where long stages and hot and high airfields made operating conditions especially difficult. BOAC indicated, in May 1957, that it would order 35 of these aeroplanes, and a further development of the design made it possible to offer transatlantic capability by the time the contract was signed in January 1958. In June 1960, an enlarged version of the VC10 was announced, known as the Super VC10, and in 1961 BOAC announced that it had reduced its VC10 order to 12 (Model 1101) and would also take 30 Super VC10s with a 13ft longer fuselage, more fuel and higher weights. The BOAC contract for Super VC10s was eventually reduced to 17 (Model 1151) with deliveries stretched out until 1969. Other airline customers for VC10s and Super VC10s were BUA, Ghana Airways, and EAA. One of the Ghana Airways aircraft was leased to MEA and was detroyed in the Israeli attack on Beirut Airport. Laker Airways purchased the prototype VC10 early in 1968, following its modification to production standard as Model 1109, and sold it subsequently to BUA. One BOAC VC10 was sold to Nigeria Airways and was subsequently destroyed, and one BOAC Super was destroyed by hijackers at Dawson's Field in 1970. British Airways had retired its last Standard VC10s by the end of 1976, but in 1979 it still had 15 Supers in service. Ghana Airways had one Standard in use, and Air Malawi was also using one, ex-BUA. Both Gulf Air and East African fleets of, respectively, Standard and Super VC10s had been sold to the British Government for conversion to flight-refuelling tankers for the RAF.

Vickers Vanguard and Merchantman

UK

Short/medium-range airliner and freighter, in service
Photo: Type 952
Silhouette: Merchantman
Data: Vanguard

Accommodation: Flight crew of 7, including cabin staff, and 76-139 passengers
Powered by: Four 5,545ehp Rolls-Royce Tyne 512 turboprops
Span: 118ft 7in (36.15m)
Length: 122ft 10.5in (37.45m)
Gross weight: 146,500lb (66,448kg)
Max payload: 37,000lb (16,783kg)
Max cruising speed: 425mph (684km/h) at 20,000ft (6,100m)
Typical range: 1,830 miles (2,945km) with max payload at 420mph (676km/h)

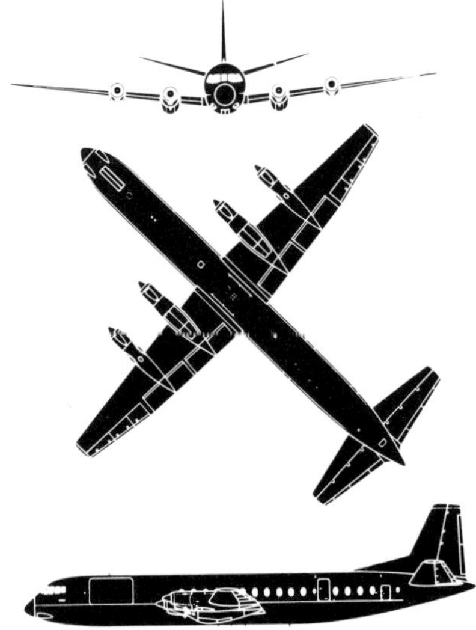

The Vanguard was evolved from a series of design studies to meet a BEA requirement for a 'big brother' to the Viscount. The design finally adopted, although new in almost every respect, relied heavily on Viscount design experience. The first Vanguard, a Vickers-owned prototype, flew for the first time on 20 January 1959, and was followed by the first of 20 ordered by BEA on 22 April 1959. The first six aircraft for BEA were Type 951s, with 4,985ehp Tyne 506 engines and 135,000lb (61,235kg) weight. They went into full service with BEA on 1 March 1961. Vickers built 23 Type 952s for TCA (Air Canada), with Tyne 512s and 146,500lb (66,448kg) weight. The first of these went into service on 1 February 1961. The BEA order was completed with 14 Type 953s which had the higher weight and payload of the 952, but Tyne 506 engines. The first of these flew on 1 May 1961, and was in service on BEA routes by the end of the same month. In October 1968, BEA began a programme to convert nine Vanguards to Merchantman freighters, with cargo doors and other modifications designed by Aviation Traders. The first conversion was flown at Southend on 10 October 1969 and five remained in service with British Airways in 1979, all its passenger Vanguards having been retired. Air Canada had also retired its Vanguards, and the principal operator had become Europe Air Service, with 11 in use. Merpati Nusantara in Indonesia had three and Air Bridge Carriers was using one.

Vickers Viscount

UK

Short/medium-range airliner, in service
Data: Viscount 810
Photo: Viscount 814

Accommodation: Flight crew of 3-4 and 52-75 passengers
Powered by: Four 1,990ehp Rolls-Royce Dart 525 turboprops
Span: 93ft 8.5in (28.56m)
Length: 85ft 8in (26.11m)
Gross weight: 72,500lb (32,886kg)
Max payload: 14,500lb (6,577kg)
Max cruising speed: 358mph (576km/h) at 15,000ft (4,575m)
Range: 1,760 miles (2,830km) with 14,500lb (6,575kg) payload at 343mph (552km/h)

The first Viscount, the Type 630 G-AHRF (first flown on 16 July 1948) was smaller than all examples which followed, but all the 700 series are dimensionally similar to the prototype 700, G-AMAV (flown on 28 August 1950). Initial production aircraft had Dart 505s and 506s and operated at a lower gross weight. With Dart 510s, provision for slipper tanks on the wings and 64,500lb (29,250kg) weight, the type was known as the 700D. 285 Srs 700 were ordered by airlines in addition to several VIP and executive variants. Each initial-customer model was distinguished by a separate type number between 700 and 799. The 810 series was developed later from the 700 series, with greater length and more powerful engines. The first of these (G-AOYV) flew on 23 December 1957. The first of the 800 series was the 802 for BEA (first flown on 27 July 1956); this had the same power plant as the 700D series but the longer fuselage of the 810 series, and was able to carry a bigger payload over shorter ranges. Large-scale production of the Viscount ended in 1959, but Vickers continued to work on a small quantity of Viscounts until the spring of 1964, the last aircraft off the line at Hurn being six for airline use in China. The grand total of all Viscount variants built was 444. Most major airline users of the Viscount have now retired their fleets of this pioneering transport — the first turboprop-engined transport in the world to enter service — but about 80 remain in airline service with subsequent owners. Others are still used for executive transport by private companies, Governments and air forces.

Yakovlev Yak-40

USSR

Short-range jet airliner, in service

Accommodation: Flight crew of 2 and 27-32 passengers
Powered by: Three 3,300lb (1,500kg) st Ivchenko AI-25 turbofans
Span: 82ft 0.25in (25.00m)
Length: 66ft 9.5in (20.36m)
Gross weight: 35,275lb (16,000kg)
Payload: 6,000lb (2,720kg)
Cruising speed: 292-342mph (470-550km/h)
Range: 1,118 miles (1,800km) with max payload (with reserves)

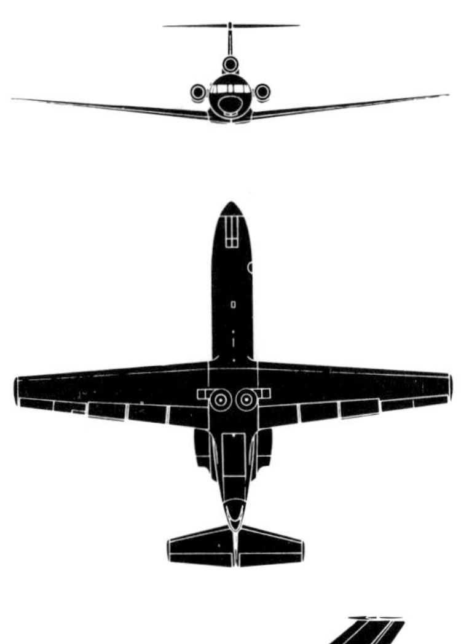

First flown on 21 October 1966, the Yak-40 was the smallest of the current range of jet airliners manufactured in Russia. It was also of particular interest as the first civil transport to come from the Yakovlev design bureau, after many years of specialisation on high-performance attack bombers and fighters. Use of three engines in so small an air-craft was an unusual feature, giving the Yak-40 the ability to take-off and climb on any two engines, and maintain height in cruising flight with two engines shut down. Production of the Yak-40 began in 1967, for Aeroflot use as a replacement for the several hundred Li-2s still in service. More than 200 were in service by April 1970, when production of 300 more was authorised, with a further 300 authorised by 1976 and a grand total of 1,000 built by the time major production ended in 1978. Efforts to export the Yak-40 were less successful than had been hoped. Aertirrena in Italy acquired an agency to market the Yak-40 in Europe and took delivery of the first European-registered Yak-40 at the end of 1970. Two were supplied to Bakhtar Afghan Airlines, 11 to Balkan Bulgarian, five to General Air in Federal Germany, 17 to CSA and two to Hang Khong in Vietnam, with others in military service with various countries. During 1979, the practicability of fitting US engines in the Yak-40 for sale on the American market was being investigated by ICX Aviation, which had obtained an option to acquire the original production jigs and proposed to rename the aircraft the X-Avia, with 3,700lb (1,680kg) st Garrett TFE 731-3 turbofans and US systems equipment throughout.

Yakovlev Yak-42

USSR

Short-to-medium-range airliner, under development

Accommodation: Flight crew of 3-4, and 100-120 passengers six-abreast in a single class layout; typical mixed class layout, 40 four-abreast and 60 six-abreast
Powered by: Three 14,200lb (6,440kg) st Lotarev D-36 high by-pass turbofans
Span: 112ft 2.5in (34.20m)
Length: 119ft 4.25in (36.38m)
Gross weight: 114,640lb (52,000kg)
Max payload: 32,000lb (14,500kg)
Cruising speed: 510mph (820km/h) at 26,250ft (8,000m)
Range: 620 miles (1,000km) with max payload

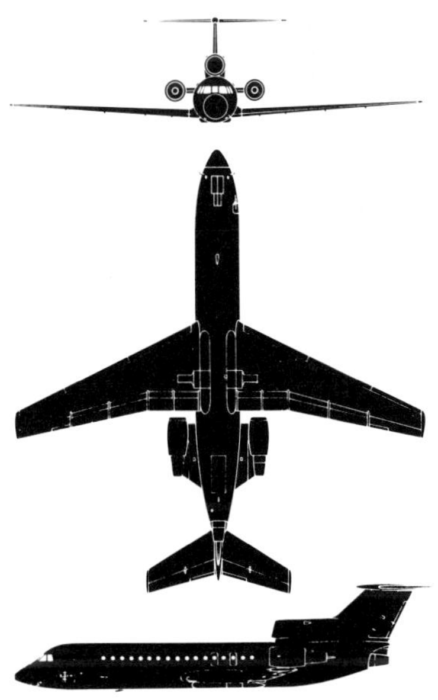

First news of the development of the Yak-42 was given in mid-1973, by which time a mock-up existed in Yakovlev's works near Moscow and detail design was under way. The aircraft was designed to operate into the less well-developed airfields in the Soviet Union, away from the trunk routes, with the ability to operate on to and off grass and to fly from runways less than 3,000ft (915m) in length. In overall configuration, the Yak-42 resembles the Yak-40, with three engines grouped in the tail; in passenger capacity it resembles the DC-9 Srs 40 and 50. The fact that it has almost 50% more power than the latter aircraft is indicative of the premium placed upon airfield performance. The Yak-42 is designed to airworthiness standards comparable with those of FAR 25 in the USA and is expected to be one of the major civil aircraft exports of the Soviet Union in the 'eighties, once Aeroflot's immediate needs have been met. The total domestic requirement is said to be for 2,000 aircraft of this type. The first Yak 42 prototype flew on 7 March 1975 and had a wing sweep-back of 11deg. The second aircraft, flown in April 1976, had 23deg of sweep-back and this standard was adopted for production aircraft after comparative testing of the prototypes. Production of an initial batch of 200 Yak-42s was reported underway in 1979, with entry-into-service planned for the second half of 1980.

Part Two

Aero Spacelines Guppies

USA

Outsize cargo transport, in service
Photo: Guppy 101
Data: Guppy 201

Accommodation: Flight crew of 3-4
Powered by: Four 4,912eshp Allison 501-D22C turboprops
Span: 156ft 3in (47.62m)
Length: 143ft 10in (43.84m)
Gross weight: 170,000lb (77,110kg)
Cruising speed: 253mph (407km/h)
Range: 505 miles (813km) with max payload

Aero Spacelines Inc originated the scheme for transporting outsize items of space hardware in conversions of the Boeing 377 Stratocruiser with enlarged fuselages. The first conversion was based on a standard Stratocruiser, the fuselage of which was lengthened by 16ft 8in (5.08m) and modified to have a new upper lobe with an inside height of 20ft 4in (6.20m). This aircraft was known as the B-377PG Pregnant Guppy and first flew on 19 September 1962. With wing span increased by 15ft (4.57m) and fuselage lengthened by 30ft 10in (9.40m), the Guppy 201 was powered by Allison 501-D22C turboprops and was the 'production' version of the Super Guppy, although still based on components of existing Boeing 377 C-97 airframes; the first example flew on 24 August 1970. Two Guppy 201s purchased by Aérospatiale and operated by Aéromaritime, are used to transport components for the Airbus A300B between the production centres in Europe, and the single Guppy 101, with a swing nose, is used by Gulfstream American.

Antonov An-2

USSR/Poland

General-purpose and utility transport
Photo: WSK-Mielec An-2R
Data: An-2P built in Poland

Accommodation: 1-2 pilots, plus 12 adult passengers and 2 small children
Powered by: One 1,000hp Shvetsov ASh-62IR piston-engine
Span: 59ft 8.5in (18.18m)
Length: 40ft 8.25in (12.40m)
Gross weight: 12,125lb (5,500kg)
Normal cruising speed: 115mph (185km/h)
Range: 560 miles (900km) with 1,102lb (500kg) payload

Designed primarily for agricultural duties, the An-2 appeared in 1947 and has subsequently been adopted for various utilitarian tasks, more than 5,000 having been built in the Soviet Union by 1962. The basic light transport for Aeroflot was the An-2P and the initial agricultural version was the An-2S. The latter was superseded by the An-2M with a number of external changes and improved performance. Other versions included the An-2V floatplane and An-2L water-bomber, also a floatplane. With the local name of Type 5 Transport Plane, or C-5, the An-2 was built in China, where the first example flew in December 1957. In Poland, the type has been in large-scale production since 1960 and over 8,200 had been built by 1979, at which time the WSK-Mielec factory was the sole source. Polish variants have included the An-2R (similar to Soviet An-2S), the An-2S ambulance, the An-2T (basic passenger or freight version), the An-2P passenger carrier and An-2M (as An-2V).

Antonov An-22 Antheus

USSR

Heavy cargo transport, in service

Accommodation: Flight crew of 5-6 and 28-29 passengers and freight
Powered by: Four 15,000shp Kuznetsov NK-12MA turboprops
Span: 211ft 4in (64.40m)
Length: 189ft 7in (57.80m)
Gross weight: 551,160lb (250,000kg)
Max level speed: 460mph (740km/h)
Max range: 6,800 miles (10,950km) with 99,200lb (45,000kg) payload

First flown on 27 February 1965, the An-22 is Russia's largest aircraft to date, and was a natural progression in the series of Antonov freighters which began with the twin-engined An-8. The basic aircraft was intended for use as a freighter and was produced in this role for Aeroflot (as well as for the Soviet military services). The rear fuselage incorporates a split door, the rear-most section hinging up into the hold, and the forward section hinging down to form a loading ramp. The NATO code-name for the An-22 is 'Cock'; Antheus is the name sometimes applied by Soviet sources to the type. About 80 were built before manufacture ended in 1974.

CCCP-56391

Antonov An-72 USSR

STOL freighter, under development

Accommodation: Flight crew of 2-3; cargo loads including vehicles, pallets or freight containers. Provision for up to 30 seats along cabin sides
Powered by: Two 14,330lb (6,500kg) st Lotarev D-36 turbofans
Span: 84ft 8.875in (25.83m)
Length: 87ft 2.25in (26.58m)
Gross weight: 67,240lb (30,500kg)
Max cruising speed: 447mph (720km/h)
Range: 620 miles (1,000km) with max payload and reserves

The Antonov An-72 was first flown on 22 December 1977, according to reports in the Soviet Union, and a second prototype flew in 1978. The first Antonov transport to feature turbofan rather than turboprop engines, the An-72 is designed to carry a useful cargo load into and out of short, unprepared fields. It has a high lift system similar to that of the Boeing YC-14, using USB (upper surface blowing) with trailing edge flaps operating in the jet exhaust for maximum lift enhancement. In addition there are triple-slotted flaps on the outer wings, full-span leading-edge flaps and upper surface spoilers. Testing of the prototypes was under way in 1979 and no decision had been taken to put the An-72 into production. The NATO code-name is 'Coaler'.

Bristol 175 Britannia UK

Medium/long-range airliner, in service
Photo: Britannia 307F
Data: Srs 310

Accommodation: Crew of 9, including cabin staff, and 82-133 passengers
Powered by: Four 4,445ehp Bristol Siddeley Proteus 765 turboprops
Span: 142ft 3.5in (43.39m)
Length: 124ft 3in (37.89m)
Gross weight: 185,000lb (83,990kg)
Max cruising speed: 402mph (647km/h) at 21,000ft (6,405m)
Range: 4,268 miles (6,867km) with max payload at 357mph (574km/h)

The Britannia was designed to a 1947 BOAC requirement for a medium-range transport for Empire routes, and the prototype (Srs 100) with Proteus turboprops flew on 16 August 1952. This version was followed by a family of long-fuselage Britannias evolved primarily to meet BOAC requirements for an Atlantic transport but including the Srs 300s which were similar to the Srs 100s in range performance. The fully developed version was the Britannia 310. As well as the longer fuselage, extra fuel capacity and higher weights, these Britannias had uprated Proteus 755 or 765 engines. A few of these original civil aircraft remained in use, primarily for cargo-carrying, in 1979 together with some of the 22 Britannias offered for sale by the RAF in 1975.

Canadair 400 and CL-44 Forty Four Canada

Long-range passenger/freighter, in service
Photo: Yukon
Data: Canadair 400

Accommodation: Flight crew of 4 and 63,272lb (28,725kg) freight (or 214 passengers)
Powered by: Four 5,730hp Rolls-Royce Tyne 515/10 turboprops
Span: 142ft 3.5in (43.37m)
Length: 151ft 9.75in (46.28m)
Gross weight: 210,000lb (95,250kg)
Max payload: 63,272lb (28,725kg)
Max cruising speed: 386mph (621km/h) at 20,000ft (6,100m)
Range: 3,260 miles (5,245km) with max payload

The Canadair CL-44D long-range freighter was based on the Bristol Britannia and the first of 12 military CL-44Ds for the RCAF (designated CC-106 Yukon) flew on 15 November 1959. This version had normal side-loading through large freight doors. A commercial version was developed as the CL-44D4, in which the entire rear fuselage hinged sideways, so that vehicles and bulky freight could be loaded straight into the cabin from the rear. The first swing-tail CL-44D4 flew on 16 November 1960. Four Canadair 400s (CL-44J) had longer fuselages and the single CL-440, first flown on 26 November 1969, had a Conroy-developed 'Guppy' type fuselage. CL-44s remain in service primarily as cargo carriers, including the CL-440 and several of the ex-CAF Yukons, sold on the civil market as CL-44-6s in 1971/72.

АЭРОФЛОТ
СССР-19774
northeast
BK
AEROLINEAS NACIONALES DEL ECUADOR
ANDES
HC-AZH

Canadair CL-215 — Canada

Water-bomber and general-purpose amphibian, in production and service

Accommodation: Flight crew of 2-4 and water tanks or up to 19 passengers
Powered by: Two 2,100hp Pratt & Whitney R-2800-83AM-12AD/CA3 piston-engines
Span: 93ft 10in (28.60m)
Length: 65ft 0.25in (19.82m)
Gross weight: 43.500lb (19,728kg)
Cruising speed: 181mph (291km/h) at 10,000ft (3,050m)
Range: 1,405 miles (2,260km) with 3,500lb (1,587kg) payload

The CL-215 was evolved as a specialised water-bomber, following several years' close study by Canadair of the requirements for this type of operation. In the water-bomber role the aircraft can carry 12,000lb (5,440kg) of water in a fuselage tank which can be emptied in less than a second, and refilled in 12 seconds during a high-speed taxi across a lake. The prototype CL-215 made its first flight on 23 October 1967 and the first four of 15 purchased by the French Protection Civile went into use during 1969. Fifteen have been delivered to the Ontario Provincial Government, 17 for use in Spain, including eight for search and rescue duties with nose radar, and 11 have gone to the Greek Air Force. Others are in service in Alaska (2), Manitoba (1), Thailand (2) and Venezuela (2).

Curtiss C-46 Commando — USA

Medium-range airliner, in service

Accommodation: Flight crew of 2 and up to 62 passengers
Powered by: Two 2,000hp Pratt & Whitney R-2800-5IMI piston-engines
Span: 108ft 0in (32.92m)
Length: 76ft 4in (23.27m)
Gross weight: 48,000lb (21,770kg) (as freighter)
Max cruising speed: 187mph (301km/h) at 7,000ft (2,133m)
Typical range: Up to 1,170 miles (1,883km) with 5,700lb (2,585kg) payload

The Curtiss-Wright CW-20 was designed in 1938 as a pressurised airliner for US operators, and a prototype made its first flight on 26 March 1940. In unpressurised form, the CW-20 was adopted for production for the USAAF as the C-46. Over 3,000 of these rugged and capacious transports were built, and hundreds survived the war to serve, primarily as freighters, with airlines in the early postwar years, particularly in South and Central America. About 70 still survive, operating mostly in more remote areas and at airfields with minimum facilities. Several different modification schemes were introduced to improve the performance of the C-46 and so allow it to meet changing civil airworthiness requirements, leading to designations such as Super 46C and C-46R.

Hawker Siddeley (AW 650) Argosy — UK

Turboprop freighter, in service
Photo: Srs 200
Data: Srs 222

Accommodation: Normally freight only, can carry up to 89 passengers
Powered by: Four 2,230ehp Rolls-Royce Dart 532-1 turboprops
Span: 115ft 0in (33.05m)
Length: 86ft 9in (26.44m)
Gross weight: 93,000lb (42,185kg)
Normal cruising speed: 280mph (451km/h) at 18,000ft (5,490km)
Range: 485 miles (780km) with max payload

The AW650 was designed by Armstrong Whitworth as a variant of the AW66 Eland-engined military freighter project. Production of an initial batch of 10 Argosy Srs 100s was inititiated as a private venture and the first of these civil aircraft, made its first flight on 8 January 1959. An improved version was developed as the Srs 200, with a new wing structure, higher weights and other refinements. The first of these new models flew on 11 March 1964 and six were built. Argosies in civil use in the UK, New Zealand, Australia and Africa in 1979 include a few of the original RAF freighters sold in 1976.

LACSA
TI-1010C
COSTARRICENSES, S. A.

Ilyushin Il-76T

USSR

Medium/long-range freight transport, in production and service

Accommodation: Basic flight crew of 3
Powered by: Four 26,455lb (12,000kg) st Soloviev D-30KP turbofans
Span: 165ft 8in (50.50m)
Length: 152ft 10.5in (46.59m)
Gross weight: 374,785lb (170,000kg)
Normal cruising speed: 466-497mph (750-800km/h)
Range: 3,100 miles (5,000km) with max payload

First flown on 25 March 1971, the Il-76 was designed to carry 40 tonnes of freight for a distance of 5,000km (3,100 miles) in under six hours. It was clear from the start that the Il-76 also had military potential and it entered service with the Soviet Air Force to replace the An-12 as a tactical transport (with a rear gun turret) as well as with Aeroflot as a freighter. For the latter, the Il-76T was introduced in 1978, featuring a higher gross weight than the originally-quoted 356,125lb (157,000kg) and this version began operating scheduled international cargo services on 5 April 1978. Two examples entered service with Iraqi Airways in 1979.

Lockheed L-100 Hercules

USA

Commercial freighter, in production and service
Photo and Data: L-100-30

Accommodation: Flight crew of 3 plus freight
Powered by: Four 4,508ehp Allison 501-D22A turboprops
Span: 132ft 7in (40.41m)
Length: 112ft 8.5in (34.35m)
Gross weight: 155,000lb (70,308kg)
Max cruising speed: 377mph (607km/h) at 20,000ft (6,100m)
Range: 2,130 miles (3,425km) with max payload (45min fuel reserve)

By 1979 Lockheed's Georgia company had sold more than 50 Hercules freighters for commercial use, in addition to over 1,500 in military guise. The first commercial variants were the Model 382B and L-100, similar to the C-130E, with 4,050ehp Allison 501-D22 engines. The Model 382E introduced a fuselage 'stretch' of 8ft 4in (2.54m) and is now known as the L-100-20, with uprated D22A engines. The first flight was made on 19 April 1968. A later development was the Model 382G, or L-100-30 with a further fuselage stretch of 6ft 8in (2.03m); the first flight was made on 14 August 1970. In 1979, Lockheed was working on development of still larger variants as the L-100-50 and L-100-60, for introduction in 1982 or later.

PZL-Mielec M-15 Belphagor

Poland

Agricultural aircraft, in production and service

Accommodation: Pilot plus provision for 21 passengers in cabin for ferry flights
Powered by: One 3,306lb (1,500kg) st Ivchenko AI-25 turbojet
Span: 73ft 6in (22.4m)
Length: 41ft 8.75in (12.72m)
Gross weight: 12,456lb (5,650kg)
Max cruising speed: 124mph (200km/h)
Range: 248 miles (400km) at 9,850ft (3,000m)

The unique M-15 — the world's only jet-powered biplane — was developed in Poland by a joint Soviet/Polish team under the terms of an agreement concluded in 1971 providing for Poland exclusively to develop new agricultural aircraft for use in the Soviet bloc countries. A prototype (known as the LLP-M15, or 'flying laboratory' prototype M-15) flew on 20 May 1973, followed by a fully representative prototype on 9 January 1974. Powered by a turbofan of Soviet origin, the M-15 can carry 640 Imp gal (2,900 litres) or 4,850lb (2,200kg) of insecticide in containers between the wings and produces a swath width of 197ft (60m). Five pre-production M-15s were sent to the Soviet Union for evaluation in April 1975 and series production began in the same year. About 100 had been built by 1977, when the production rate was still increasing to meet Soviet requirements, which are reported to total about 3,000 M-15s.

АЭРОФЛОТ
366
СССР-15598

Shorts Belfast

UK

Turboprop freighter, in service

Accommodation: Flight crew of 2-3 and up to 78,000lb (35,400kg) of freight.
Powered by: Four 5,730eshp Rolls-Royce Tyne RTy. 12 turboprops
Span: 158ft 9.5in (48.82m)
Length: 136ft 5in (41.69m)
Max gross weight: 230,000lb (104,300kg)
Max cruising speed: 352mph (566km/h) at 24,000ft (7,300m)
Max range: 5,300 miles (8,530km) at 336mph (540km/h)

Design of the Shorts Belfast was based upon that of the Bristol Britannia and the first of the 10 examples built for the RAF flew for the first time on 5 January 1964. The Belfasts served with No 53 Squadron until 1976; they were then phased out of RAF service and three were subsequently acquired for use as heavylift freighters by Eurolatin. After modification and certification in 1979 they entered service in TAC HeavyLift colours in 1980.

Transall C-160P

International

Mail carrier, in service

Accommodation: Flight crew of 3 and up to 29,735lb (13,500kg) load of mail
Powered by: Two 6,100ehp Rolls-Royce Tyne RTy 20 Mk 22 turboprops
Span: 131ft 3in (40.0m)
Length: 106ft 3.5in (32.40m)
Gross weight: 112,440lb (51,000kg)
Cruising speed: 306mph (492km/h) at 26,250ft (8,000m)
Range: 730 miles (1,175km) with max payload

The C-160 was developed as a medium-sized tactical transport to meet the requirements of the Luftwaffe and the Armée de l'Air and the first prototype flew on 25 February 1963. Production was shared between France and Germany and 169 were built. During 1973, four of the French C-160Fs were modified by SOGERMA for the carriage of mail; re-designated C-160Ps, they were loaned to the Centre d'Exploitation Postal Metropolitan (CEPM), to be operated by Air France on night mail services within France. After production of the Transall had been resumed in France in 1979, to meet military orders, the Indonesian government announced plans to acquire three to carry migratory workers between the Indonesian islands.

Part Three

Aérospatiale Corvette

France

Executive jet and air taxi, in service
Data: SN 601

Accommodation: Flight crew of 1-2, and 6-13 passengers
Powered by: Two 2,300lb (1,043kg) st Pratt & Whitney JT15D-4 turbofans
Span: 42ft 2.5in (12.87m)
Length: 45ft 4.5in (13.83m)
Gross weight: 13,890lb (6,300kg)
Max payload: 2,248lb (1,000kg)
Max cruising speed: 472mph (760km/h) at 30,000ft (9,144m)
Range: 910 miles (1,465km) with 12 passengers at 391mph (628km/h) (with reserves)

The Corvette is a multi-purpose light transport suitable for business use or as an air taxi, ambulance, freighter or training aircraft. The prototype (with JT15D-1 engines) made its first flight on 16 July 1970, but was destroyed in March 1971. It was followed by two pre-production models, the first of which flew on 20 December 1972, with JT15D-4 engines, and the first production example flew in November, 1973. Initial orders included four for Air Alpes, one for Air Alsace, one for Protection Civile and one for Africair; deliveries began in September 1974 following certification on 28 May. Production ended in 1976 when 40 had been built but the marketing effort continued into 1979, to sell the last few aircraft in the batch.

Ahrens AR-404

USA

Utility transport, in production

Accommodation: Flight crew of 2 and up to 30 passengers
Powered by: Four 420eshp Allison 250-B17B turboprops
Span: 66ft 0in (20.12m)
Length: 52ft 9in (16.08m)
Gross weight: About 17,000lb (7,710kg)
Max cruising speed: 195mph (315km/h)
Range: 978-1,473 miles (1,575-2,370km)

A prototype of the AR-404 light utility transport was designed and built by Ahrens Aircraft Corp at Oxnard, California, in 1976, and it made its first flight on 1 December 1976. After a brief period of flight testing in the USA, the prototype was transferred to Ramey AFB, Puerto Rico, where certification was to be completed and production launched. The Puerto Rican government was providing finance for an initial batch of 18 aircraft, the first of which was ready to fly before the end of 1979. The AR-404 is designed for civil or military use in the general category of a DC-3 replacement featuring a rear-loading ramp and a rectangular section fuselage that can seat three-abreast or carry mixed loads of passengers and freight. Production aircraft, to which the data apply, have a 1ft (0.30m) greater span and are 4ft 5in (1.35m) longer than the first prototype (shown in the photograph) with twice as many cabin windows.

Antonov An-14

USSR

General-purpose light transport, in production and service

Accommodation: Pilot and up to 8 passengers
Powered by: Two 300hp Ivchenko AI-14RF piston-engines
Span: 72ft 2in (21.99m)
Length: 7ft 6.5in (11.44m)
Gross weight: 7,935lb (3,600kg)
Cruising speed: 112mph (180km/h) at 6,560ft (2,000m)
Range: 404 miles (650km) with max payload

First flown on 15 March 1958, the An-14 underwent a prolonged flight development and improvement programme, eventually going into service in the form illustrated during 1965. Changes since the prototype appeared include the use of uprated engines (the 260hp AI-14R was used initially), an enlarged wing and revised fins and rudders. The An-14 is used by Aeroflot for air-taxi, ambulance (six stretchers), and agricultural duties and can be operated on floats. An executive version has been developed, seating five passengers. More than 300 An-14s had been built by 1976.

Beagle B206

UK

Business twin, in service
Photo: B206 Srs I
Data: B206S

Accommodation: 5-8 seats
Powered by: Two 340hp Rolls-Royce/Continental GTSIO-520 turbo-supercharged piston-engines
Span: 49ft 9.5in (13.96m)
Length: 33ft 8in (10.26m)
Gross weight: 7,500lb (3,400kg)
Cruising speed: 187-209mph (301-336km/h)
Max range: 1,600 miles (2,575km) at 187mph (301km/h) (no reserves)

First aircraft of original design produced by Beagle, the prototype B206X (G-ARRM) had 260hp Continental IO-470-A engines and spanned 38ft (11.58m). Deliveries of production 5/8-seat B206Cs began in 1965, together with the first of 20 similar B206Rs for the RAF, which named them Basset CC Mk 1. The B206S (or Srs II) with supercharged engines first flew on 23 June 1965, and features an enlarged rear door as well as other refinements. Forty Beagle 206s were sold in civil guise and in 1975 the RAF sold its Bassets, most of which were then acquired for civil use.

Beechcraft Model 18

USA

Light transport, in service
Photo: Volpar Turboliner
Data: Super H18

Accommodation: 2 pilots and 5-7 passengers
Powered by: Two 450hp Pratt & Whitney R-985-AN-14B piston-engines
Span: 49ft 8in (15.14m)
Length: 35ft 2.5in (10.70m)
Gross weight: 9,900lb (4,490kg)
Max cruising speed: 220mph (354km/h) at 10,000ft (3,050m)
Range: 1,530 miles (2,460km)

First flown on 15 January 1937, the Beech 18 remained in production continuously until the end of 1969 and over 9,000 were built. Many changes were introduced in the Super 18 series of postwar business aircraft, over 700 of which were built, and a Volpar nosewheel gear was made available as an alternative to the tail-down type. The Beech 18 also provided the basis of a number of major modification schemes, with turboprop engines and other features. Many original Beech 18s remain in airline service — SMB Stage Lines alone having 24 in 1979 as well as four Hamilton Westwinds with turboprops. The Volpar Turboliner conversions have TPE 331-1 turboprops and lengthened fuselages

Beechcraft Twin Bonanza

USA

Light business twin, in service
Photo: E50
Data: J50

Accommodation: 6 seats
Powered by: Two 340hp Lycoming IGSO-480-A1B6 piston-engines
Span: 45ft 11.5in (13.99m)
Length: 31ft 6.5in (9.61m)
Gross weight: 7,300lb (3,311kg)
Cruising speed: 172-223mph (277-359km/h)
Max range: 1,650 miles (2,655km)

The first example of the Twin Bonanza was flown on 15 November 1949, as a straightforward development of the Bonanza (qv) and became the first light twin of modern configuration to achieve production status after the war. The early models had 260hp engines, successive development bringing 275hp, 295hp and eventually 340hp engines. The final production version, J50, had a more pointed nose than its predecessors, and other refinements. The type eventually gave way to the Travel Air and Baron after 974 had been built. Modernised variants include the Excalibur with 380hp IGSO-540-A1A engines and the Excalibur 800 with 400hp Lycoming IO-720-A1B engines and other refinements.

Beechcraft Queen Air

USA

Business twin, in production and service
Photo: Queen Air B80
Data: Model B80

Accommodation: Flight crew of 1-2 and 4-9 passengers
Powered by: Two 380hp Lycoming IGSO-540-A1D piston-engines
Span: 50ft 3in (15.32m)
Length: 35ft 6in (10.82m)
Gross weight: 8,800lb (3,992kg)
Cruising speed: 183-224mph (294-360km/h)
Max range: 1,517 miles (2,442km)

The first Queen Airs were 6/9-seaters designated Model 65 (first flight 28 August 1958), followed by A65s with swept-back fins; both had 340hp Lycoming IGSO-480-A1E6 engines. Queen Air 70s had greater span and the same power plant as the A65s. Production of these models ended in 1971 with a total of 444 built, including 71 military U-8Fs, and some 11-seat Queen Airliner versions. A prototype Queen Air 80 flew on 22 June 1961 with more power and went into production as the A80 and B80 with increased span. Over 500 of the Queen Air 80 series, including Queen Airliners, had been built by early 1978. Excalibur Aviation offer modified versions as the Queenaire 800 (early models) and Queenaire 8800 (A80 and B80) with 400hp Lycoming IO-720-A1B engines and other refinements.

Beechcraft Baron (and Travel Air)

USA

Business twin, in production and service
Photo: Baron B58
Data: Baron B58P

Accommodation: 4-6 seats
Powered by: Two 310hp Continental TSIO-520-L piston-engines
Span: 37ft 10in (11.53m)
Length: 29ft 10in (9.09m)
Gross weight: 5,700lb (2,585kg)
Cruising speed: 231-251mph (372-404km/h)
Cruising range: 1,300 miles (2,090km)

Beech introduced the Model 95-55 Baron in November 1960 to succeed the lower-powered Model 95 Travel Air (719 built), which had an unswept fin and rudder. Originally a 4/5-seater, the Baron evolved into the 4/6-seat B, C, D and E55, with more powerful engines. Introduced in late 1969, the Baron 58 is 10in (25cm) longer and has the same engines as the E55. Subsequently, the pressurised Baron 58P and turbo-supercharged Baron 58TC have been added to the range. Over 4,400 Barons of all types have been built.

Beechcraft King Air 90, 100

USA

Business twin and third-level airliner, in production and service
Photo: Super King Air F90
Data: King Air B100

Accommodation: 2 pilots and up to 13 passengers
Powered by: Two 715shp Garrett AiResearch TPE331-6-252B turboprops
Span: 45ft 10.5in (13.98m)
Length: 39ft 11.25in (12.17m)
Gross weight: 11,800lb (5,352kg)
Max cruising speed: 306mph (493km/h) at 10,000ft (3,050m)
Cruising range: 1,575 miles (2,438km)

Beech developed the pressurised King Air as an outgrowth of the piston-engined Queen Air, by way of the military NU-8F, which had PT6A turboprops. A production prototype of the commercial model flew on 20 January 1964, and entered production during the same year as the Model 90 with PT6A-6 engines. A switch to -20 engines was made in the Model A90, announced in 1966. The King Air C90 is the economy member of the family, with 550shp PT6A-21 engines, a span of 50ft 3in (15.32m), length of 35ft 6in (10.82m) and gross weight of 9,650lb (4,377kg). The King Air 100 appeared in 1969 with 680shp PT6A-28 engines and dimensions as quoted alongside. The same PT6A-28 engines crossed with the earlier airframe produced the King Air E90 in 1972 and in 1979 the Super King Air F90 appeared with a T-tail and PT6A-135 engines. TPE331 engines in the A100 airframe produced the B100 in 1975. The same engine can be retrofitted in any King Air 90 by Jetcrafters Inc in its Taurus modification.

Beechcraft Duke

USA

Business twin, in production and service
Photo and data: B60

Accommodation: 4-6 persons in individual seats
Powered by: Two 380hp Lycoming TIO-541-E1C4 piston-engines
Span: 39ft 3in (11.96m)
Length: 33ft 10in (10.31m)
Gross weight: 6,775lb (3,073kg)
Cruising speed: 229-268mph (369-417km/h)
Typical cruising range: 1,291 miles (2,079km) at 20,000ft (6,100m)

First flown on 29 December 1966, the Duke was designed to complete the Beech twin-engined range and fits between the Baron light twin and the heavier family of Queen Airs. It is pressurised for operation above 20,000ft and has turbo-supercharged engines. Deliveries began early in 1968, following certification on 1 February and about 500 had been built by January 1979. The current model is designated B60 and introduced a number of refinements including an improved pressurisation system.

Beechcraft Super King Air 200 USA

Business transport, in production and service

Accommodation: Two seats on flight deck and 6-8 passengers in the cabin
Powered by: Two 850shp Pratt & Whitney PT6A-41 turboprops
Span: 54ft 6in (16.6m)
Length: 43ft 10in (13.36m)
Gross weight: 12,500lb (5,670kg)
Max cruising speed: 320mph (515km/h) at 25,000ft (7,620m)
Range: 1,370-2,172 miles (2,204-3,495km)

The Super King Air was developed by Beech (with the engineering designation of Model 101) over a period of four years and was first marketed in 1974. Compared with the King Air the Super has more powerful engines, a T-tail, lengthened fuselage and increased wing span, more fuel capacity and a higher cabin pressurisation level. Two prototypes were used for flight development, first flights being made on 27 October and 15 December 1972 respectively. FAA certification was obtained on 14 December 1973. Deliveries totalled more than 500 by early 1979 including military C-12 models. Wing-tip tanks can be fitted to special-duty Model 200Ts, as delivered to French IGN and Japanese Maritime Safety Agency.

Beechcraft Duchess USA

Light twin transport, in production and service

Accommodation: Pilot plus three passengers
Powered by: Two 180hp Lycoming O-360-A1G6D piston-engines
Span: 38ft 0in (11.59m)
Length: 29ft 0.5in (8.86m)
Gross weight: 3,900lb (1,769kg)
Cruising speed: 182mph (293km/h)
Range: 818-898 miles (1,317-1,445km)

Beech Aircraft Corp developed the Model 76 under the project designation PD 289 during 1974 as an addition to its twin-engined range of aircraft at the lighter end of the scale, providing competition for the Piper Seneca and Cessna 310. Following the adoption of a T-tail for the Beech Super King Air 200, this same feature was used on the PD 289, which first flew in September 1974 with 160hp engines. After 180hp engines had been substituted Beech decided to launch production of the new light twin as the Model 76 Duchess. First flight was made on 24 May 1977 and deliveries began in May 1978. More than 200 Model 76s were ordered by Beech distributors when it was launched in 1976 and that total had more than doubled by mid-1979.

British Aerospace (HS) 125 UK

Business jet transport, in production and service
Photo and data: Srs 700

Accommodation: Crew of 2 and 8-14 passengers
Powered by: Two 3,700lb (1,680kg) st Garrett AiResearch TFE731-3-1H turbofans
Span: 47ft 0in (14.33m)
Length: 50ft 8.5in (15.46m)
Gross weight: 24,200lb (10,977kg)
Cruising speed: 449-502mph (723-808km/h)
Range: 2,210 miles (3,556km) with max payload and reserves

A prototype of the HS125 Srs 700 made its first flight on 28 June 1976, followed by the first production model before the end of the year and deliveries in the first half of 1977. This variant of the biz-jet originally developed by de Havilland and produced by Hawker Siddeley, differed from its predecessors primarily in having turbofan engines, with a number of drag-reducing refinements and other improvements. The original 125 prototype (as a de Havilland product) flew on 13 August 1962 and more than 420 of all versions had been sold by mid-1979, all except the Srs 700 with Rolls-Royce (Bristol) Viper turbojets. From the original Srs 1 evolved the Srs 3A and 3B (A=North American market, B=rest of the world) with increased power, the 3A-RA and 3B-RA with flush-fitting ventral fuel tank, the Srs 400A and 400B with uprated Vipers and higher weights, and the Srs 600A with lengthened fuselage and other refinements. A Srs 800 was projected in 1979, with enlarged fuselage and new engines.

British Aerospace Jetstream 31 UK

Feeder-liner and business transport, in production and service
Photo: Century Jetstream III
Data: Jetstream 31

Accommodation: Flight crew of 1-2 and 12-18 passengers
Powered by: Two 940shp Garrett AiResearch TPE-331-10 turboprops
Span: 52ft 0in (15.85m)
Length: 47ft 1.5in (14.37m)
Gross weight: 14,110lb (6,400kg)
Cruising speed: 291mph (469km/h)
Max range: 1,275 miles (2,053km) with six passengers and reserves

Development of the Jetstream was undertaken by the former Handley Page company early in 1966 and the first of four test aircraft flew on 18 August 1967. Deliveries of the Jetstream Mk 1, with Astazou XIV engines, began in the spring of 1969, and 36 were built by HP. Scottish Aviation subsequently built 26 more as trainers for the RAF and RN and in 1979 British Aerospace announced that the Scottish Division would relaunch production of a version with Garrett AiResearch TPE 331s as the Jetstream 31, for delivery in 1981. Several original HP Jetstreams have been re-engined in the USA with these engines or PT6A-34s.

Canadair CL-600 Challenger

Canada

Business twin-jet, in production

Accommodation: Flight crew of 2 and 8-14 passengers
Powered by: Two 7,500lb (3,405kg) st Avco Lycoming ALF-502L turbofans
Span: 61ft 10in (18.85m)
Length: 68ft 5in (20.85m)
Gross weight: 36,000lb (16,330kg)
Cruising speed: 547mph (882km/h)
Range: 4,140 miles (6,667km) with eight passengers and IFR reserves

The original version of this aircraft, known as the LearStar 600, was designed by William P. Lear in the USA in 1974/75, and an option on design and manufacturing rights was acquired by Canadair in mid-1976. Canadair received Canadian government approval on 29 October 1976 to proceed with full-scale development and production of what is now named the Challenger. This is intended primarily for the top end of the biz-jet market and also has applications in the third level/commuter market. The first Challenger was flown on 8 November 1978 at Montreal, temporarily with 6,700lb (3,042kg) st ALF502H engines. It was then moved to California for flight testing, where it first flew with ALF502L engines on 12 March 1979. The second aircraft flew on 17 March and in 1979 Canadair announced development of a stretched version with CF-34 engines, known as the Challenger E, for 1983 delivery.

Canadian Car and Foundry Norseman

Canada

Utility transport, in service
Data: Norseman V

Accommodation: Pilot and 7-9 passengers
Powered by: One 600hp Pratt & Whitney S3H1 or R-1340-AN-1 Wasp piston-engine
Span: 51ft 8in (15.74m)
Length: 33ft 4in (10.16m)
Gross weight: 7,400lb (3,357kg)
Cruising speed: 141mph (227km/h)
Range: 464 miles (747km)

The rugged Norseman was designed in 1934 specifically for Canadian 'bush' flying, and a prototype flew in 1935 with a 450hp engine. Prewar production models were the Norseman II and IV, built by the Noorduyn company, which also produced 746 of these aircraft for the USAAF during the war, with the designation UC-64. In 1946, CCF acquired the design and produced an improved version, the Norseman V, until 1950, by which time about 850 of all models had been built. Many still operate in Canada, often on floats or skis.

CASA C-212 Aviocar

Spain

Light general purpose transport, in production and service
Data: C-212CB

Accommodation: 2 pilots and up to 19 passengers
Powered by: Two 776ehp Garrett AiResearch TPE331-5-251C turboprops
Span: 62ft 4in (19.0m)
Length: 49ft 10.5in (15.20m)
Gross weight: 14,330lb (6,500kg)
Cruising speed: 171mph (275km/h)
Range: 300 miles (400km) with max payload

First flown on 26 March 1971, the Aviocar was designed initially to meet Spanish Air Force requirements for a multi-role transport, with potential for later development in civil guise. A second prototype flew on 23 October 1971, and the first of a production batch for the Spanish Air Force flew on 17 November 1972. Civil certification was then obtained for the C-212C variant, first sales of which were made to Pelita Air Service in Indonesia, where PT Nurtania company also assembles the Aviocar for military and civil customers in the Far East. The C-212C had a gross weight of 12,500lb (5,675kg) to comply with FAA certification as a third-level airliner but the C-212B was approved later at the weights shown above. The C-212-10 or Srs 200 has 865shp TPE 331-10 engines and a gross weight of 16,534lb (7,500kg).

Cessna Stationair and Skywagon

USA

Single-engined utility aircraft, in production and service
Photo: Stationair 7
Data: Turbo-Stationair 7

Accommodation: Pilot and up to 6 passengers.
Powered by: One 310hp Continental TSIO-520-M flat-six piston engine.
Span: 35ft 10in (10.92m)
Length: 31ft 9in (9.68m)
Gross weight: 3,800lb (1,723kg)
Max cruising speed: 185mph (298km/h) at 20,000ft (6,100m)
Range: 443-702 miles (713-1,130km)

The Cessna U206 and turbo-charged TU206 were originally known as Skywagons but were renamed Stationair 6 (300hp Continental IO-520F) and Turbo-Stationair 6 (310hp TSIO-520-M) to distinguish them from the smaller Model 185 Skywagon. They incorporate double cargo doors to facilitate freight loading. By early 1978, 4,802 Model 206s had been delivered, including 643 de luxe versions known as Super Skylanes, no longer in production. The Model 207 Skywagon and T207 Turbo-Skywagon, now Stationair 7 and Turbo-Stationair 7 with the same engine, are generally similar but have a lengthened centre fuselage and seat up to seven. The prototype Model 207 flew on 11 May 1968, and over 370 have been built.

Cessna 337 Skymaster USA

Light transport, in production and service
Photo and data: Reims pressurised Skymaster

Accommodation: 4-6 seats
Powered by: Two 225hp Continental TSIO-360-C piston-engines
Span: 38ft 2in (11.63m)
Length: 29ft 10in (9.09m)
Gross weight: 4,700lb (2,132kg)
Cruising speed: 228mph (367km/h) at 16,000ft (4,877m)
Range: 1,320-1,810 miles (2,124-2,913km)

The prototype of this revolutionary 'push-and-pull' twin-boomed four-seat business aircraft flew on 28 February 1961, and production deliveries began in May 1963. Powered by two 210hp Continental IO-360 engines, the Skymaster combined the advantages of a normal light twin with simpler handling characteristics, especially after a failure of one engine. The original Model 336 Skymaster had a fixed undercarriage and 195 were built. The Model 337, with retractable undercarriage, replaced it in 1965 and introduced a number of other new features. The Turbo-System Skymaster, with turbo-supercharged engines, was announced in April 1967, and over 2,900 Model 337s had been built by 1978, including 544 O-2 military versions. Added to the range in 1972 was a pressurised version, the P337, data for which are quoted here. Reims Aviation has sold more than 90 Skymasters assembled in France as well as about 70 of its own FTB 337 STOL variant.

Cessna 310/340/335 USA

Business twin, in production and service
Photo: Model 340
Data: Model 340A

Accommodation: 6 including pilot
Powered by: Two 285hp Continental TSIO-520-B piston engines
Span: 38ft 1.33in (11.62m)
Length: 34ft 4in (10.46m)
Gross weight: 5,990lb (2,717kg)
Cruising speed: 231-267mph (372-430km/h)
Max range: 1,586 miles (2,552km) (with reserves)

Cessna's popular Model 310 made its first flight on 3 January 1953, and went into production in 1954, since when more than 5,000 have been built. Early models had an unswept fin; the present swept fin was introduced on the Model 310D in 1960 and the current 310P has 285hp Continental IO-520-M engines and a ventral fin. The similar Turbo-System T310 has turbo-supercharged TSIO-520-B engines. This variant took the place of the Model 320 Skynight, production of which ended in 1968 after 575 had been delivered. In 1972, Cessna introduced the pressurised Model 340, derived from the basic 310 design with the Model 414's wing and Turbo-System 310's power plant. The Model 340A, which followed in 1976, has 310hp Continental TSIO-520-N engines and the Model 335, introduced in 1980, is an unpressurised version of the 340. About 700 Model 340s have been built.

Cessna 401/402

USA

Business twin and air taxi, in production and service
Photo: Model 402 Businessliner
Data: Model 402B

Accommodation: Up to 10 seats
Powered by: Two 300hp Continental TSIO-520-E turbo-supercharged piston-engines
Span: 39ft 10.25in (12.15m)
Length: 36ft 1in (11.0m)
Gross weight: 6,300lb (2,858kg)
Cruising speed: 215-240mph (346-386km/h) at 20,000ft (6,100m)
Range: 633-1,639 miles (1,018-2,637km)

Cessna announced these additions to its twin engined range late in 1966, having flown the 401 prototype on 26 August 1965. They were closely related to the Model 411, which was subsequently dropped, but lighter and cheaper. The 6/8-seat Model 401 was aimed specifically at the executive market and production ended in 1973 with more than 400 built. The Model 402 Businessliner and Utililiner, with similar dimensions, weights and performance, have a re-designed interior for use as a 9/10-seat commuter or for light freighting. The Model 402B, introduced in 1971, has a longer nose than the original Model 401. About 1,000 have been built to date. American Jet Industries produced a small number of turboprop conversions of the Model 402, with 400shp Allison 250-B17 engines, as the Turbo Star 402A.

Cessna Titan

USA

Business twin and commuter/light freighter, in production and service

Accommodation: Up to 10 including pilot
Powered by: Two 375hp Continental GTSIO-520-M turbo-supercharged piston-engines
Span: 46ft 0in (14.02m)
Length: 39ft 5in (12.04m)
Gross weight: 8,300lb (3,765kg)
Cruising speed: 246mph (396km/h) at 20,000ft (6,100m)
Range: 1,020-2,060 miles (1,641-3,315km)

As the Model 404, the Titan joined the Cessna range of business twins during 1976, being similar in general size and characteristics to the Model 421 but without cabin pressurisation. Consequently, the type was expected to appeal more especially to the commuter/air cargo market, with its large cabin and its ability to fly good loads out of short, rough fields. A large cargo door was available as an option, permitting the loading of freight containers or items of unusual size. The Model 404 designation has now been dropped and the Titan is offered in three versions: the Ambassador for the business/executive market, the Courier for the commuter and the Freighter for cargo operations. Over 100 had been built by early 1978.

Cessna 414A Chancellor, 421 Golden Eagle and Corsair — USA

Business twin and air taxi, in production and service
Photo and Data: Model 414A Chancellor

Accommodation: Pilot and 5 passengers
Powered by: Two 310hp Continental TSIO-520-N turbo-supercharged piston-engines
Span: 44ft 1.5in (13.45m)
Length: 36ft 4.5in (11.09m)
Gross weight: 6,750lb (3,062kg)
Max cruising speed: 259mph (417km/h) at 25,000ft (7,620m)
Range: 1,500 miles (2,414km)

First flown on 18 July 1962, the Cessna 411 entered production as the largest member of the Cessna range and deliveries began in February 1965. Production ended in June 1968, when 301 had been built, and the top end of the range was filled instead by the Model 421 which was similar but with pressurisation. The 421B had tip-tanks but was followed in 1976 by the 421C with a new wing incorporating extra fuel capacity. More than 1,400 Model 421s have been sold. First flown on 1 November 1968, the Model 414 combined the pressurised fuselage and tail unit of the Model 421 with the wing and power plant of the Model 401. The Model 414A Chancellor in 1978 introduced a bonded 'wet' wing. For 1980, Cessna introduced the Corsair; this being basically the 421 Golden Eagle with 450shp Pratt & Whitney PT6A-112 turboprops.

Cessna 441 Conquest — USA

Business twin and light transport, in production and service

Accommodation: Up to 11 including pilot
Powered by: Two 620shp Garrett AiResearch TPE331-8-401 turboprops
Span: 49ft 4in (15.05m)
Length: 39ft 0.25in (11.89m)
Gross weight: 9,850lb (4,468kg)
Cruising speed: 337mph (543km/h)
Max range: 2,382 miles (3,833km) with five passengers at 33,000ft (10,060m)

The Cessna 441 was first flown on 26 August 1975 and was added to the company's range of business twins in 1977 as its first turboprop aircraft. Of typical Cessna configuration and similar in overall appearance to the 404 Titan, it originally had an almost identical wing, but after initial specifications had been released, the aspect ratio was increased by adding 18in (46cm) to each semispan; this also allowed an increase in fuel capacity and improved the service ceiling and cruising speed. Deliveries began at the end of 1977 and more than 100 had been sold by 1979.

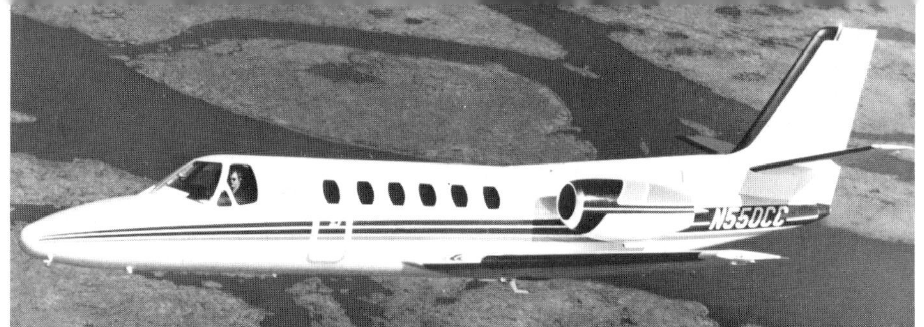

Cessna Citation I & II

USA

Business jet transport, in production and service
Photo and data: Citation II

Accommodation: Flight crew of 2 and up to 8 passengers
Powered by: Two 2,500lb (1,135kg) st Pratt & Whitney JT15D-4 turbofans
Span: 51ft 8in (15.75m)
Length: 47ft 2in (14.38m)
Gross weight: 13,500lb (6,033kg)
Max cruising speed: 420mph (675km/h)
Normal range: 1,968 miles (3,167km)

Cessna announced preliminary details of its first jet-powered design for the commercial market in October 1968, when the type was known as the Fanjet 500. The prototype made its first flight on 15 September 1969, and production deliveries began late in September 1971 following certification to FAR Pt 25 standards. Engines were JT15D-1s and span 43ft 9in (13.33m) After production of 349 Citations, a switch was made at the end of 1976 to the Citation I with increased span and uprated engines; the Model 501 Citation I/SP is certificated for single pilot operation. The Citation II (Model 550 and 551SP) first flew on 31 January 1977 and deliveries began in April 1978.

Cessna Citation III

USA

Business jet transport, under development

Accommodation: Crew of 2 and up to 13 passengers
Powered by: Two 3,650lb (1,655kg) st Garrett AiResearch TFE 731-3-100s turbofans
Span: 53ft 4.25in (16.3m)
Length: 55ft 5.25in (16.9m)
Gross weight: 17,000lb (7,711kg)
Max cruising speed: 540mph (868km/h)
Range: 2,190-2,875 miles (3,525-4,625km) (with reserves)

Cessna announced in late-1976 that it would proceed with development of the Citation III for 1980 deliveries after earlier studies for Citation derivatives that had included the Citation 600 and the three-engined straightwing Citation 700. The Citation III is larger than those projects, with stand-up aisle height, and retains little of the basic Citation beyond the name. The wing has a supercritical section and, with the different turbofan engines, helps to give the aircraft an intercontinental range. The prototype made its first flight on 31 May 1979 and deliveries were to begin in early 1981.

Dassault-Breguet Falcon 10 (Mystère 10) France

Business jet transport, in production and service

Accommodation: Crew of 2 and 4-7 passengers
Powered by: Two 3,230lb (1,465kg) st Garrett AiResearch TFE 731-2 turbofans
Span: 42ft 11in (13.08m)
Length: 45ft 5in (13.85m)
Gross weight: 18,740lb (8,500kg)
Max cruising speed: 568mph (915km/h)
Range: 2,210 miles (3,555km) wiht 4 passengers (with reserves)

Development of the Mystère 10 was first announced by Dassault in June 1969, when the type was known as the Minifalcon. As that name suggested, it is a scaled-down version of the Mystère/Falcon 20, of about three-quarters the power and two-thirds the weight. First flight of the prototype was made on 1 December 1970, with 2,954lb st General Electric CJ610-6 engines, pending availability of the AiResearch turbofans planned for production models and fitted in the second prototype, flown on 15 October 1971. This aircraft subsequently became a test-bed for the Larzac, flying with one of these engines (and one TFE 731) on 22 May 1973. The first production Falcon 10 flew on 30 April 1973, and deliveries began in November. By late-1979, total sales of the Falcon 10 stood at 194.

Dassault-Breguet Falcon 20 (Mystère 20) France

Business jet transport, in production and service
Data: Falcon F

Accommodation: Crew of 2 and up to 14 passengers
Powered by: Two 4,500lb (2,043kg) st General Electric CF700-2D-2 turbofans
Span: 53ft 3in (16.30m)
Length: 56ft 3in (17.15m)
Gross weight: 28,660lb (13,000kg)
Cruising speed: 466-536mph (750-862km/h)
Max range: 2,080 miles (3,350km) with 1,600lb (725kg) payload (with reserves)

Construction of a prototype Mystère 20 executive jet transport was started by Dassault in January 1962, and the first flight was made on 4 May 1963, with 3,300lb st Pratt & Whitney JT12A-8 turbojets; GE turbofans were selected for production and the prototype flew with these engines on 10 July 1964. The aircraft is known in the USA, and generally outside of France, as the Falcon 20. The Standard Falcon was followed by the C, D, E and F versions, the latest of these having uprated engines, more fuel, new high-lift devices and other improvements. For the US Coast Guard, Dassault developed the Falcon G (HU-25A Guardian) with 5,300lb (2,406kg) st Garrett AiResearch ATF3-6 turbofans and the Falcon H was launched in 1979 for commercial use with these engines and increased fuel capacity. More than 450 Falcon 20s had been sold by late-1979.

Dassault-Breguet Falcon 50 (Mystère 50) France

Business jet transport, in production and service

Accommodation: Flight crew of 2 and 8 passengers in standard layout
Powered by: Three 3,700lb (1,680kg) st Garrett AiResearch TFE 731-3 turbofans
Span: 61ft 10.5in (18.85m)
Length: 60ft 9in (18.52m)
Gross weight: 37,480lb (17,000kg)
Cruising speed: 552mph (889km/h)
Range: 3,910 miles (6,295km) at Mach 0.75 with eight passengers

The Dassault-Breguet company decided to add the Falcon 50 to its range of biz-jets during 1974, finding that the market for such an aircraft was more promising than for the larger Falcon 30 twin-jet, which was then dropped. The Falcon 50, a prototype of which made its first flight on 7 November 1976, uses many components of the Falcon 20, having the same basic fuselage cross-section, but introduced an improved wing, and a third engine in the rear fuselage. The latter is lengthened, to provide extra space for fuel and baggage; passenger accommodation remains unchanged. The wing first flown on the Falcon 50 was replaced by one of more advanced (supercritical) design with which the prototype first flew on 6 May 1977. The second and third aircraft flew on 16 February and 13 June 1978 and the fourth on 2 March 1979, a few days after French certification. Sales totalled 117 by late-1979.

De Havilland DHC-2 Beaver and Turbo Beaver Canada

Light utility transport, in service
Photo: Beaver Mk I
Data: DHC-2 Mk III Turbo-Beaver

Accommodation: Pilot and up to 10 passengers
Powered by: One 578ehp Pratt & Whitney PT6A-6 or -20 turboprop
Span: 48ft 0in (14.64m)
Length: 35ft 3in (10.75m)
Gross weight: 5,370lb (2,435kg)
Cruising speed: 140-157mph (225-252km/h)
Range: 260-677 miles (418-1,090km) (with reserves)

The Beaver was the first of de Havilland's family of STOL utility aircraft, and made its first flight in August 1947. It was designed particularly to meet local Canadian requirements for a rugged 'bush' aircraft, but found a wide market overseas. A total of 1,657 Mk 1s were built, with 450hp P&W R-985 engine, including 968 for the US Army and USAF and 46 for the British Army. A single Beaver Mk II had an Alvis Leonides engine. On 30 December 1963, DHC flew the prototype Mk III Turbo-Beaver, powered by a PT6A turboprop, and a few examples were built. A Garrett AiResearch TPE331 has been fitted in a Beaver in New Zealand.

De Havilland DHC-3 Otter

Canada

Utility transport, in service
Photo: DHC-3 Amphibian

Accommodatipn: Pilot and up to 11 passengers
Powered by: One 600hp Pratt & Whitney R-1340-S1H1-G piston-engine
Span: 58ft 0in (17.69m)
Length: 41ft 10in (12.80m)
Gross weight: 8,000lb (3,629kg)
Cruising speed: 121-132mph (195-212km/h)
Range: 875 miles (1,410km) with 2,100lb (953kg) payload

Second of the de Havilland utility line, the Otter was first flown on 12 December 1951, and was an extrapolation of the successful Beaver formula into a larger size. Deliveries began at the end of 1952 and 460 were built, including large batches for the US Army and the RCAF. Land, sea or snow undercarriages can be fitted and a later development was an amphibious version featuring retractable wheels in standard Edo floats. During 1978, Cox Air Resources of Edmonton, Alberta, completed a prototype conversion of an Otter with 600hp PT6A-27 turboprop, giving a cruising speed of 150mph (241km/h) and range of 1,045 miles (1,681km).

De Havilland DHC-5 Transporter

Canada

STOL passenger/cargo transport, in production

Accommodation: Flight crew of 2 and 44-48 passengers or 13,500lb (6,130kg) cargo
Powered by: Two 3,133shp General Electric CT64-820-4 turboprops
Span: 95ft 0in (29,26m)
Length: 79ft 0in (24.08m)
Gross weight: 41,000lb (18,597kg)
Cruising speed: 288mph (463km/h)
Range: 230 miles (370km) with max payload, 1,035 miles (1,665km) with 6,000lb (2,724kg) payload.

The DHC-5 was first flown on 9 April 1964, as the prototype of the Buffalo tactical STOL transport for military use. Since that date, more than 100 have been built for the Canadian Armed Forces and for export to a number of countries in South America, the Middle East and Africa. These include a number of the more powerful DHC-5D versions, first flown on 1 August 1975 and with gross weight increased to 49,200lb (22,316kg). In 1979, de Havilland announced its intention of offering a civil version of the DHC-5D as the Transporter, and a prototype was shown publicly for the first time at the Paris Air Show in that year. The Transporter differs from the military Buffalo in having a lower gross weight and in interior arrangements, which include quick-change provision between passenger and cargo layouts.

Dornier Do27

Germany

Light utility transport, in service
Data: Do27A-4

Accommodation: 2 pilots and up to 6 passengers
Powered by: One 270hp Lycoming GO-480-B piston-engine
Span: 39ft 4.5in (12.00m)
Length: 31ft 6in (9.6m)
Gross weight: 4,070lb (1,850kg)
Cruising speed: 109-130mph (175-210km/h)
Max range: 685 miles (1,100km) (no reserves)

Dornier's Do27, a development of the Do25 which was built in Spain to Prof Dornier's designs in 1954, was the first aircraft of indigenous design to be produced in Germany after World War II. The prototype, built by CASA in Spain, flew on 27 June 1955, followed by the first genuine German specimen on 17 October 1956. A total of 620 were built, of which 478 were for the Luftwaffe and Spanish Air Force (the latter built in Spain). Prototypes were flown on floats and with an Astazou turboprop engine.

Dornier Do28

Germany

Utility transport, in service
Data: Do28-1

Accommodation: Pilot and up to 7 passengers
Powered by: Two 290hp Lycoming IO-540-A piston engines
Span: 45ft 3.5in (13.80m)
Length: 29ft 6in (9.00m)
Gross weight: 6,000lb (2,720kg)
Cruising speed: 150-170mph (242-274km/h)
Normal range: 768 miles (1,235km) with max payload (no reserves)

Derived from the Do27, the Do28 has virtually the same fuselage and an extended version of the same wing. The two engines are carried on stub wings. The prototype, with a standard Do27 wing and 180hp Lycoming O-360 engines, flew on 29 April 1959. The first production model was the Do28A-1 with 250hp O-540 engines; 60 were built. First flown in April 1963, the Do28B-1 has more power, a larger tailplane, higher weights and other changes. A total of 60 were built, of which six were converted to Do28B-1-S floatplane configuration by the Job-master Company for service in Canada, following one Do28A-1-S prototype.

Dornier Do28 D Skyservant

Germany

STOL utility transport, in production and service
Data: Do28D-2
Accommodation: Pilot and up to 14 passengers
Powered by: Two 380hp Lycoming IGSO-540-A1E piston engines
Span: 51ft 0.5in (15.55m)
Length: 37ft 5.25in (11.41m)
Gross weight: 8,853lb (4,015kg)
Cruising speed: 150-170mph (241-273km/h)
Max range: 656 miles (1,050km) (with max payload)

Despite its designation, the Skyservant inherits only the basic configuration of the Do28 which preceded it. The wing is similar but of greater span. The new fuselage is much longer and of bigger cross-section than that of the Do28, and embodies a larger freight loading door. Developed with financial assistance from the German government, the prototype flew for the first time on 23 February 1966, and certification was obtained in February 1967. Following delivery of seven initial production aircraft designated Do28D, manufacture switched to the D-1 with a 1ft 7.5in (50cm) increase in wing span and higher gross weight. The Do28D-2 appeared after the first 50 Skyservants and had a number of improvements, no inboard leading-edge slats, slab tailplane, more fuel and higher weight. On 9 April 1978, Dornier flew the Do28D-5X with Lycoming LTP101-600 turboprops and in 1979 announced the Do28D-6 Turbo-Skyservant with 400shp PT6A-110 turboprops.

EMBRAER EMB-121 Xingu

Brazil

Business twin-jet, in production and service

Accommodation: Flight crew of 2 and up to 6 passengers
Powered by: Two 680shp Pratt & Whitney PT6A-28 turboprops
Span: 47ft 5in (14.45m)
Length: 40ft 1.25in (12.25m)
Gross weight: 12,500lb (5,670kg)
Cruising speed: 280mph (450km/h)
Range: 1,460 miles (2,382km)

The Brazilian state factory EMBRAER has been steadily expanding the family of designs based on the Bandeirante (qv) since this light transport was first developed for the Brazilian Air Force. Several prospects were studied in the EMB-120 series and the first of these, flown in prototype form on 10 October 1976, is the EMB-121 Xingu. This has essentially the same wing (with slightly extended tips) and powerplant as the EMB-110, but a shortened, pressurised fuselage and a T-tail. The first production Xingu flew on 20 May 1977 and six were delivered to the Brazilian Air Force as VU-9 VIP transports in 1978. Civil certification was obtained in May 1979 and deliveries began on 1 June. Starting with the 49th aircraft in September 1981, the Xingu 2 will have a 33in (84cm) fuselage stretch for two more seats, and PT6A-42 engines.

Foxjet ST600 USA

Business twin-jet, under development

Accommodation: 6 seats including pilot in three pairs
Powered by: Two 800lb (363kg) st Williams Research WR44-800 turbofans
Span: 31ft 7in (9.63m)
Length: 31ft 6in (9.60m)
Gross weight: 4,449lb (2,018kg)
Max cruising speed: 409mph (659km/h)
Range: 1,099 miles (1,768km) with 45min reserve

Foxjet International, under the presidency of businessman Tony Fox, announced in the spring of 1977 that it was developing a completely new four-seat twin-jet aircraft for the business market, the principal feature of which was to be its small size and economy of operation. Williams WR19-3 turbofans were initially specified but the WR44-800s were later adopted, with a 40% increase in thrust that allowed the ST600 to be enlarged and redesigned for six seats instead of four. This also made redundant an alternative three-engined version that had been studied. A first flight target of May 1979 was announced when the Foxjet was launched but this was not achieved and the prototype was still being assembled in late-1979.

Gates Learjet Models 23, 24, 25, 28 and 29 USA

Business twin-jet, in production and service
Photo: Model 28/29 Longhorn
Data: Model 28 Longhorn

Accommodation: 2 pilots and up to 6 passengers
Powered by: Two 2,950lb (1,340kg) st General Electric CJ610-8A turbojets
Span: 43ft 9.5in (13.35m)
Length: 47ft 7in (14.50m)
Gross weight: 15,000lb (6,804kg)
Max cruising speed: 534mph (859km/h)
Max range: 1,577 miles (2,538km) with reserves

The Learjet was designed in Switzerland by the late Bill Lear Sr (as the SAAC-23) and a prototype, built in the USA, was first flown on 7 October 1963; deliveries began in October 1964. A total of 104 of the original Model 23 were built before a switch was made to the Model 24, with modifications to meet Part 25 of the Federal Air Regulations. The Model 24 first flew on 24 February 1966, and 80 were built before a switch was made in 1968 to the Model 24B, with -6 engines replacing the lower-rated -4s and a higher gross weight. This version was followed in 1970 by the 24D, with greater range and without the bullet fairing at the junction of the tailplane and fin. Current versions are the short-field 24E and, with increased fuel capacity, 24F. Lengthened by 4ft 2in (1.27m), to seat eight passengers, the Model 25 flew for the first time on 12 August 1966. Current versions are the improved Learjet 25D and the Model 25F with extra fuel. All these versions have a span of 35ft 7in (10.84m) but the Model 28 and Model 29 Longhorn version have a longer span with NASA winglets. The wing was first flown on a Learjet 25D on 24 August 1977 and the first production Learjet 28 flew on 21 August 1978.

Gates Learjet Models 35 and 36 USA

Business twin-jet, in production and service
Photo: Century III
Data: Model 35A

Accommodation: 2 pilots and up to 7 passengers
Powered by: Two 3,500lb (1,588kg) st Garrett AiResearch TFE 731-2 turbofans
Span: 39ft 4in (12.04m)
Length: 48ft 8in (14.83m)
Gross weight: 17,000lb (7,711kg)
Max cruising speed: 534mph (859km/h)
Max range: 2,775 miles (4,466km)

Announced at the 1973 Paris Air Show, the Learjet Models 35 and 36 differ only in payload/range characteristics. The Model 35A carries seven passengers in its main cabin, plus an eighth on the flight deck when flown with a single pilot. The Model 36A carries only five passengers in its cabin but has an increased fuel capacity to extend its range to 3,305 miles (5,318km) with four passengers. Both aircraft represent slightly 'stretched' versions of the basic Learjet airframe. The switch to turbofans enables them to offer both improved payload/range and lower noise levels. First to fly with TFE 731 engines, on 4 January 1973, was a modified Learjet 25, followed by the Model 35 prototype on 22 August 1973. Deliveries began in the summer of 1974 and by mid-1979 a total of over 900 Learjets of all models (including the 20-series, see previous entry) had been delivered.

Gates Learjet Models 54, 55 and 56 Longhorn USA

Business twin-jet, in production
Data: Learjet 55

Accommodation: Crew of 2 and up to 10 passengers
Powered by: Two 3,650lb (1,657kg) st Garrett AiResearch TFE731-3 turbofans
Span: 42ft 9.5in (13.35m)
Length: 55ft 1in (16.79m)
Gross weight: 18,500lb (8,391kg)
Max cruising speed: 534mph (859km/h)
Range: 3,000 miles (4,830km) with 1,200lb (544kg) payload

While sales of the earlier Learjet models continued to exceed those of all other biz-jets by a substantial margin, the Gates Learjet company announced in June 1977 that it was developing a new family of Longhorn variants featuring a fuselage both lengthened and deepened plus the advanced technology wing, with winglets, already developed for the Learjet 28/29 Longhorns. The new variants were the Model 54, 55 and 56, dimensionally similar but with different cabin lengths and fuel capacities; the Model 56 has a gross weight of 20,000lb (9,080kg). The prototype of the Longhorn 54/55/56 was first flown on 19 April 1979 and certification was expected by mid-1980, by which time production was expected to reach four a month.

Grumman (and McKinnon) Goose

USA

Light transport amphibian, in service
Photo: Standard Goose
Data: G-21G Turbo-Goose

Accommodation: Pilot and up to 11 passengers
Powered by: Two 680shp Pratt & Whitney (Canada) PT6A-27 turboprops
Span: 50ft 10in (15.49m)
Length: 39ft 7in (12.07m)
Gross weight: 12,500lb (5,670kg)
Max speed: 243mph (391km/h)
Max range: 1,600miles (2,575km)

The Grumman G-21 first flew in June 1937 and production was initiated to meet orders from commerical users. The majority of over 250 built, however, were for military use during World War II, although many of these were later sold in the civil market and are still used for specialised airline operations. McKinnon Enterprises engineered a conversion scheme for the Goose, soon after the war, in which four 340hp Lycoming GSO-480s replaced the original pair of 450hp R-985 Wasps, and many other changes were made to improve the performance of the Goose and its suitability as an executive aircraft. In 1966, McKinnon flew the prototype of a further refined conversion, with PT6A turboprops. This conversion is available to owners of Goose amphibians, current versions being the G-21C, with short bow, and the lengthened G-21C, with further improvements to enhance comfort and performance.

Grumman Mallard (and Albatross)

USA

Light transport amphibian, in service
Photo: Mallard

Accommodation: Crew of 2 and 10 passengers
Powered by: Two 600hp Pratt & Whitney R-1340-S3H1 piston engines
Span: 66ft 8in (20.32m)
Length: 48ft 4in (14.73m)
Gross weight: 12,750lb (5,790kg)
Cruising speed: 180mph (290km/h) at 8,000ft (2,438m)
Range: 730-1, 380 miles (1,175-2,220km)

The Grumman G-73 was developed postwar as an attempt to continue the tradition of the Goose (qv) and small Widgeon. The prototype first flew in 1946 and deliveries began in 1947, most of the 61 built being delivered initially for business use. In 1979, at least 10 Mallards were in airline service in the USA — three with Trans Catalina and seven with Chalks International Airlines. The latter company also was planning to introduce a fleet of up to 12 converted HU-16 Albatross amphibians after flight testing of a prototype G-111 began on 13 February 1979. These would operate as 28-seat commuter airliners.

Grumman Gulfstream I

USA

Business transport, in service

Accommodation: Crew of 2 and 10-14 passengers
Powered by: Two 2,210ehp Rolls-Royce Dart 529-8X turboprops
Span: 78ft 4in (23.88m)
Length: 63ft 9in (19.43m)
Gross weight: 36,000lb (16,330kg)
Cruising speed: 357mph (575km/h)
Max range: 2,740 miles (4,410km)

The Gulfstream was developed as the first of the larger, long-range corporate transports to take advantage of turbine power plants. In all respects a 'baby airliner', with standards of comfort and performance equal to those experienced on scheduled airline flights, the Gulfstream was intended primarily for the US domestic market, where it gained a ready acceptance. The first flight was made on 14 August 1958 and certification was obtained in the following year. Production ended early in 1969, when the 200th aircraft had been delivered. During 1979, Gulfstream American Corp was considering launching a stretched version of the Gulfstream I for the commuter airline market, and one existing airplane was converted to this new standard as the G-159C, making its first flight on 25 October 1979.

Grumman GA-7 Cougar

USA

Light business and private twin, in service

Accommodation: Pilot plus 3-5 passengers
Powered by: Two 160hp Lycoming O-320-D1D piston engines
Span: 36ft 10.5in (11.25m)
Length: 29ft 10in (9.10m)
Gross weight: 3,800lb (1,725kg)
Max cruising speed: 184mph (296km/h)
Max range: 1,336 miles (2,150km)

The Cougar was the first twin-engined aircraft developed by Grumman American, designed, like the Beech Model 76, to meet the requirements of that portion of the market left unfilled when Piper stopped production of the Twin Commanche. A four-seat prototype of the Cougar first flew on 20 December 1974, and a pre-production prototype flown on 1 December 1976 differed from the prototype in having a wider fuselage, outward rather than inward retracting undercarriage, and a cabin entry door in place of a sliding canopy. Delivery of production aircraft began in February 1978, six months before the company was taken over by AJI and renamed Gulfstream American.

Gulfstream American Gulfstream II and III — USA

Business twin-jet in production and service
Photo: Gulfstream II
Data: Gulfstream III

Accommodation: Flight crew of 2-3 and up to 19 passengers
Powered by: Two 11,400lb (5,171kg) st Rolls-Royce Spey Mk 511-8 turbofans
Span: 77ft 10in (23.7m)
Length: 83ft 1in (25.3m)
Gross weight: 68,200lb (30,936kg)
Max cruising speed: 577mph (928km/h)
Max range: 4,785 miles (7,699km)

The Gulfstream II, developed originally by Grumman, was designed to carry up to 19 passengers in executive comfort over long ranges. The first Gulfstream II flew on 2 October 1966 and the first 82 aircraft had a lower gross weight of 57,500lb (26,080kg) thereafter increased to 65,500lb (29,711kg); with effect from aircraft No 166 delivered July 1975, hush-kits are fitted on the engines and Grumman also introduced tip tanks for the Gulfstream II, adding 3,120lb (1,415kg) of fuel. After Gulfstream American acquired the company in September 1978 work continued on the Gulfstream III with a 2ft (0.61m) fuselage stretch and improved wing with winglets. First flight was made on 2 December 1979 by which time over 250 Gulfstream IIs had been delivered.

Gulfstream American Model 500 Hustler — USA

Business transport, under development
Photo: Hustler 400
Data: Hustler 500

Accommodation: Flight crew of 1-2 plus up to 7 passenger seats in cabin
Powered by: One 900shp Garrett AiResearch TPE331-10-501 and one 2,200lb (1,000kg) st Pratt & Whitney JT15D-1 turbofans
Span: 34ft 5in (10.49m)
Length: 41ft 3in (12.57m)
Gross weight: 10,000lb (4,540kg)
Max cruising speed: 460mph (770km/h)
Range: 2,300-2,762 miles (3,700-4,444km)

The Hustler was conceived by American Jet Industries as a new-type business aircraft, with a basic turboprop engine plus a turbojet in the rear fuselage to provide power for emergency use. The prototype Model 400 Hustler flew for the first time on 11 January 1978, powered by the PT6A-41 turboprop only and the company subsequently decided that the Williams WR 19-3-1 turbofan in the rear fuselage (Hustler 400A) would be replaced by the Pratt & Whitney JT15D-1 (Hustler 500). After AJI acquired the Grumman American company in September 1978, the Hustler was added to the range of aircraft to be built by the Gulfstream American and in 1979 the company decided to replace the nose-mounted PT6A with a Garrett AiResearch engine.

Hawker Siddeley (DH104) Dove and Riley Turbo-Exec 400

UK/USA

Light transport and business twin, in service
Photo: Riley Turbo-Exec 400
Data: Dove 8

Accommodation: Crew of 2 and 8-11 passengers
Powered by: Two 400hp Gipsy Queen 70 Mk 3 piston-engines
Span: 57ft 0in (17.37m)
Length: 39ft 3in (11.96m)
Gross weight: 8,950lb (4,060kg)
Cruising speed: 187-210mph (301-338km/h)
Range: 880 miles (1,416km) at 187mph (301km/h) with reserves

The Dove was the first civil transport to fly in Britain after World War II, on 25 September 1945; production eventually totalled about 540, mostly for export. The early series had 340hp Gipsy Queen 70-3 (Dove 1 and 2) or Gipsy Queen 70-4 (Dove 1B and 2B) engines and 8,500lb (3,855kg) gross weight. Dove 5 and 6 executive versions have 380hp Gipsy Queen 70 Mk 2s and 8,800lb (3,991kg) weight. Doves 7 and 8 have ejector exhausts, a Heron-type canopy and, respectively, airline-type and executive interiors. Known also as the Dove Custom 600, the executive 8A was built for the US market. US conversions built in small numbers included the Riley Turbo-Exec 400 with 300hp Lycoming IO-720s and other refinements, with an optional swept fin; and the Carstedt Jet Liner 600 and 605ehp AiResearch TPE 331-101E turboprops and a longer fuselage seating 18 passengers; the latter variant was being marketed as the CJ600 by Texas Airplane Mfg Co in 1977.

Israel Aircraft Industries 1123/1124 Westwind

Israel

Business twin-jet transport, in production and service
Photo: Westwind II
Data: Westwind I

Accommodation: 1-2 pilots and up to 10 passengers
Powered by: Two 3,700lb (1,680kg) st Garrett AiResearch TFE 731-3-1G turbofans
Span: 44ft 9.5in (13.65m)
Length: 52ft 3in (15.93m)
Gross weight: 22,850lb (10,364kg)
Max level speed: 542mph (872km/h) at 19,400ft (5,900m)
Range: 2,785 miles (4,490km) with seven passengers

The Aero Commander company in the USA flew the prototype of its Model 1101 Jet Commander business transport on 27 January 1963. The second prototype, with longer fuselage and higher weights, flew on 14 April 1964; deliveries of production aircraft, to the same standard with General Electric CJ610 turbojets, began in January 1965. The complete programme was sold by Rockwell International to Israel Aircraft Industries which renamed the aircraft the Commodore Jet and began developing 'stretched' and improved models. A total of 150 Jet Commanders and Commodore Jets were built in three models, the 1121, 1121A and 1121B. They were superseded by the 1123 Westwind with uprated engines, wingtip tanks, lengthened fuselage and other improvements. Production totalled 36, of which two became prototypes of the Westwind 1124 (first flight, 21 July 1975) and described alongside. Production of this model exceeded 100 by late-1979, when IAI introduced the Westwind II with improved wing and winglets.

L-200 Morava

Czechoslovakia

Light business twin, in service
Data: L-200D

Accommodation: 4-5 seats
Powered by: Two 210hp M337 piston-engines
Span: 40ft 4.5in (12.31m)
Length: 28ft 3in (8.61m)
Gross weight: 4,300lb (1,950kg)
Normal cruising speed: 159mph (256km/h) at 8,200ft (2,500m)
Max range: 1,063 miles (1,710km)

First flown on 8 April 1957, the Morava was developed as a successor to the Aero 145, and like the earlier type was sold in quantity to the Soviet Union for use as an air taxi. The original L-200 had 160hp Walter Minor 6-III engines. The M337 engines were introduced on the L-200A, and three-blade vp propellers and other refinements distinguished the L-200D. More than 1,000 examples of the L-200 were built, but few examples are seen outside of the Eastern European countries.

Learavia Learfan 2100

USA

Twin-engined business transport, under development

Accommodation: 2 pilots and up to 8 passengers
Powered by: Two Pratt & Whitney PT6B-35F turboshaft engines flat rated to 650shp each
Span: 39ft 4in (11.99m)
Length: 39ft 7in (12.06m)
Gross weight: 6,000lb (2,724kg)
Cruising speed: 350mph (564km/h) at 30,000ft (9,150m)
Range: 2,150 miles (3,462km) with 1,500lb (680kg) payload

The Learfan 2100 was the last design initiated by William Lear Sr, who had previously been responsible for the concept and preliminary design of the Learjet and Learstar business twins, the latter now being in production as the Canadair Challenger.

The Learfan is highly unconventional both in layout — with two engines coupled to drive a single pusher propeller — and in construction, which is almost wholly of graphite epoxy composites. The Learavia company was proceeding with construction of a prototype during 1979, with first flight expected in mid-1980, and had recorded 79 firm orders and letters of intent for 50 more. However, the Reno-based company lacked resources to launch production and was negotiating during 1979 for participation by another company, possibly in Britain.

Lockheed JetStar and JetStar II — USA

Business twin-jet, in service
Photo and data: JetStar II

Accommodation: Flight crew of 2 and up to 10 passengers
Powered by: Four 3,700lb (1,680kg) st Garrett AiResearch TFE 731-3 turbofans
Span: 54ft 5in (16.60m)
Length: 60ft 5in (18.42m)
Gross weight: 43,750lb (19,844kg)
Cruising speed: 508-547mph (817-880km/h)
Range: 2,994-3,189 miles (4,818-5,132km), with reserves

Lockheed developed the JetStar as a private venture, to meet a USAF requirement for a utility jet transport, and flew two prototypes each powered by two Bristol Siddeley Orpheus turbojets. The first flight was made on 4 September 1957. Production models swiched to four JT12As, initially in the 2,400lb (1,088kg) st -6 version and later the 3,300lb (1,497kg) JT12A-8. Production of 162 JetStars ended in 1973. In 1974 Garrett AiResearch developed the JetStar 731 conversion with TFE 731 turbofans (first flown on 10 July 1974) and Lockheed subsequently built 40 of the similar JetStar II version. This was first flown on 18 August 1976 and production ended late-1979.

Martin 4-0-4 — USA

Short-range airliner, in service

Accommodation: Crew of 2 and 40-52 passengers
Powered by: Two 2,400hp Pratt & Whitney R-2800-CB-16 piston engines
Span: 93ft 3.5in (28.44m)
Length: 74ft 7in (22.75m)
Gross weight: 44,900lb (20,385kg)
Cruising speed: 276mph (442km/h) at 18,000ft (5,486m)
Range: 310 miles (500km) with max payload

This conventional twin piston-engined airliner had its origins in the Martin 2-0-2, which first flew on 22 November 1946 to become the first new commercial transport certificated in the US after the end of the war. The prototype of a pressurised version flew as the Martin 3-0-3 on 20 June 1947, and further improvements were made in the Martin 4-0-4, first flown on 21 October 1950. Delivery of 103 production examples began in July 1951, almost all for airline use. Southern Airways was the last major user of the Martin 4-0-4 but retired its fleet in 1978; in 1979, Florida Airlines was using seven, Naples Airlines had eight, and Marco Island Airways, three.

Messerschmitt-Bölkow-Blohm HFB320 Hansa Germany

Business twin-jet and light transport, in service

Accommodation: Crew of 2 and up to 12 passengers
Powered by: Two 3,100lb (1,406kg) st General Electric CJ610-9 turbojets
Span: 47ft 6in (14.49m)
Length: 54ft 6in (16.61m)
Gross weight: 20,280lb (9,200kg)
Cruising speed: 420-513mph (675-825km/h)
Range: 1,472 miles (2,370km) with 6 passengers (with reserves)

Development of the Hansa began in 1961 as the first original product of the resurrected Blohm und Voss concern in Hamburg. The company was then known as Hamburger Flugzeugbau and the new aircraft, identified as HFB320, made its first flight on 21 April 1964. Although having the typical rear-engine layout of other business jets, the HFB320, later named Hansa, was distinguished by its unique swept-forward wings. Certification of the Hansa was obtained during 1967, and the first commercial delivery was made on 26 September in that year. The first 15 Hansas had CJ610-1 engines and the next 20 had CJ610-5s. Subsequent aircraft have -9s as indicated above. Production totalled 46 aircraft, of which 12 were for Luftwaffe use. Among commercial Hansa users are the Dutch Training School at Eelde, Midwest Air Charter in the USA and MBB for executive flights.

Mitsubishi MU-2 Solitaire and Marquise Japan

General-purpose and business transport, in production and service
Photo: Solitaire
Data: Marquise

Accommodation: 2 pilots and up to 11 passengers
Powered by: Two 778ehp AiResearch TPE 331-10-501M turboprops
Span: 39ft 2in (11.95m)
Length: 39ft 5in (12.02m)
Gross weight: 11,575lb (5,250kg)
Cruising speed: 357mph (574km/h) at 16,000ft (4,880m)
Max range: 1,725 miles (2,780km) with reserves

The Mitsubishi company began studies of a small business twin in September 1959. The first of four prototypes, with Astazou engines, flew on 14 September 1963. Two more with French engines followed as MU-2A; the MU-2B switched to TPE 331 engines, and first flew on 11 March 1965. Production totalled 34. The MU-2D (18 built) introduced integral tanks and higher weights, and the MU-2F (95 built) had uprated engines and larger wingtip tanks. On 10 January 1969 Mitsubishi flew the prototype MU-2G, which differed from the 7/9-seat MU-2F primarily in having a 6ft 2.75in (1.90m) stretch in length and external fairings on the fuselage sides to house the main undercarriage. The MU-2J has the same long fuselage, with uprated engines. The MU-2K is an 'F' with these same engines, while the MU-2L and MU-2M are respectively similar to the 'J' and 'K' with increased gross weights. The MU-2N and MU-2P have larger diameter, slow-running propellers to reduce cabin noise and have been superseded by the Marquise and Solitaire with uprated engines and larger fuel tanks. Orders for all versions were approaching 600 by the autumn of 1979.

Mitsubishi MU-300 Diamond I

Japan

Business twin-jet, under development

Accommodation: 2 pilots and up to 9 passengers
Powered by: Two 2,500lb (1,135kg) st Pratt & Whitney JT15D-4 turbofans
Span: 43ft 5in (13.23m)
Length: 48ft 4in (14.73m)
Gross weight: 13,890lb (6,300kg)
Max cruising speed: 501mph (806km/h)
Range: 1,440 miles (2,315km) with reserves

Mitsubishi flew the prototype of its new biz-jet on 29 August 1978 and a second prototype was completed early in 1979. The name Diamond I was adopted in June 1979, by which time the two prototypes had completed more than 300hr of flight testing and the company had decided to put the new type into production to complement the successful MU-2 series (qv). Certification was handled by Mitsubishi's subsidiary company at San Angelo, Texas, the two prototypes being transferred to this location in July 1979, and production deliveries were expected to begin in 1981. The Diamond I was designed with special emphasis upon speed, comfort, low cabin noise levels and economy.

Partenavia P68 Victor

Italy

Twin-engined light transport, in production and service
Photo: P68C/TC
Data: P68B

Accommodation: Pilot and 5 passengers
Powered by: Two 200hp Lycoming IO-360-A1B6 piston-engines
Span: 39ft 4.5in (12.00m)
Length: 30ft 8in (9.35m)
Gross weight: 4,320lb (1,960kg)
Cruising speed: 168-188mph (270-302km/h)
Max range: 1,045 miles (1,681km) at 9,000ft (2,750m)

Partenavia developed this light twin to supplement its well-established Oscar family of single-engined 2/4-seaters. The first of two prototypes flew on 25 May 1970. Thirteen pre-production aircraft, three of them equipped for air survey, were manufactured initially. The front fuselage of the production version is lengthened by 6in (15cm). Sportavia-Pützer in Germany developed the P68 Observer variant with a new Plexiglas nose and observation position. The P68C, introduced in 1979, has a lengthened nose and other refinements and P68B/TC and P68C/TC turbosupercharged versions are available. A P68R with retractable undercarriage flew in December 1976 and the AP68TP, developed jointly with Aeritalia, has retractable gear and Allison 250-B17B turboprops; the prototype flew on 11 September 1978. More than 200 P68s had been sold by mid-1979.

Piaggio P166 — Italy

Light transport, in production and service
Photo and data: P166-DL3

Accommodation: Pilot and 5-9 passengers
Powered by: Two 587hp Avco Lycoming LTP 101 turboprops
Span: 48ft 2.5in (14.69m)
Length: 39ft 3in (11.90m)
Gross weight: 9,480lb (4,300kg)
Cruising speed: 186-250mph (300-404km/h) at 10,000ft (3,050m)
Range: 460-1,667 miles (741-2,687km) according to payload, with reserves

Powered by two 340hp Lycoming GSO-480 engines, the original 6/8-seat P166 was a development of the P136 amphibian and flew for the first time on 26 November 1957. Several of the total of 94 built were purchased for use as executive transports and for service as feeder and charter airliners. The P166B Portofino (first flown 27 March 1962) has more power and up to 10 seats; five were built. The 12-passenger P166C (first flown 2 October 1964) (two built) was similar with a modified undercarriage. The P166-DL2 (first flown on 2 May 1975) introduced wing-tip tanks and higher gross weight, four were built for air survey duties. P166-DL3 (first flown 3 July 1976) is similar, with larger cabin windows and turboprop engines.

Pilatus PC-6 Porter and Turbo-Porter — Switzerland

Light transport, in production and service
Photo: PC-6 Porter
Data: PC-6/B2-H2 Turbo-Porter

Accommodation: Pilot plus 7-9 passengers
Powered by: One 550shp Pratt & Whitney (Canada) PT6A-27 turboprop
Span: 49ft 10.5in (15.20m)
Length: 36ft 1in (11.00m)
Gross weight: 4,850lb (2,200kg)
Cruising speed: 150-161mph (240-259km/h) at 10,000ft (3,050m)
Max range: 634 miles (1,020km) with normal fuel

The Porter was designed as a STOL transport with the ability to operate safely from small, high airfields in Switzerland. The first of five prototypes flew on 4 May 1959, and deliveries began at the end of that year. Production models are the PC-6 with 340hp Lycoming GSO-480-B1A6 and PC-6/350 (first flown in December 1961) with 350hp IGO-540-A1A. Three different types of turboprop engine have been offered in the Turbo-Porter which, apart from the power plant, is identical with the Porter. First to fly, on 2 May 1961, was the PC-6/A with 523shp Astazou IIE or IIG; the A1 and A2 have 573shp Astazou XII and XIVE respectively. The PC-6/B, with 550shp PT6A engine, first flew on 1 May 1964, and was followed by the PC-6/B1 and /B2 with A-20 and A-27 engine. The PC-6/C and C1 have 575shp AiResearch TPE 331-25D and 1-100 respectively. Variants of all models with H1 or H2 suffix have increased gross weights. Overall production of Porters and Turbo-Porters exceeded 450 by mid-1979, including those built by Fairchild in the USA.

Pilatus Britten-Norman BN-2 Islander — UK

Light feeder-line transport, in production and service
Data: BN-2B Islander II

Accommodation: Pilot and up to 9 passengers
Powered by: Two 260hp Lycoming O-540-E4C5 piston-engines
Span: 49ft 0in (14.94m)
Length: 35ft 7.75in (10.86m)
Gross weight: 6,300lb (2,857kg)
Cruising speed: 160mph (257km/h)
Max range: 1,193 miles (1,920km)

Over 800 of these simple and sturdy light transports had been sold by mid-1979. The prototype first flew on 13 June 1965, with 210hp Continental IO-360-B engines, but production aircraft, the first of which flew on 20 August 1966, had 260hp Lycomings as standard equipment. The BN2A, starting with the 25th aircraft, had increased payload and gross weight, and was produced in several configurations, the most distinctive of which had extra fuel in tanks forming extensions to the wing-tips. Also available are a 'hot and high' version with 300hp Lycoming IO-540-K1B5 engines, and a supercharged version with TIO-540-H engines rated at 270hp each. Other optional modifications include a longer nose with extra baggage space and crop-spraying or dusting equipment. The original company based in the Isle of Wight was acquired by Pilatus in 1979; production continued with the BN-2B Islander II featuring higher landing weight and many internal improvements.

Piper PA-23 Aztec (and Apache) — USA

Light business twin, in production and service
Photo and data: Turbo Aztec F

Accommodation: Pilot and 5 passengers
Powered by: Two 250hp Lycoming TIO-540-C1A piston-engines
Span: 37ft 2.5in (11.34m)
Length: 31ft 2.75in (9.52m)
Gross weight: 5,200lb (2,360kg)
Cruising speed: 179-241mph (289-389km/h)
Max range: 1,018-1,317 miles (1,639-2,120km)

The Apache was Piper's first major entry in the twin-engined market, the prototype making its first flight on 2 March 1952, when it was known as the Twin-Stinson. Successive development of the type led to the Apache H by 1962. The more powerful Aztec was developed from the later models of the Apache, both types sharing the Piper PA-23 designation. As a 5-seater, the Aztec could originally be distinguished by its angular swept-back fin and was originally type-approved by the FAA in September 1959, the 6-seat version following two years later. The Aztec's tail unit and some other features were adopted on the Apache 235 from which the Aztec could be distinguished primarily by a longer nose. Normally-aspirated and turbosupercharged versions of the Aztec were still in production in 1979, by which time nearly 5,000 Aztecs had been built.

Piper PA-30 and PA-39 Twin Comanche — USA

Light private and business twin, in service
Photo: PA-30B Twin Comanche B
Data: PA-39 Twin Comanche C/R

Accommodation: Pilot and 3-5 passengers
Powered by: Two 160hp Lycoming IO-320-B1A piston-engines
Span: 36ft 9.5in (11.22m) over tip-tanks
Length: 25ft 2in (7.67m)
Gross weight: 3,725lb (1,690kg)
Cruising speed: 178-198mph (286-319km/h)
Max range: 1,200 miles (1,930km) at 178mph (286km/h)

As the name suggests, this aircraft was based on the design of the Comanche, especially in respect of the main fuselage structure and cabin layout. The prototype flew on 7 November 1962, and the PA-30 Twin Comanche entered production to supersede the Apache H in 1963. Twin Comanches B and C followed in 1965 and 1968 respectively, before being superseded in 1970/71 by the PA-39 series with opposite-rotating propellers. All variants had the same power plant and were available in Standard, Custom and Sportsman models with different standards of equipment. PA-30/PA-39 Turbo Twin Commanches differed in having 160hp IO-320-C1A engines and Rajay turbosuperchargers.

Piper PA-31T Cheyenne — USA

Twin-turboprop executive aircraft and air taxi, in production and service
Photo and data: Cheyenne II

Accommodation: Pilot and 5-7 passengers
Powered by: Two 620shp Pratt & Whitney (Canada) PT6A-28 turboprops
Span: 42ft 8.25in (13.01m)
Length: 34ft 8in (10.57m)
Gross weight: 9,000lb (4,082kg)
Cruising speed: 244-326mph (393-524km/h)
Max range: 1,739 miles (2,798km) at 244mph (393km/h) with reserves

Top aircraft in the Piper range, the original Cheyenne combined the basic airframe of the Pressurised Navajo with PT6 turboprop engines, retaining the Navajo's PA-31 designation. The prototype first flew on 20 August 1969. Production was under way by 1974, when full details were first released, the first production Cheyenne having flown on 22 October 1973. Deliveries began on 27 March 1974, the standard model becoming designated Cheyenne II in 1978, with wingtip tanks as standard equipment. The Cheyenne I, introduced in 1978, is a low-cost model with 500shp PT6A-11s and optional tip-tanks. The stretched 6/10-seat Cheyenne III with 680shp PT6A-41 engines and a T-tail was announced in 1977 but after the prototype flight testing Piper announced the production model would have a longer cabin and market introduction was delayed until early 1980.

Piper PA-31 Navajo and Chieftain USA

Twin-engined executive aircraft and air taxi, in production and service
Photo: Navajo C/R
Data: PA-31-350 Chieftain

Accommodation: 2 pilots and up to 10 passengers
Powered by: Two 350hp Lycoming TIO-540-J2BD piston-engines
Span: 40ft 8in (12.40m)
Length: 34ft 7.5in (10.55m)
Gross weight: 7,000lb (3,175kg)
Cruising speed: 253mph (407km/h)
Max range: 1,020 miles (1,640km) at 251mph (404km/h) at 20,000ft (6,100m)

Piper flew the prototype PA-31 on 30 September 1964 and deliveries began in April 1967. Original versions, no longer in production, were the 6/9-seat PA-31-300 Standard Navajo, the Executive Navajo, furnished to VIP standards, and the commuter Navajo, seating 8 persons. These three models had 300hp IO-540-M engines. The current Navajo has 310hp supercharged Lycoming TIO-540-A2C engines, while the Navajo C/R has 325hp counter-rotating TIO-540-F2BD engines. Production of the PA-31P pressurised Navajo has been completed. The PA-31-350 Chieftain is a version of the Navajo lengthened by 2ft (0.61m) to seat up to 10 persons. More than 2,000 Navajos had been built by autumn 1977. EMBRAER builds the PA-31-350 in Brazil as the EMB-820C.

Piper PA-34 Seneca USA

Twin-engined light transport and trainer, in production and service
Data: Seneca II

Accommodation: Pilot and 5-6 passengers
Powered by: Two 200hp Continental TSIO-360-E piston-engines
Span: 38ft 10.75in (11.85m)
Length: 128ft 7.5in (8.73m)
Gross weight: 4,570lb (2,073kg)
Cruising speed: 177-219mph
Typical range: 700 miles (1,128km) at 177mph (285km/h)

Announced in September 1971, the Seneca is a light twin developed from the Cherokee Six. Piper claimed that it was the lowest-priced aircraft of its class on the US market and uses it as a standard twin-engine transition trainer at its Flite Centers, now numbering well over 400. The centre and rear rows of seats are removable for cargo-carrying. With the seats in place, 200lb (91kg) of baggage or freight can be carried in nose and rear-cabin compartments. The 1974 model introduced a fourth window on each side of the cabin and the 1975 model, Seneca II, switched from Lycoming to Continental engines. Licence production of the Seneca II began in Poland in 1979, as the PZL-M20 Mewa. In Brazil, EMBRAER builds the Seneca II as the EMB-810C

Piper PA-44 Seminole

USA

Light business and private twin, in production and service

Accommodation: Pilot and 3 passengers
Powered by: Two 180hp Lycoming O-360-E1AD piston engines
Span: 38ft 6.5in (11.75m)
Length: 27ft 7.25in (8.41m)
Gross weight: 3,800lb (1,723kg)
Cruising speed: 170-187mph (274-300km/h)
Range: 820-960 miles (1,320-1,545km)

Piper flew the prototype of this new light twin in May 1976, to take the place of the Twin Comanche in its range of products. Featuring the T-tail that is increasingly favoured by the American general aviation manufacturers, the Seminole has a number of components fabricated from composites, including a glassfibre one-piece nosecone that can be removed to give easy access to the undercarriage retraction mechanism. Details of the PA-44-180, as the Seminole is designated in its initial version, were first announced by Piper in February 1978 and deliveries began later in the same year.

Piper (Ted Smith) Aerostar

USA

Twin-engined light transport, in production and service
Photo: Aerostar 600A
Data: Aerostar 601B

Accommodation: Pilot and 5 passengers
Powered by: Two 290hp Lycoming IO-540-S1A5 piston-engines
Span: 36ft 8in (11.18m)
Length: 34ft 9.75in (10.61m)
Gross weight: 6,000lb (2,721kg)
Normal cruising speed: 270mph (434km/h) at 25,000ft (7,620m)
Max range: 1,435miles (2,309km) at 25,000ft (7,620m)

The name Aerostar was common to a family of high-speed light transports designed by the late Ted R. Smith, who was responsible for the original Aero Commander light twins. Production was undertaken initially by Butler Aviation, but was taken over by Ted R. Smith and Associates (later Ted Smith Aerostar Corp) in 1972; Piper acquired the company by outright purchase in 1978. Manufacture was concentrated initially on the Aerostar 600 which had first flown in prototype form in October 1967, and the similar Aerostar 601 with turbochargers. The 600 has a shorter wing span, of 34ft 2in (10.41m). The 601P is pressurised, with 300hp Lycoming TIO-541 engines. A further development stage was represented by the slightly larger Aerostar 700, with 350hp IO-540-M engines, which flew for the first time on 22 November 1972, and its pressurised version, the 700P; these are no longer in production.

Rockwell Shrike Commander, Courser Commander and Commander 685

USA

Twin-engined light transport, in production and service
Photo and data: Commander 685

Accommodation: Pilot and up to 8 passengers
Powered by: Two 435hp Continental GTSIO-520-F flat-six engines
Span: 46ft 6.25in (14.19m)
Length: 42ft 11.75in (13.10m)
Gross weight: 9,000lb (4,082kg)
Cruising speed: 175-256mph (281-412km/h)
Max range: 1,766 miles (2,842km) at 175mph (281km/h) at 20,000ft (6,100m) with reserves

Since the merger which brought together the former Rockwell Aero Commander and North American Aviation companies, the twin-engined Aero Commander transports have been marketed under new names. The Shrike Commander 500S with 290hp Lycoming IO-540-E1B5 engines is the current production version of the original Aero Commander 500; the Shrike Commander Esquire was a de luxe 6-seat executive version. Until production was suspended, the former Grand Commander was produced as the Courser Commander, with 380hp IGSO-540 engines and up to 11 seats in a lengthened fuselage. The later Commander 685 was a 7/9-seater, combining the Turbo Commander 690 airframe with piston-engines.

Rockwell Turbo Commander

USA

Business twin, in production and service
Photo: Commander 840
Data: Turbo Commander 690B

Accommodation: 1-2 pilots and up to 11 passengers
Powered by: Two 700ehp AiResearch TPE 331-5-251K turboprops
Span: 46ft 6.5in (14.19m)
Length: 44ft 4.25in (15.52m)
Gross weight: 10,325lb (4,683kg)
Cruising speed: 289-330mph (465-532km/h)
Max range: 1,693 miles (2,725km), with reserves

First flown on 31 December 1964, the original Turbo Commander made use of a Grand Commander (Courser Commander) airframe in all major respects other than the engines. Production deliveries began in April 1965. After the Aero Commander/North American merger, the nose was lengthened and the name changed for a time to Hawk Commander. The name Turbo Commander was revived in 1971, when the basic Model 681B, with 605ehp engines and up to nine seats, was joined by the new Turbo Commander 690, with increased span and uprated engines, weights and performance. The Turbo Commander 690B was a further improvement in 1976; itself superseded in 1979 by the Commander 840 and 980 featuring small winglets, more fuel and, respectively, TPE 331-5 or TPE 331-10 engines.

Rockwell Sabreliner Srs 40, 60 and 75 — USA

Business twin-jet, in production and service
Photo: Srs 60
Data: Sabreliner 75A

Accommodation: Flight crew of 2 and 6-10 passengers
Powered by: Two 4,500lb (2,043kg) st General Electric CF700-2D-2 turbofans
Span: 44ft 8in (13.61m)
Length: 47ft 2in (14.38m)
Gross weight: 23,000lb (10,432kg)
Max cruising speed: 528mph (850km/h)
Max range: 1,957 miles (3,149km) with 4 passengers (with reserves)

The Sabreliner was developed as a private venture to meet USAF requirements for a combat readiness trainer and utility aircraft. The prototype flew on 16 September 1958 with General Electric J85 engines and initial production models, for the USAF as T-39s, had Pratt & Whitney JT12A turbojets. The same engines were used in the original commercial version, the Sabreliner 40. The Sabreliner 60 had the same engines, with fuselage lengthened by 3ft 2in (0.97m); the Sabreliner 75 introduced a deepened cabin and the similar Sabreliner 75A has CF700-2D turbofans. The designations Sabreliner 40A and Sabreliner 80A refer to versions of the Sabreliner 75A fitted with Raisbeck Mark Five wing improvements.

Rockwell Sabreliner 65 (and 60A, 80A) — USA

Business twin-jet, in production and service
Photo: Srs 65

Accommodation: 2 pilots and up to 10 passengers
Powered by: Two 3,700lb (1,680kg) st Garrett AiResearch TFE731-3-1D turbofans
Span: 50ft 5.25in (15.37m)
Length: 46ft 11in (14.30m)
Gross weight: 24,000lb (10,886kg)
Max cruising speed: 530mph (850km/h)
Max range: 3,350 miles (5,393km)

The Sabreliner 65, first flown on 29 June 1977, combines the advanced wing developed by the Raisbeck Group as the Mark Five system with a new airframe powered by Garrett AiResearch turbofans but otherwise similar to the Sabreliner 60. Raisbeck wing development was undertaken in 1976 in a number of progressive steps on a Sabreliner 60 and a second, fully-modified aircraft, flew on 15 December 1976. Certification of the Mark Five was obtained in the late summer of 1978 and the first 'production conversion' of a Sabreliner 60 to 60A with this wing flew on 8 September 1978. The first production Sabreliner 65 flew on 8 April 1979 and deliveries began mid-year; at about the same time, Raisbeck obtained certification of the Sabreliner 80A, this being the Sabreliner 75A (qv) with the Mark Five wing, first flown on 28 April 1978. Sabreliner 40s retrofitted with the new wing are designated Sabreliner 40A.

Rockwell Commander 700/710 — USA/Japan

Business twin, in production and service
Photo and data: Commander 700

Accommodation: 2 pilots and up to 6 passengers
Powered by: Two 325hp Lycoming TIO-540-R2AD piston-engines
Span: 42ft 5.5in (12.94m)
Length: 39ft 4.5in (12.00m)
Gross weight: 6,750lb (3,062kg)
Cruising speed: 252mph (405km/h) at 24,000ft (7,315m)
Max range: 1,197 miles (1,926km)

Fuji in Japan began development of this business twin in 1971, as the FA-300, and three years later concluded an agreement with Rockwell International for the latter to market an Americanised version in the USA as the Commander 700, using Japanese-built components assembled and furnished in the USA. The prototype first flew on 13 November 1975 in Japan, followed by a second on 25 February 1976 in the USA. Deliveries of certificated aircraft began in the summer of 1978. On 22 December 1976, a more powerful version made its first flight. Known as the FA-300-Kai or Commander 710, it has 450hp Lycomings.

Siai-Marchetti SF-600 Canguro — Italy

Light utility transport, under development

Accommodation: Crew of 2 and up to 10 passengers
Powered by: Two 350hp Avco Lycoming TIO-540J piston-engines
Span: 47ft 6.5in (14.50m)
Length: 39ft 10in (12.15m)
Gross weight: 6,828lb (3,100kg)
Cruising speed: 168mph (270km/h) at 12,000ft (3,657m)
Range: 310-995 miles (500-1,600km) according to payload

The Canguro is the latest design of Dott Ing Stelio Frati, well-known Italian designer of light aircraft. First flown on 30 December 1978, it is intended as a simple and cheap to operate utility transport that is particularly suitable for use in developing countries. The prototype was built by General Avia in Milan, a company formed by Stelio Frati to undertake initial development and flight testing of his designs; marketing of the Canguro is handled by Siai-Marchetti (a member of the Agusta Group) and if production ensues, it will be handled by the latter group. A turboprop version of the Canguro has been planned, to be powered by 400shp Allison 250B-17 engines, and the prototype was to be re-engined for comparative trials. Cruising speed was expected to increase to 193mph (310km/h), the useful load would be increased and economy of operation improved.

Shenyang C-11

China

Light utility transport, in production and service

Accommodation: Flight crew of 2 and 6-8 passengers
Powered by: Two 285hp Type 6 bis Sinshi-liyu Jia Hou-Sai piston-engines
Span: 55ft 9.25in (17.00m)
Length: 39ft 4.5in (12.00m)
Gross weight: 7,715lb (3,500kg)
Cruising speed: About 102mph (165km/h)
Range: About 500 miles (805km)

The C-11, or Sinshi-shi Yuong-shu Chi (Type 11 Transport Plane), is one of the few aircraft of original design to have reached quantity production in China since the Communist regime came to power in 1949. It first flew during 1975/6, and subsequently entered production to complement or replace the several hundred Antonov An-2s that had previously been built in China with the designation C-5. Like the C-5, the C-11 is produced at the State Aircraft Factory at Shenyang (formerly Mukden) and is powered by engines built locally but based on the AI-14RF of Soviet origin. One role for the C-11 is agricultural spraying, for which purpose individual rotary atomisers are carried under the wings and fuselage.

Swearingen Merlin II and III

USA

Business twin, in production and service
Photo and data: Merlin IIIB

Accommodation: Flight crew of 2 and 6-9 passengers
Powered by: Two 900shp AiResearch TPE 331-10U-501G turboprops
Span: 46ft 3in (14.10m)
Length: 42ft 2in (12.85m)
Gross weight: 12,500lb (5,670kg)
Max cruising speed: 345mph (556km/h) at 14,000ft (4,270m)
Max range: 2,792 miles (4,494km) with IFR reserves

To produce the original Merlin IIA, Swearingen Aircraft combined the basic wing structure of the Beech Queen Air and undercarriage of the Twin Bonanza with an entirely new pressurised fuselage of its own design and two 578shp Pratt & Whitney PT6A-20 turboprops instead of the Queen Air's Lycomings. The first Merlin IIA flew on 13 April 1965, and production deliveres began in August 1966. The IIA was superseded by the IIB with 665shp AiResearch engines; but production is now centred on the Merlin III, with a slightly longer fuselage, new tail unit and the wings, undercarriage and engines of the Metro. A total of about 100 IIIs, IIIAs and IIIBs had been delivered by mid-1979.

Part Four

AAMSA Quail Commander (and Rockwell Sparrow and Snipe Commanders) / Mexico

Photo: Quail Commander
Data: Quail A-9B
Span: 34ft 9in (10.59m)
Length: 23ft 6in (7.16m)
Gross weight: 3,800lb (1,725kg)
Operating speed: 90-100mph (145-161km/h)
Max range: 300 miles (483km)

The Commander family of agricultural sprayer/dusters have had a long and involved history. Early, low-powered versions were developed and produced by the CallAir company from 1956 to 1962, when CallAir was taken over by Intermountain Manufacturing Co (IMCO). IMCO evolved the A-9, with 235hp Lycoming O-540-B2B5 engine and 1,250lb (567kg) payload; the A-9 Super, with 290hp Lycoming IO-540-G1C5 and 1,600lb (726kg) payload; and the scaled-up B-1, with span of 42ft 8in (13.00m), 400hp Lycoming IO-720-A1A engine and 2,000lb (907kg) payload. After a subsequent period of production by Aero Commander as Ag Commanders, the three types became, respectively, Rockwell's Sparrow Commander, Quail Commander and Snipe Commander, the Snipe being re-engined with a 450hp Pratt & Whitney R-985 radial. The Quail programme has been transferred to Aeronautica Agricola Mexicana SA in Mexico, which now builds the Quail AA-9B version with 300hp Lycoming IO-540-K1A5 engine. Production of the Sparrow and Snipe Commanders has ended.

Aero Boero 95/115/150/180 / Argentina

Photo and data: Aero Boero 95
Span: 35ft 2in (10.72m)
Length: 23ft 10.25in (7.27m)
Gross weight: 1,860lb (844kg)
Max cruising speed: 131mph (211km/h)
Max range: 733 miles (1,180km)

The prototype of this family of three-seat lightplanes flew for the first time on 12 March 1959. Initial production Aero Boero 95s had a 95hp Continental C90-8F engine; they were followed by the Aero Boero 95A De Lujo and its agricultural dusting/spraying counterpart, the 95A Fumigador, each with a 100hp Continental O-200-A. Standard production model from July 1969 was the Aero Boero 95/115, with 115hp Lycoming O-235-C2A engine, followed by the AB 115 BS, with swept fin, increased span and more fuel. Twenty-five 115 BS were built. Production is now centred on the 180 RV (data above) with 180hp Lycoming O-360-A1A and higher performance; the generally similar 180 RVR glider-towing version; the 180 Ag agricultural sprayer; the 150 RV with 150hp Lycoming O-320-A2B; and its agricultural counterpart, the 150 Ag. Nearly 70 of the 180hp models had been built by spring 1979.

Aero Boero 260 Ag / Argentina

Span: 35ft 9in (10.90m)
Length: 24ft 5.25in (7.45m)
Gross weight: 2,976lb (1,350kg)
Max cruising speed: 125mph (201km/h)
Range: 683 miles (1,100km)

The Aero Boero company, which previously had built only high-wing lightplanes, began design of this agricultural aircraft in 1971. A prototype made its first flight on 23 December 1972, powered by a 260hp Lycoming O-540 engine. A second prototype was completed in mid-1977. Production 260 AG sprayer/dusters will be similar, except that the rear fuselage will be cut down to give the pilot an all round view.

Aeronca 7 Champion (and Champion Traveler and Challenger) / USA

Photo: Model 7AC
Data: Model 7EC

Span: 35ft 0in (10.67m)
Length: 21ft 6in (6.55m)
Gross weight: 1,450lb (658kg)
Range: 350 miles (563km) at 100mph (161km/h)

More than 10,000 Champions were built by Aeronca in 1946-51. All were tandem 2-seaters, with engines ranging from the 65hp Continental A65-8 (Model 7AC) to the 90hp Continental C90-12F (Model 7EC). Manufacture of the 7EC was resumed by Champion Aircraft from 1955 to 1964, under the names Traveler and Traveler Deluxe. The 7FC TriTraveler is similar, but with tricycle undercarriage. Developments, built in quantity, were the 3-seat 7GC Sky-Trac with 140hp Lycoming O-290-D2B engine, and the 2-seat 7GCB Challenger with 150hp Lycoming O-320-A2B engine. The Champion-built models have shorter, more square wingtips than the original Aeronca machines (see also Bellanca Champ and Citabria).

Aeronca 15AC Sedan / USA

Span: 37ft 6in (11.43m)
Length: 25ft 3in (7.69m)
Gross weight: 2,050lb (930kg)
Max cruising speed: 114mph (183km/h)
Range: 455 miles (732km)

A very large number of these 4-seat light aircraft are still in service. First flown in 1947, the Sedan has a metal structure, with metal-skinned wings and fabric covered fuselage. Standard power plant is a 145hp Continental C145; but a few Sedans have a 165hp Franlin engine.

Aerospace (NZAI) Airtourer / New Zealand

Photo: Airtourer T2
Data: Airtourer T5

Span: 26ft 0in (7.92m)
Length: 22ft 0in (6.71m)
Gross weight: 1,750lb (793kg)
Max range: 670 miles (1,075km) at 134mph (216km/h)

The Airtourer beat 103 other designs to win a Royal Aero Club design competition for a 2-seat light aircraft in 1953. A wooden prototype, with 65hp engine, flew in Australia in March 1959. Victa Ltd, of Milperra, New South Wales, then built 170 all-metal production Airtourers with 100hp Continental O-200-A or 115hp Lycoming O-235 engine. Manufacture in New Zealand by Aero Engine Services Ltd (now New Zealand Aerospace Industries) began in October 1967. Variants were the Airtourer T2 (115hp O-235-C2A), T3 (130hp engine), T4 (150hp O-320-E2A), T5 (O-320-E1A engine with constant speed propeller and needle-type spinner) and T6, as T5 with 1,900lb (862kg) gross weight. Over 100 were built in New Zealand, in addition to similar CT/4 Airtrainers for military use. Production has now ended.

Aerospace (NZAI) Air Parts Fletcher FU-24 (and Cresco) / New Zealand

Photo: FU-24-950
Data: Cresco

Span: 42ft 0in (12.81m)
Length: 36ft 4in (11.07m)
Gross weight: 7,000lb (3,175 kg)
Max cruising speed: 140mph (226km/h)
Max range: 430 miles (692km)

The FU-24 was designed originally by Fletcher Aviation Co of America for agricultural top-dressing duties in New Zealand. The first 100 production machines were built by the parent company in 1954-64. Air Parts (NZ) Ltd then acquired all rights in the FU-24 and continued manufacture in New Zealand. The basic version is operated as a single-seater, with 300hp Continental IO-520-F and hopper for 1,610lb (730kg) of chemicals aft of the cockpit. The FU-24A is a dual-control version. Now available is the FU-24-950 with 400hp Lycoming IO-720 engine, which carries a 2,320lb (1,052kg) payload in agricultural form and has a ferry seat for a loader/mechanic. It can be flown in utility form, carrying up to seven passengers or freight. Prototypes have flown with both AiResearch TPE 331 and Pratt & Whitney PT6A turboprops, and New Zealand Aerospace Industries, formed by a merger between Air Parts and AESL, was producing in 1979 the Cresco as a version of the FU-24-950 with an Avco Lycoming LTP 101 turboprop. First flight of the prototype was made on 28 February 1979.

Aerotec A-122B Uirapuru / Brazil

Span: 27ft 10.75in (8.50m)
Length: 21ft 8in (6.60m)
Gross weight: 1,825lb (840kg)
Max cruising speed: 121mph (195km/h)
Max range: 495 miles (800km) at 108mph (174km/h)

The prototype of this side-by-side 2-seat all-metal trainer flew on 2 June 1965, with a 108hp Lycoming O-235 engine. The A-122A Uirapuru was ordered into production for the Brazilian Air Force as the T-23, with a 160hp Lycoming O-320-B2B engine, a total of 100 being delivered, followed by 18 for Bolivia and eight for Paraguay. A 2-seat civil version has been developed as the A-122B, with a modified cockpit, and 18 were delivered to Brazilian civil flying clubs in 1975.

Aircoupe (and Ercoupe, Fornaire and Mooney M-10 Cadet) / USA

Data: M-10 Cadet

Span: 30ft 0in (9.14m)
Length: 20ft 4in (6.19m)
Gross weight: 1,450lb (657kg)
Max cruising speed: 124mph (200km/h)
Max range: 455 miles (732km)

This series of 2-seat all-metal light aircraft began with the Erco Ercoupe of 1940, featuring a then-unique two-control system without rudder pedals. Manufacturing rights passed subsequently to Forney, who produced the same design as the Fornaire, and then to Alon, who introduced several changes in the A-2 Aircoupe and offered optional conventional controls. The Alon company was acquired by Mooney in 1967, the final versions of this aircraft being produced subsequently as the A-2 with new spring-steel main undercarriage legs and the M-10 Cadet with new rear fuselage and single tail-fin. Standard engine in the later versions was the 90hp Continental C90-16F.

Air Tractor Model AT-301 (and AT-302) / USA

Photo: AT-302
Data: AT-301

Span: 45ft 0in (13.72m)
Length: 27ft 0in (8.23m)
Gross weight: 6,900lb (3,130kg)
Range: 350 miles (563km) at 140mph (225km/h)

The design of this agricultural sprayer/duster originated in the Snow S-2B, certificated in 1958. Aero Commander acquired the Snow range of aircraft, which eventually formed the basis of some of Rockwell's agricultural types. Leland Snow, designer of the S-2B, began work on the AT-301 Air Tractor in 1971. The prototype flew in September 1973. By 1979, over 200 production models had been delivered and production was continuing at the rate of six aircraft a month. The AT-301 is a conventional single-seater, of all-metal construction, except for fabric-covered tail control surfaces, and powered by a 600hp Pratt & Whitney R-1340 piston-engine. In June 1977, Air Tractor flew a prototype with an Avco Lycoming LTP 101 turboprop engine and this version entered production as the AT-302.

AISA I-11B / Spain

Span: 30ft 7in (9.32m)
Length: 21ft 3in (6.47m)
Gross weight: 1,474lb (668kg)
Range: 403 miles (649km) at 110mph (177km/h)

The prototype I-11, which flew in 1950, had a tricycle undercarriage. All production I-11Bs have a tailwheel; the first one flew on 16 October 1953, and a total of 180 have been delivered, some to the Spanish Air Force for liaison and training duties. Standard engine is the 90hp Continental C90-12F, but some I-11Bs have a 93hp ENMA Flecha of Spanish design. All are side-by-side two-seaters of wooden construction.

Anahuac Tauro / Mexico

Photo and data: Tauro 350

Span: 37ft 6.5in (11.44m)
Length: 26ft 11.25in (8.21m)
Gross weight: 4,545lb (2,062kg)
Cruising speed: 85-90mph (137-145km/h)
Max range: 233 miles (375km)

The Anahuac company was founded to develop aircraft suited particularly to Mexican needs. Its first product is this single-seat agricultural aircraft, which flew on 3 December, 1968. The first of a test batch of seven production Tauro 300s followed on 5 June 1970, with a 300hp Jacobs R-755-A2M1 engine. On the basis of experience with these aircraft, an improved version known as the Tauro 350, with 350hp Jacobs R-755-SM engine, was developed and is in series production.

Arctic Aircraft Interstate S1B2 Arctic Tern / USA

Span: 35ft 6in (10.82m)
Gross weight: 1,900lb (862kg)
Max cruising speed: 117mph (188km/h)
Max range: 650 miles (1,045km)

The Arctic Tern is an updated and improved version of the Interstate S-1 Cadet, which first entered production in 1940. Cadets began life as S-1As with 65hp Continental or Franklin engines. Variants with 85hp and 90hp Franklins followed. Then, when America came into World War II, 250 S-1Bs were acquired for the US Army as L-6s for liaison and observation roles. As well as having a 102hp Franklin O-200-5 engine, the L-6s had their cabin glazing extended back to a point about halfway between the wing trailing edge and the fin. Several Cadets remain airworthy in the US. In addition, Arctic Aircraft is building the tandem two-seat Arctic Tern in Alaska, with a 150hp Lycoming O-320 engine, optional underbelly cargo pack, and a removable rear seat to provide space for bulky freight inside the cabin.

Auster J/1 Autocrat (and J/1B Aiglet, J/1N Alpha, J/2 Arrow, J/4 and J/5 Adventurer) / UK

Photo: J/1N
Data: Autocrat

Span: 36ft 0in (10.98m)
Length: 23ft 5in (7.14m)
Gross weight: 1,850lb (839kg)
Range: 320 miles (515km) at 100mph (161km/h)

The Autocrat was Auster's first postwar lightplane, powered by a 100hp Cirrus Minor II engine. Others have been converted from 3- to 4-seaters (J/1A), or to have a 130hp Gipsy Major I engine and larger vertical tail surfaces, when they become J/1N Alphas. Aircraft built from the start with a Gipsy Major I and enlarged tail are J/1B Aiglets; of the 90 or so built, those registered in the UK were equipped mainly for crop-spraying. The J/2 Arrow (75hp Continental) and J/4 (90hp Cirrus Minor) are similar to the J/1 but seat only two. The J/5 Adventurer differed from the Aiglet in not having enlarged tail surfaces. The J/5F Aiglet Trainer has a wider fuselage and shorter span, and is aerobatic.

Auster J/5B, J/5G and J/5P Autocar (and J/5Q and J/5R Alpine) / UK

Photo: J/5Q Alpine
Data: J/5G Autocar

Span: 36ft 0in (10.98m)
Length: 23ft 4in (7.11m)
Gross weight: 2,400lb (1,088kg)
Range: 260 miles (418km) at 106mph (171km/h)

First full 4-seater put into production by Auster, the Autocar made its maiden flight in August 1949 and about 100 were built, mostly for export. Variants are the J/5B with 130hp Gipsy Major I engine, J/5G with 155hp Cirrus Major 3, and J/5P with 145hp Gipsy Major 10. The somewhat similar Alpine is a cross between the Autocar and the Aiglet Trainer, offering improved performance as a 3-seater. Variants are the J/5Q with Gipsy Major I and J/5R with Gipsy Major 10.

Ayres (Rockwell) Thrush Commander / USA

Data: Thrush Commander 500

Span: 44ft 5in (13.54m)
Length: 29ft 4.5in (8.95m)
Gross weight: 6,900lb (3,130kg)
Operating speed: 105-115mph (169-185km/h)
Max range: 403 miles (698km)

Largest of the former range of Rockwell (North American) agricultural aircraft, and the only one still manufactured by the parent company, this aircraft was produced originally with a variety of engines by the former Snow Aeronautical Corp from 1958 until 1965. Snow was then taken over by Aero Commander, which continued building the S-2D version, with 600hp Pratt & Whitney R-1340-S3H1 engine, as the Ag Commander S-2D. Following Aero Commander's merger with North American, the same basic design became the Thrush Commander 600 with R-1340-AN-1 engine and Thrush Commander 800 with 800hp Wright R-1300-1B engine. Ayres Corporation took over the manufacturing and marketing rights in 1977 and production continues. In addition, Ayres was developing a two-seat version in 1979 and offered the PZL-35 engine as an alternative.

Ayres (and Marsh) Turbo-Thrush / USA

Photo: Ayres S-2R
Data: Marsh S-2R-T

Span: 44ft 5in (13.54m)
Length: 30ft 5in (9.27m)
Gross weight: 7,800lb (3,538kg)
Cruising speed: 146mph (235km/h)
Range: 320 miles (515km)

Ayres Corporation markets a conversion kit for the Thrush Commander (qv) fit a 750shp Pratt & Whitney PT6A-34 engine. The conversion was engineered for Ayres by Serv-Aero Engineering and the prototype flew on 9 September 1975. About 60 conversions had been made by 1979 and a two-seat version was also available. A similar conversion engineered by Marsh Aviation Co uses the 600shp Garrett AiResearch TPE331-1-101 turboprop. Two prototypes were built and Marsh began delivering production conversions in September 1976; about 20 have been made.

Beagle (Auster) 'D' Series and A113 Husky / UK

Photo and data: A113

Span: 36ft 0in (10.98m)
Length: 22ft 2in (6.76m)
Gross weight: 2,400lb (1,088kg)
Cruising speed: 95-110mph (153-177km/h)
Range: 580 miles (933km) at 95mph (153km/h)

The cleaned-up Auster 'D' series, introduced in 1960, have basically identical airframes, with new metal wing spars and Lycoming engines. The D4 2-seater has 108, 150/160 or 180hp engine and 32ft (9.75m) or 36ft (10.98m) wing. D5 3-seater has 150/160 or 180hp engine and 32ft or 36ft wing. D6 4-seater has 160 or 180hp engine and 36ft wing. Production of the D5/160 and D5/180 was continued by Beagle, the latter aircraft, with 180hp Lycoming O-360-A2A engine, being redesignated A113 Husky. Some were equipped with agricultural spray gear. The specialised J/1U Workmaster agricultural aircraft, first flown in 1958, is similar, with 180hp Lycoming engine. In addition, 150 D4/108, D5/160 and D5/180 aircraft were built by OGMA in Portugal for air force and local club use.

Beagle A61 Srs 2 Terrier / UK

Span: 36ft 0in (10.98m)
Length: 23ft 8in (7.21m)
Gross weight: 2,400lb (1,088kg)
Cruising speed: 108-115mph (174-185km/h)
Range: 300 miles (483km) at 108mph (174km/h)

This 2/3-seat touring and training lightplane, first flown on 25 April 1962, was produced by rebuilding and refurbishing ex-Army Auster AOP6 and T7 monoplanes. The normal 145hp Gipsy Major 10 Mk 1-1 engine is retained, but cabin noise is reduced by fitting a lengthy exhaust and silencer. The Terrier is an excellent glider tug and had its origin in the less-refined, but generally similar, Auster 6A Tugmaster.

Beagle A109 Airedale / UK

Span: 36ft 4in (11.07m)
Length: 26ft 4in (8.02m)
Gross weight: 2,750lb (1,247kg)
Cruising speed: 108-115mph (174-185km/h)
Max range: 830 miles (1,335km) at 115mph (185km/h)

First flown on 16 April 1961, the 4-seat Airedale was a refined development of the traditional Auster monoplane. The 180hp Lycoming O-360 engine gives a top speed of 141mph (227km/h). More modern features include a car-type cabin, wheel controls, swept fin, spatted tricycle undercarriage, and provision for complete airline-standard instrumentation for all-weather flying. 42 were built.

Beagle B121 Pup / UK

Photo and data: Pup-100

Span: 31ft 0in (9.45m)
Length: 22ft 9in (6.93m)
Gross weight: 1,600lb (726kg)
Range: 540 miles (870km) at 100mph (161km/h)

First flown on 8 April 1967, the Pup-100 is a fully-aerobatic lightplane, powered by a 100hp Rolls-Royce/Continental O-200-A engine and able to carry two adults and, optionally, two children. Deliveries of production aircraft began in April 1968. Meanwhile, the first of two prototypes of the 2/4-seat Pup-150, with 150hp Lycoming O-320-A2B engine, had flown on 4 October 1967. This aircraft was re-engined subsequently with a 160hp Lycoming, to fly as the prototype Pup-160 on 5 September 1968. The first Pup-200 flew in 1969 with a 200hp Continental engine. Early in the following year the Beagle company went into liquidation and production ended. 128 Pups of all models were built. The Scottish Aviation Bulldog military trainer is derived from the same design.

Beechcraft Model 17 / USA

Photo: D17S
Data: G17

Span: 32ft 0in (9.75m)
Length: 25ft 9in (7.85m)
Gross weight: 4,250lb (1,928kg)
Max cruising speed: 198mph (319km/h)
Max range: 1,400 miles (2,253km)

The famous Beechcraft 'Staggerwing' first flew in 1932 and remained in production, in various versions, until 1948. Many remain in use. Early models included the 4-seat 17R (420hp Whirlwind), A17F (700hp Cyclone) and B17L (225hp Jacobs), of which the first two had fixed spatted undercarriages and the B17L a retractable gear. Hundreds built prewar were supplemented by 270 UC-43s and GB-1s (D17S variants), delivered to the US services with 450hp Pratt & Whitney R-985 engine. About 90 civil G17S 5-seaters were produced postwar, also with R-985 engine.

Beechcraft Bonanza (V-tail series) / USA

Photo and data: Model V35B

Span: 33ft 5.5in (10.20m)
Length: 26ft 4.5in (8.04m)
Gross weight: 3,400lb (1,542kg)
Cruising speed: 164-203mph (264-327km/h)
Range: 520-1,010 miles (836-1,625km) (with reserves)

The prototype of this V-tail 4/6-seat light plane flew on 22 December 1945, and more than 10,100 had been built by February 1979. The design has undergone continuous refinement, with increasingly-powerful engines, and the current Model V35B Bonanza has a 285hp Continental IO-520-B fuel-injection engine. The V35B TC is similar except for having a turbosupercharger and oxygen system. Conventional-tailed Bonanzas are also in production and are described below.

Beechcraft Bonanza (conventional tail) and Debonair / USA

Photo: Model A36
Data: Model F33A

Span: 33ft 5.5in (10.20m)
Length: 25ft 6in (7.77m)
Gross weight: 3,400lb (1,542kg)
Cruising speed: 156-200mph (251-322km/h)
Range: 515-980 miles (828-1,577km) (with reserves)

Except for having a conventional tail unit and different engine, this family of Bonanzas is generally similar to the V-tail series. The prototype flew on 14 September 1959, and production models were known as Debonairs until 1967. Production of the G33, with 260hp Continental IO-470-D engine, ended in 1973, after 49 had been delivered. Current models are the F33A with 285hp IO-520-B and aerobatic F33C. Altogether, some 2,200 Model 33s had been built by the beginning of 1979. The Model A36 Bonanza is generally similar to the F33A, but is lengthened to make it a full six-seater, and has a double-door for easier cargo loading; about 1,300 had been built by January 1979.

Beechcraft Musketeer (and Sierra, Sundowner and Sport / USA

Photo: Sundowner 180
Data: Sierra 200

Span: 32ft 9in (9.98m)
Length: 25ft 9in (7.85m)
Gross weight: 2,750lb (1,247kg)
Cruising speed: 132-158mph (213-254km/h)
Range: 790 miles (1,271km) (with reserves)

The prototype of this family of low-cost all-metal light aircraft flew on 23 October 1961. Initially, all Musketeers had a fixed undercarriage, the 1971 models of this type being the 4/6-seat Musketeer Custom with 180hp Lycoming O-360-A4G engine; two-seat (optional four-seat) Musketeer Sport with 150hp O-320-E2C; and 4/6-seat Musketeer Super with 200hp IO-360-A2B. There were aerobatic versions of the Custom and Sport; the Super R differed from the Super in having a retractable undercarriage and constant-speed propeller. In 1972, the Musketeer range was renamed, becoming the Sierra (Super R); the Sundowner (Custom) and Sport (Sport). Subsequently, suffix numbers were added to these names to indicate the engine power. Some 3,900 Musketeers and later models had been built by the beginning of 1979.

Beechcraft Model 77 Skipper / USA

Span: 30ft 0in (9.14m)
Length: 24ft 0in (7.32m)
Gross weight: 1,675lb (760kg)
Cruising speed: 78-110mph (158-177km/h) at 8,500ft (2,590m)
Range: 475 miles (764km/h)

In late 1974 Beech announced that it was building the prototype of a single-engined trainer designated PD 285 for potential use at its Aero Centers. New constructional methods were to be used to keep manufacturing costs to a minimum. The wing, of GAW-1 aerofoil section, resulted from combined NASA/Beech research into supercritical aerofoils with high-lift characteristics. Emphasis was also to be placed on providing a spacious cabin, with good all-round field of view, for the two side-by-side occupants. The prototype PD 285 flew for the first time on 6 February 1975, powered by a 115hp Lycoming O-235 engine. After a time, the original low-mounted tailplane was exchanged for a T-tail and the aircraft was redesignated Beech Model 77. Production deliveries began in mid-1979, with the name Skipper then adopted, against outstanding orders for more than 600.

Bellanca (and Downer) 14-19-2 Cruisemaster / USA

Data: Downer 14-19-2

Span: 34ft 2in (10.41m)
Length: 22ft 10.75in (6.98m)
Gross weight: 2,700lb (1,225kg)
Range: 800 miles (1,287km) at 196mph (315km/h)

Development of this aircraft began with the 3-seat Bellanca 14-9 of 1937, with alternative 90hp Rearwin and 100hp Lycoming engines. First postwar models were the 4-seat 14-13 Cruisair and 14-19 Cruisemaster, of which large numbers are still flying. Final version was the Model 14-19-2, with 230hp Continental O-470-K engine, of which 104 were built by Downer Aircraft Co after it acquired manufacturing rights from Bellanca.

Bellanca 260 (and Super Viking 300) / USA

Photo: Viking 300
Data: Super Viking 300

Span: 34ft 2in (10.41m)
Length: 23ft 6in (7.16m)
Gross weight: 3,325lb (1,508kg)
Cruising speed: 190-194mph (306-312km/h)
Max range: 940 miles (1,513km)

On 15 November 1958, Downer Aircraft flew the prototype of an improved version of the Cruisemaster (see previous entry) known as the Bellanca 260 Model 14-19-3, with 260hp Continental IO-470-F engine and tricycle undercarriage. After a period of quantity production, the design was refined further to substitute a single square-cut fin and rudder for the original triple-tail. Manufacturing rights in the new version were taken over by Bellanca Aircraft Corp, which is currently manufacturing a refined version as the Super Viking 300 with 300hp Continental IO-530-D or Lycoming IO-540-KE5 engine and the Turbo-Viking with 310hp Lycoming TIO-540.

Bellanca Aries T-250 / USA

Span: 31ft 4in (9.55m)
Length: 26ft 2in (7.98m)
Gross weight: 3,150lb (1,430kg)
Max cruising speed: 208mph (335km/h)
Max range: 1,170 miles (1,883km)

The prototype of this 4-seat lightplane was designed and built by Ben Anderson and Marvin Greenwood, who are remembered best for the AG-14 high-wing twin-boom light aircraft of 1948, with pusher engine, of which four examples were completed. Known as the AG-51, this new prototype first flew on 10 July 1973 and received FAA Type Approval in July 1976. Production under the name Aries T-250, has been launched by Bellanca Aircraft Corporation, following this company's acquisition by Anderson, Greenwood & Co and deliveries were to begin in 1980. Construction is all-metal, with a T-tail and retractable landing gear. Power plant is a 250hp Lycoming O-540-A4D5 engine.

Bellanca Model 7ACA Champ / USA

Span: 35ft 1.5in (10.70m)
Length: 21ft 9.5in (6.63m)
Gross weight: 1,220lb (553kg)
Max cruising speed: 86mph (138km/h)
Max range: 300 miles (483km)

Cheapest lightplane built in recent times in America, this wooden-sparred metal fuselage 2-seater was a 1971 reincarnation of the Aeronca 7AC, of which more than 7,200 were built in 1946-48 and some examples of which still survive. Main difference was the use of a 60hp Franklin 2A-120-B engine, in place of the original 65hp Continental which was no longer available. This was enclosed by a new cowling, which improved visibility; and the Champ also had lightweight cantilever spring-steel main undercarriage legs. Production has now ended.

Bölkow (Klemm) Kl 107C and Bölkow BO207 / Germany

Photo and data: Bolkow 207

Span: 35ft 6in (10.82m)
Length: 27ft 3in (8.30m)
Gross weight: 2,645lb (1,200kg)
Range: 775 miles (1,247km) at 124mph (200km/h)

The basic design of the Kl 107 was evolved by Klemm during the war, but the prototype, with 90hp Continental C90 engine, did not fly until 1955. A year later, the 3-seat Kl 107B appeared with 150hp Lycoming engine. Manufacturing rights were acquired by Bölkow, which built 150 improved Kl 107Cs with the same engine. Final production model was the further refined four-seat Bölkow BO207, as described and illustrated, with 180hp Lycoming O-360-A1A engine, modified wing and redesigned canopy and tail unit. All of these aircraft are of wooden construction.

Bölkow BO208/MFI-9 Junior / Germany/Sweden

Photo and data: BO208C

Span: 26ft 4in (8.02m)
Length: 19ft 0in (5.79m)
Gross weight: 1,390lb (630kg)
Max cruising speed: 127mph (204km/h)
Max range: 620 miles (1,000km)

The prototype of this ultra-light 2-seater was amateur-built in the USA by Bjorn Andreasson and first flew on 10 October 1958. Andreasson later became head of the Aircraft Division of the Swedish Malmo company, which put the aircraft into production as the MFI-9 Junior, with 100hp Rolls-Royce/Continental O-200 engine. Licence rights were acquired by Bölkow, which built about 200, under the basic designation BO208, before ending production in 1969/70. Malmo completed 25 before switching to the MFI-9B Trainer variant, mainly for military use.

Bücker Bü133 Jungmeister / Germany

Photo and data: Bü133D-1

Span: 21ft 7.75in (6.60m)
Length: 19ft 9in (6.02m)
Gross weight: 1,410lb (640kg)
Cruising speed: 87-124mph (140-200km/h)
Range: 310 miles (500km) (with reserves)

Although its design dates back to 1935, the Jungmeister is still rated so highly as a single-seater for advanced aerobatics that it was put back in production for a time in Germany by Aero Technik Canary. Two versions were available. The Bü133D-1 with 160hp Siemens Halske Sh-14A4 (Bramo) was virtually unchanged from the prewar variant but the Bü133F, first flown on 1 October 1969, has a more modern 220hp Franklin 6A-350-C1 horizontally-opposed engine and improved performance, whilst retaining the traditional 'radial' cowling.

CAC (Windecker) Eagle / USA

Span: 32ft 0in (9.75m)
Length: 28ft 6in (8.69m)
Gross weight: 3,400lb (1,542kg)
Max cruising speed: 204mph (328km/h)
Range: 1,230 miles (1,979km)

The Eagle was developed by Drs L. J. and F. M. Windecker between 1959 and 1969 to exploit glassfibre-reinforced plastics construction, which was used throughout the airframe. The first flight was made on 26 January 1969 and a second prototype was flown on 29 September 1969. Six of the seven production Eagles built by Windecker were still flying in 1979, in which year Mr G. P. Dietrick formed Composite Aircraft Corp with a view to resuming production. The engine is a 285hp Continental IO-520C.

Cessna Models 120, 140 and 170 / USA

Photo: Model 120
Data: Model 140 (65hp)

Span: 32ft 10in (10.0m)
Length: 20ft 11.75in (6.39m)
Gross weight: 1,450lb (658kg)
Range: 450 miles (724km) at 102mph (164km/h)

The side-by-side two-seat Model 120 was the first of Cessna's postwar designs for the civil market, a total of 2,164 being built in 1946-48, each powered by an 85hp Continental C85-12 or 12F engine. In parallel production was the Model 140, which differed in having manually-operated flaps, a starter and generator. The Model 140 could also be fitted, optionally, with a 90hp Continental C90-12F engine. Both the 120 and 140 were superseded in 1948 by the Model 140A, with the same choice of engines, metal instead of fabric covering on the wings and a single bracing strut each side in place of the former Vee struts. A total of 5,560 140/140As were built and many hundreds are still flying, together with large numbers of 120s. Also in production from 1948 to 1956 was the Cessna 170, a 4-seat counterpart of the Model 120/140 with 145hp Continental C145-2 engine. A considerable proportion of the 5,171 built remain airworthy.

Cessna Model 150 and 152 / USA

Photo and data: Model 152

Span: 32ft 8.5in (9.97m)
Length: 24ft 1in (7.34m)
Gross weight: 1,670lb (757kg)
Cruising speed: 123mph (198km/h)
Range: 403-794 miles (648-1,278km)

A total of 23,836 of these side-by-side club trainers had been built by 1977, when production ended. The appearance of the prototype, in September 1957, had marked Cessna's re-entry into the 2-seat market after a seven-year lapse. Powered by a 100hp Continental O-200-A piston engine, it followed the familiar Cessna all-metal high-wing, tricycle undercarriage formula. Detail refinements introduced after some years included a sweptback fin, stepped-down rear fuselage with panoramic rear window, and an optional rear 'family' seat for two small children. Versions built in France by Reims Aviation were designated F-150 and FRA-150 Aerobat; others were built in Argentina. During 1977, the Cessna 150 was superseded by the Cessna 152 with a 110hp Lycoming O-335-L2C engine operating on 100-octane low-lead fuel. More than 2,000 Model 152s had been built by 1979 and, like the Model 150, it was available also in an aerobatic version as the A152.

Cessna Model 172 and Skyhawk, 175, Skylark, 182, Skylane, Reims Rocket, Hawk and Cutlass / USA

Photo: Model F-172
Data: Hawk XP

Span: 35ft 10in (10.92m)
Length: 27ft 2in (8.28m)
Gross weight: 2,550lb (1,157kg)
Cruising speed: 150mph (241km/h)
Range: 553-662 miles (890-1,066km)

The 172 and other types listed above represent Cessna's 'middle line' of 4-seat all-metal aircraft with optional 'family seat' for two small children. The late model 172 had a 150hp Lycoming O-320-E2D engine and was built in France as the F-172, by Reims Aviation. The Skyhawk is a de luxe version of the 172 with 160hp engine. The 175 and Skylark, no longer in production, have a 175hp GO-300 engine. The 182 and Skylane are standard de luxe models with 230hp Continental O-470-R and the retractable gear Skylane RG was added in 1977. By January 1979, a total of 28,728 172/Skyhawks and 17,300 182/Skylanes had been delivered, including French-built F-172s and Reims Rockets (210hp Continental IO-370-D). A further derivative of the Model 172 is the R-172 Hawk XP with 195hp Continental IO-360-K, also assembled by Reims in France. Introduced in 1979, the Cutlass RG is in effect, the 172 Skyhawk with a retractable undercarriage.

Cessna Model 177 (and Cardinal) / USA

Photo and data: Cardinal RG

Span: 35ft 6in (10.82m)
Length: 27ft 3in (8.31m)
Gross weight: 2,800lb (1,270kg)
Cruising speed: 140-171mph (225-275km/h)
Range: 785-1,005 miles (1,260-1,615km)

Introduced into the Cessna range in September 1967, the Model 177 and de luxe Cardinal are basically four-seaters (plus optional seat for two children) with a cantilever wing and fixed tricycle undercarriage. The original versions had a 150hp Lycoming engine, but this gave way to a 180hp Lycoming O-320-A2F in the 1969 Model 177A. The latest version has an O-360-A1F and a new wing leading-edge of gull-wing concept with a further series of improvements made with the 1978 model Cardinal Classic. The series was supplemented in December 1970 by the Cardinal RG, which differs from the standard model by having a retractable undercarriage and 200hp IO-360-A1A engine. By the beginning of 1979, 2,680 Model 177/Cardinals and 1,390 RGs had been delivered, including 172 RGs assembled by Reims Aviation.

Cessna Models 180 and 185 Skywagon / USA

Photo: Model 185
Data: Model 180

Span: 35ft 10in (10.92m)
Length: 25ft 9in (7.85m)
Gross weight: 2,800lb (1,270kg)
Cruising speed: 121-162mph (195-261km/h)
Range: 695-1,215 miles (1,118-1,955km)

The two versions of the Skywagon are generally similar except for power plant, the 180 having a 230hp Continental O-470-R engine, while the 185 has a 300hp Continental IO-520-D. Each can carry up to six persons, in pairs. Alternatively, all the passenger seats can be removed to permit use of the aircraft for cargo carrying. A detachable cargo pack, with a capacity of 300lb (136kg) can be carried under the fuselage of the 185, and the A185 version is for agricultural use, named the AGcarryall. Deliveries by January 1979 totalled 5,885 Model 180s, 3,410 Model 185s (including military U-17 variants) and 92 AGcarryalls.

Cessna Model 188 AGwagon, AGtruck and AGhusky / USA

Photo and data: AGtruck

Span: 41ft 8in (12.70m)
Length: 26ft 3in (8.00m)
Gross weight: 4,200lb (1,905kg)
Range: 295 miles (475km) at 113mph (182km/h)

The prototype AGwagon flew for the first time on 19 February 1965, and two versions went into production. The basic AGwagon 'B' had a 230hp Continental O-470-R engine and a more powerful model was available optionally with a 300hp Continental IO-520-D engine and gross weight of 4,000lb. The basic model was renamed AGpickup in 1971; the 300hp version became the AGwagon and a version with enlarged hopper became the AGtruck. Deliveries totalled 1,498 AGwagons, 1,539 AGtrucks and 53 AGpickups by 1979. AGpickup production ended in 1975 but in 1978 Cessna added the AGhusky to the range, this being the AGwagon with a turbosupercharged 310hp Continental TSIO-520-T engine.

Cessna Model 195 (and 190) / USA

Photo and data: Model 195

Span: 36ft 2in (11.02m)
Length: 27ft 4in (8.33m)
Gross weight: 3,350lb (1,520kg)
Range: 750 miles (1,207km) at 165mph (265km/h)

Between 1947 and 1954, Cessna produced a total of 890 Model 195s and 195As, powered by a 300hp Jacobs R-775-A2 and 245hp Jacobs R-744-A2 engine respectively. Simultaneously, it built 233 Model 190s, which were generally similar except for their 240hp Continental R-670-23 engine. All were 4/5-seaters, with the now familiar Cessna cantilever spring-steel main undercarriage legs designed by Steve Wittman. Many examples are still current in the USA.

Cessna Stationair 6 (and Model 206 Skywagon/Super Skylane) / USA

Photo: Turbo Stationair 6 Amphibian
Data: Stationair

Span: 35ft 10in (10.92m)
Length: 28ft 0in (8.53m)
Gross weight: 3,600lb (1,633kg)
Cruising speed: 131-164mph (211-264km/h)
Range: 650-1,020 miles (1,045-1,640km)

In 1970 Cessna introduced the names Stationair and Turbo-Stationair in place of the earlier U206 Skywagon and TU206 Turbo-Skywagon, to emphasise the differences between these 6-seat cargo/utility aircraft and the Models 180 and 185 Skywagon. The suffix '6' was added in 1978. They have a swept fin, tricycle undercarriage, bigger flaps and tailplane, and a double cargo-door. The Stationair (and earlier U206) has a 300hp Continental IO-520-F engine; the Turbo-Stationair (and TU206) is similar except for its 310hp Continental TSIO-520-M. Other models, no longer in production, are the P206 and TP206 Super Skylanes, de luxe passenger versions minus the cargo-door and with 285hp IO-520-A and TSIO-520-C engine respectively. All of these aircraft can carry an under-fuselage cargo-pack. Deliveries by January 1979 totalled nearly 5,000 Model 206 Skywagons and Stationairs, and 643 Super Skylanes.

Cessna Model 210 Centurion / USA

Span: 36ft 9in (11.20m)
Length: 28ft 3in (8.61m)
Gross weight: 3,800lb (1,724kg)
Cruising speed: 154-188mph (248-303km/h)
Range: 765-1,250 miles (1,231-2,010km)

The prototype Cessna 210, flown in January 1957, was the first Cessna high-wing lightplane with a retractable undercarriage. FAA Type Approval was obtained on 23 August 1966. The 1967 models set a further new fashion by dispensing with wing-struts to give a full cantilever wing. The current basic versions are the Model 210 Centurion with 300hp Continental IO-520-L engine and six seats in pairs, with the T210 Turbo Centurion which differs in having a 310hp TSIO-520-R supercharged engine. In 1978, Cessna added to the range the Pressurised Centurion, with 310hp TSIO-520-P engine and pressurised cabin. Over 6,000 Model 210s of all types had been delivered by January 1979.

Champion (Bellanca) Citabria (and Scout and Decathlon) / USA

Photo: Decathlon
Data: Model 7GCAA Citabria

Span: 33ft 5in (10.19m)
Length: 22ft 8in (6.91m)
Gross weight: 1,650lb (748kg)
Max cruising speed: 129mph (207km/h)
Range: 503 miles (810km) at 129mph (207km/h)

Citabria is 'airbatic' spelled backwards, emphasising the manoeuvrability of this advanced development of the old Aeronca Champion family (qv). It is a tandem 2-seater, with composite wood and metal wings and steel-tube fuselage, all fabric-covered. Current models are the 7ECA with 115hp Lycoming O-235-C1 engine and optional floats or skis; Model 7GCAA with 150hp Lycoming O-320-A2D; and Model 7GCBC with increased wing span. The Model 8GCBC Scout is a utility/crop sprayer with span of 34ft 5.5in (10.50m), flaps and 180hp O-360-C2E engine. The similar Model 8KCAB Decathlon is an unlimited aerobatic competition aircraft and has a 150hp AEIO-320-E1B engine and 32ft (9.75m) wing span. All Champion aircraft are marketed by Bellanca and by 1979 sales totalled about 9,000 Citabrias, 300 Scouts and 350 Decathlons.

De Havilland DH82A Tiger Moth (and Thruxton Jackeroo) / UK

Photo and data: Tiger Moth

Span: 29ft 4in (8.94m)
Length: 23ft 11in (7.29m)
Gross weight: 1,825lb (828kg)
Range: 285 miles (460km) at 90mph (145km/h)

A few prewar civil Tiger Moths, after service with the RAF throughout the war, are still flying, together with a dwindling number of the wartime trainers which were demobilised by the score after RAF use. The engine is the 130hp Gipsy Major 1. A few veteran DH60 Moths, without wing sweepback, are also still flying. The Jackaroo is a Tiger Moth in which the centre fuselage has been widened and enclosed to accommodate two pairs of seats in an enclosed cabin. The wider fuselage increases the span to 30ft 4.5in (9.25m). Relatively few were converted and only a handful remain.

De Havilland DHC-1 Chipmunk / Canada/UK

Photo: Chipmunk 10

Span: 34ft 4in (10.47m)
Length: 25ft 8in (7.82m)
Gross weight: 2,200lb (997kg)
Cruising speed: 124mph (199km/h)
Range: 292 miles (470km)

De Havilland's Canadian company designed the Chipmunk as its first exercise in original aircraft design. The prototype was first flown on 22 May 1946, and Canadian production totalled 158 for civil use and 60 for the RCAF as Chipmunk T30. Another 60 were produced under licence in Portugal by OGMA. To meet RAF needs for a new primary trainer, the Chipmunk entered production in the UK as the T10. The 2-seat Chipmunk 21 was built from scratch in the UK for civil use, with 145hp Gipsy Major 10 Mk 2 engine; Chipmunk 22s are ex-RAF Mk 10 trainers. Chipmunk 22As have extra fuel and the Chipmunk 23 was a modified single-seat agricultural version. Also occasionally to be seen are Bristol 'tourer conversions' of the Mk 22A with blown hood and other refinements, giving a 130mph (209km/h) cruising speed.

DINFIA IA 46 Model 66 Super Ranquel / Argentina

Photo: Ranquel
Data: Super Ranquel

Span: 38ft 1.5in (11.61m)
Length: 24ft 5in (7.44m)
Gross weight: 2,775lb (1,260kg)
Range: 405 miles (652km/h) at 106mph (171km/h)

The original prototype Ranquel flew on 23 December 1957, and 100 had been built by April 1966. Final production versions were the standard Ranquel with 150hp Lycoming O-320-A2B engine and Super Ranquel with 180hp Lycoming O-360-A2A. An 88gal belly tank for agricultural chemicals could be attached to the Super Ranquel without encroaching on space inside the 3-seat cabin. DINFIA flew the prototype of an improved version known as the IA 51 Tehuelche, with O-360 engine and metal skin instead of fabric on the wing; but all Ranquel production ended in December 1968 and no more IA 51s were built.

Eagle (Bellanca) Eagle / USA

Span: 55ft 0in (16.76m)
Length: 26ft 0in (7.92m)
Gross weight: 5,211lb (2,364kg)
Working speed: 65-101mph (105-163km/h)

Eagle Aircraft Co, of Boise, Idaho, developed this unusual agricultural biplane between 1976 and 1979. After obtaining FAA certification, arrangements were made for the Eagle to be put into production by Bellanca Aircraft Corp while the original designers remained responsible for marketing. Featuring wings of unusually high aspect ratio, the Eagle is available with a number of alternative engines, including the 240hp Continental W670, 275hp Page-Jacobs R-755B1, 300hp Page-Jacobs R-755, 350hp Page-Jacobs R755S and 300hp Lycoming IO-540. The hopper has a capacity of 250 US gal (9,461 litres), with spray booms forming the trailing edge of the lower wing.

Emair MA-1B Diabolo 1200 / USA

Span: 41ft 8in (12.70m)
Length: 30ft 0in (9.14m)
Gross weight: 8,400lb (3,810kg)
Max cruising speed: 117mph (188km/h)

The prototype of this agricultural biplane was built in New Zealand under contract to Murryair Ltd of Hawaii, and first flew on 27 July 1969. After certification by the FAA, the aircraft was put into limited production in the USA as the Emair MA-1. After 25 had been built, Emair introduced the MA-1B with a 900hp Wright R-1820 engine and about 40 had been built by the end of 1978. The name Diabolo 1200 was adopted in 1979.

EMBRAER EMB-200 and 201 Ipanema / Brazil

Photo and data: EMB-201A

Span: 38ft 4.25in (11.69m)
Length: 24ft 4.5in (7.43m)
Gross weight: 3,968lb (1,800kg)
Max cruising speed: 127mph (204km/h)
Max range: 545 miles (878km)

Development of this single-seat agricultural aircraft was started in May 1969 by the national Aerospace Technical Centre, to specifications laid down by the Brazilian Ministry of Agriculture. When EMBRAER was formed a few months later it took over responsibility for the Ipanema. The prototype flew for the first time on 30 July 1970, and 73 of the initial EMB-200 and 200A versions, with 260hp Lycoming O-540 engine, were built before they were superseded by the EMB-201 in mid-1974. A total of 188 EMB-201s were delivered, with 300hp Lycoming IO-540 engine. This version was replaced by the current EMB-201A, with modified wings and other refinements from March 1977 and more than 100 have been built. The Brazilian Air Force Academy has three EMB-201Rs, adapted for gliding-towing.

Fairchild F-24W / USA

Photo: F-24R
Data: F-24W-41A

Span: 36ft 4in (11.07m)
Length: 23ft 9in (7.24m)
Gross weight: 2,562lb (1,162kg)
Range: 640 miles (1,030km) at 117mph (188km/h)

Many F-24Ws remain in civil use throughout the world, mostly of the F-24W-41/41A series, built during World War II for communications duties with the USAAF and its allies, under the designation UC-61/61A. These, and postwar civil F-24W-46s, are 4-seaters with the 165hp Warner Super Scarab 165 radial air-cooled engine. Earlier models, with 145hp Super Scarab, 175hp Ranger (F-24R) and other engines, can also be seen, particularly in the USA. British name for the F-24 was Argus.

FFA (REPAIR AG) AS202 Bravo / Switzerland

Photo and data: AS202/18A

Span: 31ft 11.75in (9.75m)
Length: 24ft 7in (7.50m)
Gross weight: 2,315lb (1,050kg)
Cruising speed: 126mph (203km/h)
Max range: 704 miles (1,134km)

This light aircraft was intended originally to be produced in both Switzerland and Italy, with joint manufacture by Flug- & Fahrzeugwerke and Siai-Marchetti. Instead, FFA now handles all production and marketing through its subsidiary Repair AG. First prototype to fly was an AS202/15, with 150hp Lycoming O-320-E2A engine and 2/3 seats, on 7 March 1969. It was followed by an Italian-assembled AS202/10 2-seater with 115hp Lycoming O-235-C2A on 7 May 1969 and another Swiss prototype on 16 June 1969. The first production AS202/15 flew on 22 December 1971 and over 30 have been built, plus more than 70 of the AS202/18A version (first flown 12 December 1975) with 180hp Lycoming. The single AS202/26A flown in 1978 has a 260hp Lycoming.

Fleet 80 Canuck / Canada

Span: 34ft 0in (10.36m)
Length: 22ft 4.5in (6.80m)
Gross weight: 1,425lb (645kg)
Range: 400 miles (644km) at 100mph (161km/h)

Designed for service in the Canadian bush and elsewhere, the Canuck is a sturdy tandem 2-seat lightplane with a fabric-covered all-metal airframe. It went into production immediately after the war and 210 were built in two years with 85hp Continental C-85-12J engine. A large number are still on register, and are able to utilise alternative wheel, float and ski undercarriages.

Flight Invert Cranfield A1 / UK

Span: 32ft 10in (10.00m)
Length: 26ft 5in (8.05m)
Gross weight: 2,505lb (1,000kg)
Max speed: 170mph (273km/h)

Design of this specialised aerobatic aircraft was started in 1968, to a specification drawn up by one of Britain's top competition pilots, Neil Williams. Lack of finance delayed completion of the prototype, which flew for the first time on 23 August 1976. By mid-1977, it had flown 60 times and was then modified to have its original 210hp Rolls-Royce Continental IO-360-D engine replaced by a 280hp Lycoming IO-540-D (Special), with which it first flew in August 1977. When flown in normal single-seat form ultimate load factors are +12g and −9g. A second person can be carried for training and ferrying.

Fournier RF-6B Club / France

Span: 34ft 5.5in (10.50m)
Length: 22ft 11.75in (7.00m)
Gross weight: 1,631lb (740kg)
Normal cruising speed: 118mph (190km/h)

As its designation implies, this two-seat aerobatic, sporting and training aircraft is related to the four-seat Sportavia RF-6 Sportsman (qv). The prototype first flew on 12 March 1974, and was followed by five pre-production RF-6Bs, the first of which flew on 4 March 1976. More than 40 aircraft had been delivered by mid-1979, the standard version being powered by a 100hp Rolls-Royce Continental O-200-A. The two seats are side-by-side, with dual controls. Construction is all-wooden, with plywood covered fuselage and fabric covering elsewhere. Development of a de luxe 120hp version was underway when financial difficulties brought further work to an end, at least temporarily.

Fuji FA-200 Aero Subaru / Japan

Photo and data: FA-200-180

Span: 30ft 11in (9.42m)
Length: 26ft 9.5in (8.17m)
Gross weight: 2,535lb (1,150kg)
Cruising speed: 104-127mph (167-204km/h)
Max range: 835 miles (1,343km)

The prototype of this 4-seat all-metal light aircraft flew for the first time on 12 August, 1965. After flight testing and some refinement of the design, two versions were put into production: the FA-200-160 has a 160hp Lycoming O-320-D2A engine; the FA-200-80 has a 180hp Lycoming IO-360-B1B. Both types are also certificated in the Aerobatic category as two-seaters as is the FA-200-180AO, which has a 180hp O-360-A5AD engine and fixed-pitch propeller instead of the normal constant-speed type. Nearly 300 Aero Subarus had been completed by 1979.

Great Lakes Sport Trainer 2T-1A / USA

Data: Model 2T-1A-2

Span: 26ft 8in (8.13m)
Length: 20ft 4in (6.20m)
Gross weight: 1,800lb (816kg)
Cruising speed: 118mph (190km/h)
Range: 300 miles (482km)

The Sport Trainer was a prewar product of the Great Lakes comapny, built in some numbers during the 1930s. A few of these survive and some examples have been built by amateur constructors, but since 1973, more than 100 new Great Lakes aircraft have been built by the Great Lakes Aircraft Company. Initially, the company built the Model 27-1A-1 with 140hp Lycoming engine but since 1978 the productive variant has been the Model 2T-1A-2 with a 180hp Lycoming AEIO-360-B1G6.

Grumman American AA-1 Yankee, Trainer, T-cat and Lynx / USA

Photo and data: Lynx

Span: 24ft 6in (7.47m)
Length: 19ft 3in (5.86m)
Gross weight: 1,600lb (726kg)
Range: 344 miles (554km) at 135mph (217km/h)

The prototype of this 2-seater family flew for the first time on 11 July 1963, as the Bede BD-1. American Aviation Corporation (subsequently acquired by Grumman) was formed in 1964 to produce the type as the AA-1 Yankee, using advanced constructional techniques such as metal-to-metal bonding and aluminium honeycomb for the fuselage panels. The first production Yankee flew on 30 May 1968, with a 108hp Lycoming O-235-C2C engine; early developments were the AA-1A/B Trainer and de luxe Tr-2. Previous models were superseded in 1977 by the AA-1C T-cat and de luxe Lynx, with a 115hp Lycoming O-235-L2C engine able to run on the new 100 octane low-lead fuel. Tailplane and elevator size were also increased. Optional extras included a spin package and 'private fighter' paint scheme. After Gulfstream American had acquired the Grumman American company, production of these two-seaters was suspended.

Grumman American AA-5, Traveler, Cheetah and Tiger / USA

Photo: Cheetah
Data: Tiger

Span: 31ft 6in (9.60m)
Length: 22ft 0in (6.71m)
Gross weight: 2,400lb (1,088kg)
Range: 637 miles (1,026km) at 160mph (258km/h)

The original AA-5, which flew on 21 August 1970, was an enlarged and more powerful four-seat version of the AA-1. It had a de luxe counterpart named the Traveler. By 1976, the standard and de luxe models had become the AA-5A and Cheetah respectively, and had been supplemented by a pair of more powerful versions known as the AA-5B and de luxe Tiger. The basic models were dropped in 1977, leaving the Cheetah and Tiger as Grumman American's only single-engined four-seaters, with 150hp Lycoming O-320-E2G and 180hp Lycoming O-360-A4K engine respectively. After the company had been acquired by Gulfstream American, plans were announced to end production late in 1979.

Gulfstream American Ag-Cat and Super Ag-Cat / USA

Photo: Super Ag-Cat
Data: Super Ag-Cat

Span: 35ft 11in (10.95m)
Length: 24ft 3in (7.39m)
Gross weight: 6,075lb (2,755kg)
Working speed: 80-100mph (129-168km/h)

The original Grumman G-164 Ag-Cat flew for the first time on 22 May 1967. Quantity production was taken on by Schweizer Aircraft, with Grumman, and later Grumman American, responsible for marketing. The initial production model had a 220-225hp Continental W-670 radial engine and loaded weight of 3,600lb (1,633kg). It was followed by versions with 240hp Gulf Coast W-670 and 245-300hp Jacobs R-755 engines, and then by the G-164A Super Ag-Cat, with a Jacobs R-755, 450hp Pratt & Whitney R-985 or 600hp Pratt & Whitney R-1340 engine. The Super Ag-Cat B had longer span wings and, optionally, the Continental R-975 engine while Super Ag-Cat C had the R-1340. The Turbo Ag-Cat D, first flown in June 1978, has a PT6A turboprop.

HAL HUL-26 Pushpak / India

Span: 36ft 0in (10.97m)
Length: 21ft 0in (6.40m)
Gross weight: 1,350lb (612kg)
Cruising Speed: 70-85mph (113-137km/h)
Range: 250 miles (402km) at 70mph (113km/h)

Hindustan Aeronautics designed this 2-seat lightplane as an inexpensive locally-built trainer for use by Indian flying clubs. The prototype flew for the first time on 28 September 1958, and a total of 150 were delivered. The airframe is a fabric-covered metal structure. Standard power plant is a 90hp Continental C90-8F, but one Pushpak was fitted experimentally with a 90hp PE90 engine of HAL's own design. The military Krishak, used by the Indian Air Force, was a derivative.

HAL HA-31 Mk II Basant / India

Span: 39ft 4.5in (12.00m)
Length: 29ft 6.25in (9.00m)
Gross weight: 5,000lb (2,270kg)
Max cruising speed: 115mph (185km/h)
Range: 400 miles (645km)

Hindustan Aeronautics designed its first agricultural aeroplane in mid-1968. This, the HA-31 Mk1, flew as a prototype in 1969 but was not a success. A completely new design was therefore evolved as the HA-31 Mk II and this, fitted with a 400hp Lycoming IO-720-C1B engine, made its first flight on 30 March, 1972. A second prototype and 20 pre-production Basants were built subsequently; and about 40 of the first series of 100 production aircraft had been completed by early 1979.

Helio Courier and Super Courier / USA

Span: 39ft 0in (11.89m)
Length: 31ft 0in (9.45m)
Gross weight: 3,400lb (1,542kg)
Cruising speed: 150-165mph (241-265km/h)
Range: 660-1,380 miles (1,062-2,220km)

Helio Aircraft Corporation was founded to develop and market a light aircraft with STOL characteristics and above-average safety. After flight tests of a converted Piper Vagabond, the company produced the prototype Courier incorporating full-span automatic leading-edge slats and high-lift flaps. More than 500 single-engined Couriers have been built, including 150 for the USAF, many of which were used for clandestine CIA-backed operations in SE Asia. Principal commercial version was the H-295 Super Courier, first flown on 24 February 1965; the HT-295, introduced in 1974, differed in having a nosewheel undercarriage; both were powered by the 295hp Lycoming GO-480-G1D6 engine.

IAR-821, 822, 826 and 827 / Romania

Photo: IAR-822
Data: IAR-826

Span: 42ft 0in (12.80m)
Length: 30ft 10in (9.40m)
Gross weight: 4,189lb (1,900kg)
Cruising speed: 103mph (165km/h)
Endurance: 1.3hr

The basic IAR-821 single-seat agricultural aircraft was designed at the former Industrial Aeronautica Romana works. The prototype flew for the first time in 1967. Production by IRMA (Aircraft Repair Factory) began in the following year and 20 were built in 1968-69, each with a 300hp Ivchenko AI-14RF radial engine. The prototype of a tandem two-seat training/utility version, known as the IAR-821B, flew in September 1968. The basic design was adapted subsequently to take a 290hp Lycoming IO-540-G1D5 engine, and a prototype of the resulting IAR-822 flew in 1970. Work on a pre-series batch of five and 200 production models was started soon afterwards, primarily for agricultural duties but suitable for a wide variety of other tasks such as highway de-icing, firefighting, aerial survey, glider towing, training and mail/freight transport. The IAR-822B is a tandem 2-seat version with the same Lycoming engine, and the all-metal IAR-826, with appeared in 1973, is generally similar to the wood and metal IAR-822. The IAR-827 is a development of the 826, first flown in 1976 with a 400hp Lycoming IO-720 engine. Installation of a 600hp PZL-35 was planned.

IAR-823 / Romania

Span: 32ft 9.75in (10.00m)
Length: 27ft 0.25in (8.24m)
Gross weight: 3,042lb (1,380kg)
Max range: 994 miles (1,600km) at 180mph (290km/h)

This 2/5-seat light aircraft was designed by a team led by Dipl Ing Radu Manicatide, one of Romania's best-known designers. The prototype flew in July 1973, followed by the first pre-production IAR-823 in 1974. At least 100 have been built for flying club and military use. Power plant is a 290hp Lycoming IO-540-G1D5, enabling the aircraft to carry up to five persons in its executive, taxi and touring roles. It is fully aerobatic as a two-seater.

Interceptor 400 (and Aero Commander 200 and Meyers 200) / USA

Photo: Meyers 200D

Span: 30ft 6in (9.29m)
Length: 26ft 11.5in (8.20m)
Gross weight: 4,005lb (1,815kg)
Max cruising speed: 281mph (452km/h)
Max range: 1,000 miles (1,610km) at 275mph (443km/h)

First product of Interceptor Corporation, this 4-seater was introduced as general aviation's first high-performance, pressurised, production aircraft powered by a single turboprop engine. The prototype flew on 27 June 1969, and received FAA certification in August 1971. Power plant is a 665shp AiResearch TPE 331-1-101, flat rated at 400shp. The airframe of the Interceptor 400 is based on that of the piston-engined aircraft known originally as the Meyers 200B and subsequently produced for a time by Aero Commander as their Model 200, with 285hp Continental IO-520-A engine. Examples of the Meyers 200 are still extant but production of the Interceptor 400 had not begun up to 1979.

Issoire IA 80 Piranha / France

Span: 30ft 10in (9.40m)
Length: 24ft 7.25in (7.50m)
Gross weight: 1,763lb (800kg)
Range: 435 miles (700km) at 118mph (190km/h)

The prototype of the Piranha, which flew for the first time in November 1975, was a two-seater designated WA-80 and developed by the Wassmer Company. Construction is all-plastics, and the fact that the fuselage is generally similar to that of the WA-51/54 series means that the cabin is unusually spacious for a 2-seater. The engine is a 100hp Rolls-Royce Continental O-200-A. After Wassmer was liquidated in 1977, Issoire Aviation took over production of the Piranha.

Jodel D11 Series / France

Photo and data: D112

Span: 26ft 10in (8.18m)
Length: 20ft 10in (6.35m)
Gross weight: 1,145lb (520kg)
Cruising speed: 93-105mph (150-169km/h)
Max range: 373 miles (600km)

The whole series of Jodel designs stemmed from the single-seat D9 Bébé, an ultra-light monoplane of such simple construction that it could be built and flown easily by amateurs. The 2-seat D11 followed and proved the starting point for a string of derivatives, including the D112 (65hp Continental), D117 (90hp Continental) and D119. Several companies acquired licences to manufacture the 2-seaters commercially. Wassmer, in France, built more than 300 D112s and de luxe D120 Paris-Nices. The improved D1190S Compostela was built in Spain by Aero-Difusion, with a 90hp Rolls-Royce/Continental C90-14F engine. Many home-built examples are also flying.

Jodel DR100 Ambassadeur Series (including Sicile and Excellence) / France

Photo: DR1050
Data: Sicile Record

Span: 28ft 7.25in (8.71m)
Length: 20ft 10in (6.35m)
Gross weight: 1,720lb (780kg)
Range: 775 miles (1,250km) at 133mph (214km/h)

One of the first manufacturers to realise the potential in the Jodel design was Pierre Robin of Centre Est Aeronautique (now Avions Pierre Robin). With the original designer, Jean Delemontez, he first evolved a high-performance 3-seater designated DR100 Ambassadeur (10 built). Successive improved versions included the DR1050 and 1051 (148 built), and DR1050/M Sicile (114 built) and Sicile Record (58 built), with 100hp Rolls-Royce/ Continental O-200-A engine. Like all Jodels, they feature all-wooden construction and considerable dihedral on the outer wings. The SAN Jodel DR1052 Excellence is similar. Production of these types has ended.

Jodel D104E Mousquetaire IV (and Abeille) and D150 Mascaret / France

Photo and data: Mousquetaire IV

Span: 33ft 8.25in (10.27m)
Length: 25ft 8in (7.82m)
Gross weight: 2,645lb (1,200kg)
Cruising speed: 125-149mph (200-240km/h)
Max range: 870 miles (1,400km)

Société Aeronautique Normande (SAN), like Avions Pierre Robin, specialised in manufacturing Jodel designs. With SAN's D140 Mousquetaire, the Jodel became a 4-seater. When SAN suspended operations, manufacture of the Mousquetaire IV was taken over by Robin, together with outstanding orders for the D140R Abeille, which is similar, but is equipped as a glider-tug and has a more extensively-glazed cabin to improve rearward view. Both types have a 180hp Lycoming O-360-A2A engine. The SAN-developed 2-seat D150 Mascaret was of similar overall appearance, with a 26ft 9in (8.15m) wing span and 100hp R-R/Continental O-200-A engine.

Lake LA-4 Buccaneer (and Colonial Skimmer IV) / USA

Photo and data: LA-4-200 Buccaneer

Span: 38ft 0in (11.58m)
Length: 24ft 11in (7.60m)
Gross weight: 2,690lb (1,220kg)
Cruising speed: 150mph (241km/h)
Max range: 825 miles (1,327km)

This amphibian began life as the 3-seat Colonial C-1 Skimmer, which flew for the first time on 7 July 1948, with a 125hp Lycoming O-290 engine. The production version had a 150hp Lycoming and was joined in 1957 by the C-2 Skimmer IV 4-seater with a 180hp Lycoming O-360-A1A. Manufacturing rights for the Skimmer IV were taken over by Lake Aircraft in 1959. From it they evolved the LA-4, with longer bow, 4ft greater span and other improvements. Several variants have been produced, the current production version being the LA-4-200 with 200hp IO-360-A1B engine. The 1,000th LA-4 was produced in 1979.

Laverda (Aviamilano) F8L Super Falco / Italy

Span: 26ft 3in (8.0m)
Length: 21ft 4in (6.50m)
Gross weight: 1,808lb (821kg)
Cruising speed: 155-180mph (250-290km/h)
Max range: 870 miles (1,400km)

This side-by-side 2-seater has the typical racey lines of a design by Stelio Frati (see Procaer Picchio and Siai-Marchetti SF260 for others). Construction is of wood, with retractable undercarriage and 160hp Lycoming O-320-B3B engine. Earlier Falcos, built by Aviamilano and Aeromere, had 135/150hp Lycomings. Production of all versions has been completed but in 1978 the Sequoia Aircraft Corp of Virginia, USA, obtained full rights in the F8L design and now offers plans and kits for home-builders.

Let Z-37 Cmelak / Czechoslovakia

Photo and data: Z-37A

Span: 40ft 1.25in (12.22m)
Length: 28ft 0.5in (8.55m)
Gross weight: 4,080lb (1,850kg)
Range: 400 miles (640km) at 114mph (183km/h) (with reserves)

This functional-looking aircraft was designed primarily for agricultural duties, with a 143gal (650 litre) chemical hopper aft of the single-seat cockpit. There is a seat for a mechanic or loader aft of the hopper, and the space occupied by this seat and the hopper can be utilised for carrying mail and freight during the winter season, when ag-planes are often unemployed. Structure is of metal, with mixed metal and fabric covering. Power plant is a 315hp M-62RF radial engine of Czechoslovakian design. The first of 10 prototype Cmelaks flew on 29 March 1963, and 600 production aircraft had been completed when production ended in 1975, including 27 Z-37A-2 two-seat trainers. The final operational version, the Z-37A, differed from the original Z-37 mainly in structural and anti-corrosive improvements to extend the time between major overhauls to as much as 4,000 flying hours.

Maule M-4 and M-5 Rocket Series (and Jetasen) / USA

Photo: M-5-210C Lunar Rocket
Data: M-5-235C

Span: 30ft 10in (9.39m)
Length: 23ft 6in (7.16m)
Gross weight: 2,300lb (1,043kg)
Max cruising speed: 172mph (277km/h)
Range: 550-800 miles (885-1,287km)

This high performance 4-seat light aircraft began as an amateur 'home-built'. The prototype, known as the Maule Bee Dee B-4, flew on 8 September 1960 and several hundred production models have since been delivered. Originally, there were M-4 variants flown as the Jetasen, Rocket, Astro-Rocket and Strata-Rocket, with various engines. Production switched in 1975 to the M-5 Lunar Rocket, with a 220hp Franklin engine. Current models have either a 210hp Continental or 235hp Lycoming engine.

MBB BO 209 Monsun / Germany

Data: BO209-160

Span: 27ft 6.75in (8.83m)
Length: 21ft 7.75in (6.58m)
Gross weight: 1,807lb (820kg)
Cruising speed: 151-158mph (243-254km/h)
Max range: 745 miles (1,200km)

The prototype of this 2-seat light aircraft, known as the MHK-101, was designed by Dipl-Ing Hermann Mylius. Technical Director of the former Bölkow company, now part of Messerschmitt-Bölkow-Blohm GmbH. It flew for the first time on 22 December 1967, and was developed into the BO209 Monsun, which first flew on 28 May 1969 and was offered in three versions. The basic BO209-150 had a 150hp Lycoming O-320-E engine; this was replaced by a 160hp Lycoming IO-320-D1A in the BO209-160. The BO209S specialised trainer, first flown in June 1971, had a 130hp Rolls-Royce/Continental O-240 engine. The BO209-150 and -160 had folding wings and an optionally-retractable nose-wheel. Production ended in 1972.

Mooney (and Aerostar) M-20 series / USA

Photo: Mooney M-20J
Data: M-20K Mooney 231

Span: 36ft 1in (11.00m)
Length: 25ft 5in (7.74m)
Gross weight: 2,900lb (1,317kg)
Max cruising speed: 210mph (338km/h)
Max range: 1,220 miles (1,963km) (with reserves)

The original Mooney company built more than 5,400 of its M20 series of 4-seaters (M-20C Mark 21 Ranger, M-20E Super-21 Chaparral and M-20F Executive) up to 1972, when financial difficulties occurred. Production resumed in 1974 and current models are the M-20J Mooney 201 with 180hp Lycoming O-360-A1D and the M-20K Mooney 231, introduced at the end of 1978, with a 210hp Continental TSIO-360-GB. Production was at the rate of more than 30 a month (combined) in 1979.

Mudry CAP 20 / France

Photo: CAP 20LS
Data: CAP 20LS-200

Span: 24ft 10in (7.57m)
Length: 21ft 2.5in (6.46m)
Gross weight: 1,433lb (650kg)
Max cruising speed: 165mph (265km/h)
Max endurance: 2hr

Avions Mudry and its now closed associated company, CAARP, developed a version of the two-seat Piel Emeraude (qv) as the CAP 10 and is responsible for a single-seat derivative of this aircraft, designated CAP 20. Intended as a specialised aerobatic type, the current CAP 20L first flew on 15 January 1976 with 180hp Lycoming AEIO-360 engine but the production model CAP 20LS-200 has a 200hp Lycoming AIO-360-B1B engine and a constant speed propeller. The CAP 21, under development in 1979, has a new wing.

Navion Rangemaster (and Navion) / USA

Photo and data: Rangemaster

Span: 34ft 9in (10.6m)
Length: 27ft 6in (8.38m)
Gross weight: 3,315lb (1,503kg)
Cruising speed: 185mph (298km/h)
Max range: 1,610 miles (2,590km)

The original 4-seat Navion was manufactured first by its designers, North American, and then by Ryan, each company building more than one thousand. Navion Aircraft then took over the design and, on 10 June 1960 flew the prototype of a 5-seat version named the Rangemaster, with engine power increased from 205 to 260hp and wingtip tanks for even-longer range. This was superseded by the further improved Mark G, with 285hp Continental IO-520-B engine, which was taken over by Janox Corporation in 1970. The rights were sold again in 1973 to Navion Rangemaster Aircraft Corp and the first production Rangemaster G flew on 16 November 1974. Six more examples of the Rangemaster G and improved Model H were built subsequently.

NDN Firecracker / UK

Span: 26ft 0in (7.92m)
Length: 25ft 3in (7.70m)
Gross weight: 2,840lb (1,288kg)
Max cruising speed: 198mph (319km/h)
Max range: 1,405 miles (2,260km) (no reserves)

The NDN-1 Firecracker is a lightweight training aircraft developed for military or civil use by a company set up by Desmond Norman, co-founder of Britten-Norman Aircraft. The prototype, powered by a 260hp Lycoming AEIO-540-B4D5 engine, made its first flight on 26 May 1977 and full civil certification was obtained just two years later. NDN Aircraft plans to licence other companies, particularly in developing countries, to produce the Firecracker, with technical and manufacturing support from the parent company.

Neiva Paulistinha 56 / Brazil

Photo and data: Paulistinha 56-C

Span: 35ft 5in (10.80m)
Length: 22ft 2in (6.76m)
Gross weight: 1,455lb (660kg)
Cruising speed: 90-99mph (145-159km/h)
Max range: 560 miles (900km)

This tandem 2-seat light aircraft was produced by Neiva for many years, in several versions. Last to be manufactured in quantity was the Paulistinha 56-C, with 90hp Continental C90 engine, of which production ended in 1964, after a total of 238 had been completed. The developed 56-D, with 150hp Lycoming O-320-A1A, did not progress beyond a single prototype. Production of an updated version, known as the Paulistão, was under consideraton in 1977 but did not proceed.

Nipper (and Tipsy Nipper) / Belgium/UK

Photo: Nipper T66 Mk2
Data: Nipper Mk III

Span: 20ft 6in (6.25m)
Length: 15ft 0in (4.57m)
Gross weight: 660lb (300kg)
Cruising speed: 90-95mph (145-153km/h)
Range: 200-450 miles (322-725km)

Two versions of the diminutive Tipsy Nipper single-seater were manufactured originally by Avions Fairey in Belgium, in the form of both kits and complete aircraft. The T66 Mk 1 Nipper had a 40hp Pollmann HEPU engine. T66 Mk 2 had a 45hp Stark Stamo, giving a range of 525 miles (845km) when wingtip tanks were fitted. Production was taken over by Nipper Aircraft Ltd of the UK in 1966, and this company evolved two improved versions. The basic Nipper Mk III has a 45hp 1,500cc Rollason Ardem (VW) engine; the Mk IIIA has a 1,600cc Rollason Ardem. These were sold in small numbers in the form of both factory-built aircraft and kits.

Nord 1101 Noralpha / France

Span: 37ft 8in (11.50m)
Length: 28ft 0in (8.53m)
Gross weight: 3,630lb (1,646kg)
Range: 745 miles (1,200km) at 172mph (277km/h)

This four-seat lightplane is a development of the Messerschmitt Bf108 with tricycle undercarriage. Two prototypes were built by Nord during World War II, with 270hp Argus engine, as Me208s. Postwar, the surviving prototype was redesignated Nord 1100. The Nord 1101 and 1102 production versions were similar, with 233hp Renault 6Q and 6Q 11 engine respectively. A total of 200 were built for military and civilian service. Many are still flying together with some Nord 1000/1001/1002 Pingouins which were versions of the Bf108 built by Nord.

Nord 1203/II Norécrin II / France

Photo and data: Norécrin II

Span: 33ft 6.25in (10.22m)
Length: 23ft 8in (7.21m)
Gross weight: 2,313lb (1,050kg)
Max cruising speed: 137mph (220km/h)
Max range: 560 miles (900km)

Despite a family likeness to the Noralpha, the Norécrin was an original Nord design to meet a French Ministry of Transport requirement. The two-seat Nord 1200 prototype had a 100hp Mathis engine and flew for the first time on 15 December 1945. Initial production model was the 3-seat Nord 1201 Norécrin 1, with 140hp Renault 4 Pei engine. A few examples are still airworthy but are outnumbered by Nord 1203/II Norécrin IIs, with 135hp Régnier 4LO engine and four seats.

North American T-6 Texan/ Harvard / USA

Span: 42ft 0in (12.80m)
Length: 29ft 6in (8.99m)
Gross weight: 5,617lb (2,547kg)
Range: 870 miles (1,400km) at 146mph (236km/h)

More than 10,000 of these famous 2-seat basic trainers were built in the USA and Canada in 1938-54 and the type still serves with many world air forces. In addition, numerous civil-registered T-6s are flying, notably as airline pilot trainers, although some have been used for such unusual jobs as skywriting and others are privately owned. Standard power plant is a 550hp Pratt & Whitney R1340-AN-1 radial engine.

Omnipol L-40 Meta-Sokol / Czechoslovakia

Span: 33ft 0in (10.06m)
Length: 24ft 9in (7.54m)
Gross weight: 2,062lb (935kg)
Max cruising speed: 127mph (204km/h)
Max range: 688 miles (1,107km)

An interesting feature of this Czech-built 4-seater is its 'reversed tricycle' retractable undercarriage, the third wheel of which is under the rear of the cabin. Normal engine is a 140hp Walter M332, but the 105hp Minor 4-III was installed in some aircraft. Wingtip fuel tanks may be fitted. Small numbers are in service in Western Europe, including the UK, and in Australia. All Czechoslovakian civil aircraft are marketed through the Omnipol organisation, and were usually referred to as Omnipol types during the period of Meta-Sokol production. The famous Zlin series of lightplanes is described under that name, however.

Partenavia P64 and P66 Oscar and P66C Charlie / Italy

Photo: P66B Oscar 150
Data: P66C-160 Charlie

Span: 32ft 9.25in (9.99m)
Length: 23ft 9in (7.24m)
Gross weight: 2,183lb (990kg)
Max cruising speed: 135mph (218km/h)
Range: 486 miles (782km) at 128mph (206km/h)

The prototype of the P64 Oscar first flew on 2 April 1965, and the type went into production as an all-metal replacement for the Fachiro. The Oscar-B of 1967 introduced a stepped-down rear fuselage and panoramic rear cabin window. Subsequently, the Oscar family was expanded to four models, and by February 1975 Partenavia had built 73 P64B Oscar-180s with 4 seats and 180hp Lycoming O-360-A1A engine; 16 4-seat P64B Oscar-200s with 200hp Lycoming IO-360-A1B, 107 2-seat P66B Oscar-100s with 115hp Lycoming O-235-C1B; and 79 3-seat P66B Oscar-150s with 150hp Lycoming O-320-E2A. The Oscar-180 was also built by AFIC in South Africa as the RSA 200 Falcon. Production of these versions has ended; but Partenavia subsequently built for the Aero Club d'Italia a batch of 70 P66C Charlie basic trainers, with two/four seats and 160hp O-320-H2AD engine.

Piaggio P149-D / Italy

Span: 36ft 6in (11.13m)
Length: 28ft 9.5in (8.78m)
Gross weight: 3,705lb (1,680kg)
Range: 680 miles (1,095km) at 145mph (233km/h)

The P149 was designed as a 4-seat civil development of the P148 primary trainer, using many components of the latter. It flew for the first time on 19 June 1953. Two years later, Piaggio received a contract for 72 modified versions (P149-D) to be used as standard Luftwaffe training aircraft; another 190 were licence-built in Germany by Focke-Wulf. Many have subsequently been released for civilian service. Powered by a 270hp Lycoming GO-480 engine, they carry up to five persons.

Piel Emeraude (and Scintex Super Emeraude and Mudry CAP 10 and Fairtravel Linnet) / France

Photo: CP 301
Data: CP 1310 Super Emeraude

Span: 27ft 0.75in (8.25m)
Length: 21ft 5.5in (6.54m)
Gross weight: 1,550lb (703kg)
Range: 620 miles (1,000km) at 137mph (220km/h)

Many companies in France and elsewhere have manufactured versions of the little Piel Emeraude side-by-side 2-seat lightplane; others have been built by amateurs. Standard Emeraudes, with 90hp Continental C90 engine, were produced in France by Rousseau and Scintex. The CP 1310 C3 Super Emeraude was produced by Scintex with a 100hp Rolls-Royce/Continental O-200-A engine. The British Fairtravel Linnet is very similar. Avions Mudry also developed the aerobatic CAP 10 from the Emeraude, and had built nearly 100 by 1979.

Piper J-3 Cub (and J-4 Cub Coupe) / USA

Photo: J-3C
Data: J-3C-65 Cub Special

Span: 35ft 2.5in (10.73m)
Length: 22ft 4.5in (6.82m)
Gross weight: 1,220lb (553kg)
Range: 300 miles (482km) at 87mph (140km/h)

First flown in 1938, the tandem 2-seat J-3 Cub became one of the most-produced aeroplanes in history. By the time production ended in 1949, a total of 14,125 civil Cubs of all versions had been delivered, plus 5,673 essentially-similar military L-4 observation aircraft. Thousands continue to fly, mainly in North America. The original J-2 Cub of 1936 had a 40hp Continental engine, and a few of these survive. The J-3 began with a 40hp Continental, but most were built with a 50hp Continental, Lycoming or Franklin engine. Postwar versions are the J-3C-65 Cub Special and PA-11 Cub Special with 65hp Continental A65 engine. Also to be seen, mainly in the USA, are J-4 Cub Coupes — more refined versions of the J-3 with side-by-side seating and a 75hp Continental A75-8 engine, built in 1938-42. Wag-Aero of Lyons, Wisconsin, markets kits of parts for an up-dated version known as the CUBy Sport Trainer, which can be powered by Continental or Lycoming engines in the 65-125hp range, and the CUBy Aero Trainer with engines of up to 150hp.

Piper PA-12 Super Cruiser (and PA-14 Family Cruiser) / USA

Photo and data: PA-12 SuperCruiser

Span: 35ft 5.5in (10.81m)
Length: 22ft 10in (6.96m)
Gross weight: 1,750lb (793kg)
Range: 600 miles (965km) at 105mph (169km/h)

The Piper Cruiser series began with the 3-seat J-5A Cruiser of 1940, with a standard J-3 wing, revised 3-seat fuselage and 75hp A75-8 engine. It was followed within a year by the J-5C Super Cruiser, with 100hp Lycoming GO-145-C2 engine. Production was resumed postwar with the generally similar PA-12, with 104hp Lycoming O-235-C. The PA-14 Family Cruiser of 1948 differed in having four seats and a 115hp Lycoming O-235-C1 engine. Many PA-12s and 14s are flying.

Piper PA-18 Super Cub / USA

Data: PA-18-150 Super Cub

Span: 35ft 2.5in (10.73m)
Length: 22ft 7in (6.88m)
Gross weight: 1,750lb (793kg)
Cruising speed: 105-115mph (169-185km/h)
Max range: 460 miles (735km)

More than 6,500 Super Cubs have been built since the original versions — the PA-18-95 (90hp Continental C90) and PA-18-105 (108hp Lycoming O-235) entered production in 1949. The PA-18-135 (135hp Lycoming O-290-D2) was introduced in 1952. Current version is the PA-18-150, with 150hp Lycoming O-320, which as been in production since 1955. All versions are tandem 2-seaters. The spruce spars of earlier Piper types gave way to all-metal structure in the Super Cub, which retained the traditional welded steel-tube fuselage and overall fabric covering. Many Super Cubs are equipped for agricultural duties, others operate on floats and skis.

Piper PA-20 Pacer / USA

Photo: PA-16 Clipper
Data: PA-20-115 Pacer

Span: 29ft 4in (8.94m)
Length: 20ft 5in (6.22m)
Gross weight: 1,650lb (748kg)
Range: 580 miles (933km) at 112mph (180km/h)

The Pacer began life in 1949 as the PA-16 Clipper, a 4-seat counterpart of the Vagabond with a 115hp Lycoming O-235-C1 engine. The name and designation were changed in 1950 and three versions were subsequently produced: the PA-20-115 (O-235-C1), PA-20-125 (125hp Lycoming O-290-D2) and PA-20-135 (135hp O-290-D2). Several hundred Clippers and Pacers remain in service.

Piper PA-22 Tri-Pacer (and Colt and Caribbean) / USA

Photo: PA-22 Colt
Data: PA-22-160 Tri-Pacer

Span: 29ft 3.25in (8.92m)
Length: 20ft 7.25in (6.28m)
Gross weight: 2,000lb (907kg)
Maximum cruising speed: 134mph (216km/h)
Max range: 536 miles (862km)

This tricycle-undercarriage version of the Pacer was introduced in 1951, initially with the same 135hp O-290-D2 engine. The PA-22-150 Tri-Pacer (150hp Lycoming O-320) appeared in 1955, followed by the PA-22-160 (160hp Lycoming O-320-B) in 1957. All Tri-Pacers are four-seaters, as is the less-elaborate Caribbean (150hp O-320), introduced in 1958. The Colt 108 was a low-price two-seat model, with the same basic airframe and a 108hp Lycoming O-235-C1B engine, intended mainly for club and training duties. All of these types remain in large-scale use.

Piper PA-24 Comanche / USA

Photo: Turbo Comanche C
Data: PA-24-260 Comanche C

Span: 36ft 0in (10.97m)
Length: 25ft 0in (7.62m)
Gross weight: 3,200lb (1,451kg)
Max cruising speed: 185mph (298km/h)
Max range: 1,225 miles (1,970km)

Piper's first all-metal low-wing monoplane, the prototype 4-seat Comanche flew on 24 May 1956. It went into production as the PA-24-180, with 180hp Lycoming O-360-A1A engine. Later production versions were the PA-24-250 (250hp Lycoming O-540-A1A5), PA-24-260 (260hp Lycoming O-540-E or IO-540-E) and PA-24-400 (400hp Lycoming IO-720). Final version was the PA-24-260 Comanche C, which had an IO-540 engine and could carry up to six persons. A version with Rajay supercharger was also produced as the Turbo Comanche C. Production ended in 1974, but many Comanches remain in service.

Piper PA-25 Pawnee (and PA-36 Pawnee Brave) / USA

Photo and Data: PA-25-235 Pawnee D

Span: 36ft 2in (11.02m)
Length: 24ft 8.5in (7.53m)
Gross weight: 2,900lb (1,315kg)
Max cruising speed: 114mph (183km/h)
Max range: 290 miles (467km) at 114mph (183km/h)

Specially developed as a safe and economical agricultural aircraft, the original PA-25 Pawnee was built in two versions, with 150hp Lycoming O-320 (PA-25-150) and 235hp Lycoming O-540-B2B5 (PA-25-235) engine. The more powerful model remains in production, as the improved Pawnee D, with optional 260hp O-540-E engine and a payload of 1,200lb (544kg) of chemicals. A mechanic or loader can be carried on a temporary seat inside the hopper during staging flights. Some 5,000 Pawnees have been built by Piper and Chincul of the Argentine. The PA-25 is now supplemented by the PA-36 Pawnee Brave, with span of 39ft (11.89m), gross weight of 4,400lb (1,996kg) and enlarged chemical hopper. The original Pawnee Brave 285 had a 285hp Continental Tiara engine but has been superseded by the Brave 300 with 300hp Lycoming IO-540-K1G5 and the Brave 375 , with gross weight of 4,800lb (2,177kg), max chemical load of 1,900lb (862kg) and 375hp Lycoming IO-720-D1CD engine.

Piper PA-28-151 Cherokee Warrior / USA

Photo and data: Warrior II

Span: 35ft 0in (10.67m)
Length: 23ft 9.5in (7.26m)
Gross weight: 2,325lb (1,055kg)
Max cruising speed: 139mph (224km/h)
Max range: 702 miles (1,130km) at 128mph (206km/h)

This junior member of the current Cherokee family introduced a completely new wing, with tapered outer panels of increased span compared with earlier Cherokee 140s. Induced drag is reduced, boosting performance, and a reflex outboard leading-edge improves stability at stall speeds. The Warrior was intended to compete directly with the Cessna 172, and had a similar 150hp Lycoming O-320-E3D engine in its original form; the current PA-28-161 Warrior II has a 160mph O-320-D3G. It is a full four-seater, with a maximum useful load of 989lb (448kg). The Warrior is one of 14 Piper types assembled by Chincul of the Argentine at the rate of 10 aircraft a month; a total of 204 had been built by April 1977.

Piper PA-28 Cherokee Series (except Warrior) / USA

Photo and Data: Archer II

Span: 35ft 0in (10.67m)
Length: 23ft 9.5in (7.26m)
Gross weight: 2,550lb (1,156kg)
Max cruising speed: 144mph (232km/h)
Max range: 725 miles (1,168km) at 119mph (191km/h)

Because of its sturdy construction and low price, the all-metal Cherokee has proved even more popular than the Tri-Pacer which it superseded. The original 4-seat prototype flew on 10 February 1961, and more than 20,000 Cherokees of all types have been built, with several versions, currently in production in the Argentine and Brazil, as well as by the parent company. Excluding the Warrior, which is described separately, models in the basic PA-28 range with fixed undercarriage have included simplified 2-seat Cherokee Flite Liner trainer and 4-seat Cruiser, with 150hp Lycoming O-320 engine; the PA-28-180 Cherokee Archer 4-seater with 180hp Lycoming O-360-A3A; the Archer II (EMB-712C Carioquinha assembled by EMBRAER in Brazil) introduced in 1976, with the same tapered wing as the Warrior; the strengthened PA-28-235 Cherokee Pathfinder now built only in Brazil as the EMB-710C Carioca with 235hp Lycoming O-540-B4B5 engine and the PA-28-236 Dakota with four seats and 235hp Lycoming O-540-J3A5D.

Piper PA-28 Cherokee Arrow Series / USA

Photo and Data: PA-28-201 Turbo Arrow IV

Span: 35ft 0in (10.67m)
Length: 25ft 0in (7.62m)
Gross weight: 2,900lb (1,315kg)
Max cruising speed: 191mph (308km/h)
Range: 933-988 miles (1,501-1,590km) at 177-188mph (284-302km/h)

Announced on 19 June 1967, the original Cherokee Arrow (PA-28-180R) was similar to the Cherokee 180 but had a retractable undercarriage, a 180hp IO-360-B1E engine and a third window on each side. To assist pilots unaccustomed to retractable gear, the legs were designed to extend automatically if power was reduced and speed fell below 105mph (170km/h). Subsequently, the PA-28-200 appeared, with 200hp IO-360-C1C engine. Piper's 1972 range brought the similarly-powered Arrow II, with 5in longer fuselage, 26in greater span and larger tailplane. In 1977, Piper introduced the Arrow III, with tapered wing as used on the Warrior and Archer II, and the similar Turbo Arrow III with turbocharged TSIO-360-F engine. The 1979-model PA-28-201 Arrow/Turbo Arrow IV have a T-tail. The Arrow is built by EMBRAER of Brazil as the EMB-711C Corisco, and by Chincul of the Argentine.

Piper PA-32 Cherokee Six / USA

Photo and Data: PA-32-300 Cherokee Six 300

Span: 32ft 8.75in (9.98m)
Length: 27ft 8.75in (8.45m)
Gross weight: 3,400lb (1,542kg)
Max cruising speed: 168mph (270km/h)
Range: 857 miles (1,379km) at 149mph (239km/h)

First flown on 6 December 1963, the Cherokee Six is a 6/7-seat version of the Cherokee, with slightly enlarged overall dimensions. It is available in two versions, the PA-32-260 with 260hp Lycoming O-540-E engine, and the PA-32-300 with 300hp Lycoming IO-540-K. Both models are available on skis; the more powerful version can be operated as a floatplane. In addition to production by Piper, the Cherokee Six is manufactured in Brazil, as the EMB-720C Minuano, and in the Argentine by Chincul.

Piper PA-32R-300 Cherokee Lance / USA

Photo: Lance II
Data: Turbo Lance II

Span: 32ft 9.75in (10.00m)
Length: 28ft 10.75in (8.81m)
Gross weight: 3,600lb (1,633kg)
Max cruising speed: 201mph (324km/h)
Range: 938 miles (1,510km) at 155mph (250km/h) (with reserves)

First flown on 30 August 1974, the 6-7 seat Cherokee Lance combines a basic Cherokee Six 300 fuselage with a wing similar to that of the Arrow but embodying Seneca spars, fuel tanks and retractable landing gear. The nose-wheel unit is like that of the Arrow, the other 'retractable' member of the Cherokee family. The first production Lance flew on 17 July 1975; within 10 months Piper had sold 186 and delivered 127 of them. For 1978, Piper introduced a T-tail and changed the name of the basic model, with 300hp Lycoming IO-540-K1G5 engine, to Lance II (PA-32RT-300). It also offered for the first time a turbocharged version, the Turbo Lance II, with 300hp TIO-540-S1AD engine. When assembled by EMBRAER in Brazil, the Lance is known as the EMB-721 Sertanejo. It is also produced in the Argentine, by Chincul.

Piper PA-38 Tomahawk / USA

Span: 34ft 0in (10.36m)
Length: 23ft 1.25in (7.04m)
Gross weight: 1,670lb (757kg)
Max cruising speed: 125mph (202km/h)
Range: 502 miles (807km) at 117mph (189km/h)

When announcing the Tomahawk, in October 1977, Piper claimed that it embodied the answers on questionnaires sent to more than 10,000 flying instructors, who were asked to describe the ideal trainer. It is an aerobatic side-by-side two-seater, powered by a 112hp Lycoming O-235-L2C engine. The wing utilises NASA's new GAW-1 aerofoil section; other features include a T-tail, 360 degree field of view from the cabin, and an engine cowling which can be removed completely without detaching the propeller. Certification was obtained in December 1977 and deliveries began in February 1978; by April 1979, over 1,500 had been built and production was continuing at the rate of about 50 a month.

Pitts Special / USA

Photo: S-1S
Data: S-2A

Span: 20ft 0in (6.10m)
Length: 18ft 3in (5.56m)
Gross weight: 1,500lb (680kg)
Max cruising speed: 140mph (225km/h)
Max range: 450 miles (725km)

The Pitts Special began as a 90hp custombuilt aerobatic single-seater, first flown in September 1944. Its designer, Curtis Pitts, developed the design to accept more powerful engines, of up to 180hp in the factory-built S-1S version. Pitts also evolved the two-seat S-2 Special (180hp Lycoming IO-360-B4A) and S-2A (200hp Lycoming). In 1972, the US national team, flying Pitts Specials, gained both the men's and women's individual prizes and the team prize at the 7th World Aerobatic Championships, in France. Britain's two Rothman's Aerobatic Teams fly S-2As, which are available only in factory-built form. Many single-seaters have been amateur-built S-1Ds from plans supplied by Curtis Pitts. On 9 December 1977 Pitts flew the prototype S-2S, an aerobatic single-seater based on the S-2A and powered by a 260hp Lycoming AEIO-540-D4A5.

Procaer/General Avia F15 Picchio (and Delfino) / Italy

Photo: F15F
Data: F15E Picchio

Span: 32ft 5.75in (9.90m)
Length: 24ft 7.25in (7.50m)
Gross weight: 3,000lb (1,360kg)
Cruising speed: 166-190mph (267-306km/h)
Max range: 994 miles (1,600km) at 166mph (267km/h)

Designed by Stelio Frati, the original versions of the Picchio were unique in having an all wood structure covered with plywood panels which had an outer skin of aluminium bonded to them. This was claimed to combine an unrivalled surface finish with the easy maintenance of wood structures and the durability of metal skinning. The prototype Picchio flew on 7 May 1959. Successive production models were the F15 with three seats and 160hp Lycoming engine (15 built), F15A with four seats and 180hp Lycoming (54 built) and F15B with increased wing area (35 built). A prototype F15C flew, with 260hp Continental IO-470-E engine, followed by the all-metal F15E, with 300hp Continental IO-520-F, on 21 December 1968. Latest in the series is the all metal 2-seat F15F Delfino, with 200hp Lycoming IO-360-A engine, which was developed by Ing Frati's General Avia company and made its first flight on 20 October 1977.

PZL-101A Gawron / Poland

Span: (over end-plates): 41ft 7.5in (12.68m)
Length: 29ft 6.5in (9.00m)
Gross weight: 3,660lb (1,660kg)
Cruising speed: 75-81mph (120-130km/h)
Max range: 708 miles (1,140km) with external tanks

Developed from the Soviet-designed Yak-12 (1,150 examples of which were built in Poland), the PZL-101 Gawron flew for the first time in April 1958 and was adopted subsequently as the standard agricultural aircraft for the countries of eastern Europe. The improved PZL-101A was powered by the 260hp Ivchenko AI-14R engine. Used mainly for agricultural work, it could be equipped also for ambulance and 4-seat communications duties; agricultural payload was 1,100lb (500kg). A prototype designated PZL-101AF, with 300hp AI-14RF engine, flew on 30 August 1966, but did not enter production. Late production Gawrons had laminar-flow wingtips instead of the former end-plates, increasing the span to 42ft 9in (13.03m). Production ended in 1970 when 330 had been built.

PZL-104 Wilga (and Lipnur Gelatik) / Poland

Photo and Data: Wilga 35A

Span: 36ft 6in (11.12m)
Length: 26ft 6in (8.10m)
Gross weight: 2,711lb (1,230kg)
Cruising speed: 80-120mph (128-193km/h)
Max range: 422 miles (680km)

The original prototype Wilga 1 flew on 24 April 1962, with a 180hp Narkiewicz WN-6B engine. The fuselage and tail unit were then redesigned completely, and the resulting Wilga 2 flew on 1 August 1963, with a 195hp WN-6RB engine. It was followed on December 30 by the Wilga C, with 225hp Continental O-470, and a modified version of this type was put into production in Indonesia as the Lipnur Gelatik. A total of 39 Gelatiks were built, the final models as Gelatik 32 with 230hp O-470-L engine. First Polish production versions, in 1966, were the Wilga 3A utility 4-seater for club use and Wilga 3S for ambulance duties, both with 260hp Ivchenko AI-14R radial engine. Improved versions, introduced in 1967, were the Wilga 32 (O-470-L or R) and Wilga 35 (AI-14R), built in 32A/35A club, 32P/35P passenger/liaison and 32S/35S ambulance models. About 430 Wilgas had been built by the end of 1979. Only the 35A/P/S remain in production.

PZL-106A Kruk / Poland

Span: 48ft 6.5in (14.80m)
Length: 29ft 10.25in (9.10m)
Gross weight: 6,614lb (3,000kg)
Range: approx 248 miles (400km) at 112mph (180km/h)

As a successor to the PZL-101 Gawron, the WSK-Okecie design team developed and flew the much modified PZL-101M Kruk (Raven), with a 260hp AI-14R engine. By early 1972 it was clear that better results would be obtained by switching to a more powerful engine and the braced low-wing monoplane layout that has become conventional for agricultural duster/sprayers. The result was the PZL-106, of which two prototypes (with T-tails) were flown with 400hp Lycoming engine (the first on 17 April 1973) followed by four more with the 600hp PZL-3S radial that is fitted in production PZL-106As. These are basically single-seaters, but have a rearward-facing seat behind the pilot to enable a mechanic/loader to be carried; a training version is also available with an extra (front) cockpit. Chemical load is 308 Imp gal (1,400 litres) of liquid or 2,204lb (1,000kg) of solids. Production of 600 is planned, for member countries of the CMEA.

PZL M-18 Dromader / Poland

Span: 58ft 0.75in (17.70m)
Length: 31ft 2in (9.50m)
Gross weight: 1,685lb (5,300kg)
Operating speed: 105-115mph (170-185km/h)
Max range: 323 miles (520km)

Despite its similarity to the PZL-106A Kruk, the M-18 is a completely new design, powered by a 1,000hp Polish-built ASh-62IR engine and able to carry a 5,732lb (2,600kg) payload. To fill the gap between the Kruk and the big turbofan M-15 Belphagor (see page 72) PZL-Mielec developed the M-18 in collaboration with Rockewell, using the cabin, outer wings and other components of the Thrush Commander. The result may inherit the ungainliness of its namesake, the Dromedary, but offers high standards of efficiency, maintainability in the field and pilot safety. The first two prototypes flew on 27 August and 2 October 1976 respectively.

Robin (CEA) DR220 '2+2' (and DR221 Dauphin, DR250 and DR253) / France

Photo: DR250
Data: DR220 '2+2'

Span: 28ft 7.25in (8.72m)
Length: 22ft 11.5in (7.00m)
Gross weight: 1,720lb (780kg)
Cruising speed: 125-130mph (201-209km/h)
Max range: 600 miles (965km)

The DR220 is a much-refined development of the Jodel DR1050 family. It retains the latter's plywood and fabric-covered wooden airframe and 100hp Rolls-Royce/Continental O-200-A engine; but, as its designation '2+2' implies, can carry one adult or two children in the rear of the cabin in addition to the pilot and passenger. 84 had been built by January 1972, including strengthened DR220As and DR220/108s with 108hp Lycoming engine. The 3/4 seat DR221 Dauphin (62 built) and DR250 (102 built) are similar in construction and appearance, but have 115hp Lycoming O-235-C2A and 160hp Lycoming O-320 engine respectively. Production has ended. The DR253 Regent, first flown on 30 March 1967, was similar with a tricycle undercarriage and 180hp Lycoming O-360-A2A.

Robin (CEA) DR300 Series / France

Photo: DR380
Data: DR340

Span: 28ft 7.25in (8.72m)
Length: 22ft 10in (6.96m)
Gross weight: 2,205lb (1,000kg)
Cruising speed: 143-158mph (230-254km/h)
Range: 850 miles (1,367km) at 158mph (254km/h)

DR300 designations cover a series of eight interrelated aircraft, of similar construction to the DR220/221/250 but with fixed tricycle undercarriage and refinements such as modified wing camber to improve performance and handling. The DR300-108 '2+2 tricycle', based on the DR220, has a 108hp Lycoming O-235-C2A engine, and first flew on 29 May 1970. The DR300/125 Petit Prince 3/4 seater has a 125hp Lycoming O-235 and flew in June 1970. The DR300/140 Petit Prince 4-seater flew on 25 March 1970. The DR300/180R Remorqueur 4-seat tourer/glider-tug has a 180hp Lycoming O-360-A2A and flew on 26 May 1970. The DR315 Cadet is a 3/4 seater with 108/115hp O-235-C2A which flew on 2 March 1968. The 4-seat DR340 Major, with 140/150hp Lycoming O-320-E, flew on 27 February 1968. The DR360 Major 160 is a de luxe version with 160hp O-360-E; and the DR380 Prince, first flown on 15 October 1968, is similar but with a 180hp O-360-D. All were superseded in production by the DR400 series.

Robin (CEA) DR400 Series / France

Photo and Data: DR400/180 Regent

Span: 28ft 7.25in (8.72m)
Length: 23ft 6.75in (7.18m)
Gross weight: 2,425lb (1,100kg)
Cruising speed: 155-166mph (249-267km/h)
Max range: 913 miles (1,470km) at 155mph (249km/h)

The DR400 series differ from the DR300 series, which they replaced in 1972/73, mainly in having a forward-sliding canopy and lowered cabin side-walls to improve access and visibility. Variants in production in 1979 were the DR400/100 2+2 2/4 seater with 100hp Lycoming O-235-H2C engine; 3/4 seat DR400/120 Petit Prince with 118hp O-235-L2A; 4-seat DR400/140B Major with 160hp Lycoming O-320-D; 4-seat DR400/160 Chevalier with 160hp O-320-D; 4/5 seat DR400/180 Regent with 180hp Lycoming O-360-A; and 4-seat DR400/180R Remorqueur glider-tug also with an O-360-A.

Robin (CEA) HR100 Series / France

Data: HR100/250TR
Photo: HR100-200

Span: 29ft 9.5in (9.08m)
Length: 24ft 10.75in (7.59m)
Gross weight: 3,086lb (1,400kg)
Max cruising speed: 185mph (297km/h)

Production of the original all-metal HR100/200, with 200hp Lycoming IO-360-A1D6, began in 1971. After 31 had been built, it was superseded by the HR100/210 Safari, a 4-seater with 210hp Continental IO-360-D engine of which 78 were built. The 4/5-seat HR100/285 Tiara, first flown on 18 November 1972, was the first Robin lightplane with retractable undercarriage. The prototype had a 320hp engine but production models had the 285hp Continental Tiara 6-285B engine. Current models in 1979 are the HR100/250TR with 250hp Lycoming IO-540 engine, and the HR100/4+2, similar to the HR100/285 Tiara but with lengthened cabin seating up to six persons without baggage and powered, in prototype form, by a 250hp Lycoming engine.

Robin (CEA) HR200 Series / France

Photo and Data: HR200/100

Span: 27ft 4in (8.33m)
Length: 21ft 9.5in (6.64m)
Gross weight: 1,719lb (780kg)
Max cruising speed: 122mph (197km/h)
Range: 652 miles (1,050km)

Intended specifically for use by clubs and flying schools, this all-metal 2-seater first flew on 29 July 1971. It entered production in 1973 and deliveries by February 1975 totalled 53 HR200/100s with 108hp Lycoming O-235-H2C; 19 HR200/120s with 118-125hp O-235; and one HR200/160 with 160hp Lycoming O-320-D. Production of all HR200 versions has ended in favour of the R2160 (below).

Robin R1180 Aiglon / France

Span: 29ft 9.5in (9.08m)
Length: 24ft 10.75in (7.59m)
Gross weight: 2,535lb (1,150kg)
Range: 932 miles (1,500km) at 130mph (210km/h)

Intended as a replacement for the HR100/210 Safari II, this fixed-undercarriage all-metal 4-seat light aircraft flew for the first time in late 1976. It was expected to receive certification before the end of 1977 and to be the forerunner of a family of touring aircraft with R1000 designations. The R1180 is powered by a 180hp Lycoming O-360-A3AD engine, as the last three figures of its designation confirm. Production began in 1978 and certification for the first production R1180 was obtained on 19 September 1978.

Robin R2000 Series (Rafale and Acrobin) / France

Photo: Robin R2100

Span: 27ft 4in (8.33m)
Length: 23ft 3.5in (7,099m)
Gross weight: 1,764lb (800kg)
Range: 590 miles (950km) at 145mph (234km/h)

To overcome certain shortcomings in the aerobatic performance of the HR200, Robin evolved from that design a new family of 2-seat trainers under the basic designation of R2000. These are conventional all-metal light aircraft with non-retractable landing gear. The wing is completely new by comparison with the HR200; the rudder has been enlarged and the aircraft are distinguished by a long ventral fin to improve spinning characteristics. First to fly, on 15 January 1976, was a prototype built to R2100 Super Club standard, with a 108hp Lycoming O-235-H engine. The same airframe was then re-engined to R2160 standard, with a 160hp Lycoming

O-320-D, with which it flew for the first time on 15 July 1976. The AEIO-320 version of the same engine powers the R2160A Rafale. New in 1979 was the R2112, a 2-seat aerobatic model with 110hp Lycoming.

Rockwell Commander Models 112 and 114 / USA

Photo: Model 114
Data: Model 112TCA

Span: 35ft 7in (10.85m)
Length: 25ft 0in (7.62m)
Gross weight: 2,950lb (1,270kg)
Max cruising speed: 188mph (302km/h)
Max range: 1,015 miles (1,633km)

The 4-seat, single-engined Aero Commander Model 112 flew on 4 December 1970, as the first of an entirely new range of light aircraft utilising many common components. The 112 is powered by a 200hp Lycoming IO-360-C1D6 engine, and has a retractable undercarriage. Deliveries began late in 1972, and this version has been followed by the improved Model 112A, 112B, 112TC (with turbo-supercharger), 112TCA and Medalist. The model 111, first flown in 1971 was similar except for having a fixed undercarriage; it did not enter production. The Commander 114, introduced in 1976, has a 260hp Lycoming IO-540-T4B5D. Production of all these single-engined Commanders ended late in 1979.

Rollason/Druine D31 Turbulent / UK

Span: 21ft 7in (6.58m)
Length: 17ft 6in (5.33m)
Gross weight: 620lb (281kg)
Cruising speed: 87-100mph (141-161km/h)
Max range: 250 miles (400km)

This ultra-light single-seater and its 2-seat counterpart, the Turbi, were designed by the late Roger Druine. Plans of both are available to amateur constructors and many have been built throughout the world. The Turbulent was also factory-built by Rollason, in England, and the data above apply to this company's basic D31 model, with 45hp Ardem 4CO 2 Mk 4 (converted Volkswagen) engine, of which 30 had been completed by 1973. Rollason have also built three D31As with Ardem Mk X engine, improved main spar and weight of 700lb (316kg); these have a full C of A instead of the usual Permit to Fly. Construction is of wood, with fabric-covered wings and plywood-covered fuselage. Some Turbulents have enclosed cockpits and wheel spats.

Rollason/Druine D62 Condor / UK

Photo: D62B Condor
Data: D62C Condor

Span: 27ft 6in (8.38m)
Length: 22ft 6in (6.86m)
Gross weight: 1,475lb (670kg)
Cruising speed: 107-115mph (172-185km/h)
Max range: 328 miles (528km)

Roger Druine intended this more refined side-by-side 2-seater primarily for factory production. After building a prototype D62, with 90hp Continental C90 engine, in 1961, Rollason Aircraft in England built two D62As with the 100hp Rolls-Royce/Continental O-200-A engine. They retained this power plant in the further-improved D62B, which became their main production type. 39 had been completed by the spring of 1973, plus nine D62Cs with 130hp Rolls-Royce/Continental O-240 engine, larger wheels and raised canopy, for glider towing. Construction is of wood, with fabric covered wings and plywood-covered fuselage.

RRA FAGA J-1 Martin Fierro / Argentina

Span: 42ft 7.75in (13.00m)
Length: 22ft 11.75in (7.00m)
Gross weight: 4,409lb (2,000kg)
Cruising speed: 131mph (211km/h)
Range: 305 miles (490km) at 131mph (211km/h)

First flown on 18 December 1975, this single-seat agricultural duster/sprayer was designed and built in the Argentine by a team headed by Ing Norberto Cobelo. Power plant of the J-1 is a 300hp Lycoming IO-540-K1JG, driving a Hartzell variable-pitch propeller. Hopper capacity is 1,874lb (850kg) of solids or 187 Imp gal (850 litres) of liquid chemicals. Five more J-1s were being built in 1978, by Ronchetti, Razzetti Aviacion of Funes, Santa Fe Province, including one for structural testing.

Saab-91 Safir / Sweden

Photo: Saab-91C
Data: Saab-91D

Span: 34ft 9in (10.59m)
Length: 26ft 4in (8.03m)
Gross weight: 2,660lb (1,206kg)
Cruising speed: 136-146mph (219-235km/h)
Max range: 660 miles (1,062km)

The prototype Safir flew on 20 November 1945, with a 130hp Gipsy Major 1C engine. Subsequently, four production versions were built. The Saab-91A (145hp Gipsy Major 10) and Saab-91B (190hp Lycoming O-435-A) are 3-seaters; the Saab-91C (O-435A) and Saab-91D (180hp Lycoming O-360-A1A) are 4-seaters. Most of the 320 or so Safirs produced went to air forces as basic trainers, but numbers of Bs and Ds have been utilised by airlines and civil authorities for pilot training.

Saab Safari / Sweden

Photo: Safari TS

Span: 29ft 0.5in (8.85m)
Length: 22ft 11.5in (7.00m)
Gross weight: 2,645lb (1,200kg)
Cruising speed: 129mph (208km/h)
Max endurance: 5hr 10min

This 2/3-seat basic training and utility aircraft was evolved from the MFI-9/Bölkow BO208 by Malmo Flygindustri before being absorbed into Saab. It was known at that stage as the MFI-15, and had a military counterpart in the MFI-17, now produced as the Saab Supporter. The Safari is powered by a 200hp Lycoming IO-360-A1B6 engine, and can carry underwing loads for airborne relief, rescue and firefighting operations. The Safari TS, introduced in 1979, has a 210hp turbo-supercharged Continental engine. More than 200 Safaris and Supporters had been sold by 1979.

SAI KZ VII Laerke (and KZ III) / Denmark

Photo and data: KZ VII Laerke

Span: 31ft 6in (9.60m)
Length: 21ft 3in (6.48m)
Gross weight: 1,910lb (866kg)
Range: 450 miles (725km) at 109mph (175km/h)

The prototype of this 4-seat light aircraft flew for the first time on 11 November 1946, and was followed by 55 production models. Standard power plant was a 125hp Continental C125-2, but seven Laerkes were supplied to Switzerland with 145hp Continental C145-2 engine. Several examples of each version remain airworthy, together with numbers of similar KZ IIIs, which are 2-seaters with a 100hp Cirrus Minor II engine. Both types have wooden wings and fabric-covered steel-tube fuselage.

Scheibe SF-25 Falke and Vickers-Slingsby T61) / Germany/UK

Photo: SF-28A
Data: SF-25C Falke

Span: 50ft 0.25in (15.25m)
Length: 24ft 9.25in (7.55m)
Gross weight: 1,345lb (610kg)
Max range: 466 miles (750km) at 81mph (130km/h)

The original SF-25B version of this side-by-side 2-seat powered sailplane, with a 45hp Stamo (Volkswagen) engine, was built in quantity by Scheibe in Germany and Slingsby built 35 in the UK, the latter as the T61. The Scheibe SF-25C introduced a more powerful (65hp) Limbach SL1700 (Volkswagen) engine; by early 1978, a total of 230 had been built by the parent company and 50 more by Sportavia. In addition, Scheibe also delivered 25 of the SF-25C-S version, with a Hoffman feathering propeller for improved engine-off gliding. Current Scheibe versions, known as Falke '76s, can be identified by a more domed canopy and larger fin. Later developments are the SF-25E Super Falke with longer span wing and SF-28 Tandem-Falke with seats in tandem, about 100 of which have been built.

Siai-Marchetti S208 (and S205 and Waco S220 Vela) / Italy/USA

Photo and data: S208

Span: 35ft 7.25in (10.86m)
Length: 26ft 3in (8.00m)
Gross weight: 3,307lb (1,500kg)
Max cruising speed: 187mph (300km/h)
Max range: 1,250 miles (2,000km)

The S205 is a 4-seat all-metal light aircraft which can have a rectractable or fixed undercarriage. Versions built in 1964-72 were the S205-18/F (=fixed undercarriage) and S205-18/R (=retractable) with 180hp Lycoming O-360-A1A engine; the S205-20/F and S205-20/R with 200hp Lycoming IO-360-A1A engine; and the S205-22/R with 220hp Franklin 6A-350-C1 engine. The 22/R was also built under licence in the USA for a time as the Waco S220 Vela. A total of 475 S205s were built, including 62 Velas. The S208 is generally similar to the 20/R, but has a 260hp Lycoming O-540-E4A5 engine and five seats. About 80 were delivered, including 44 for the Italian Air Force. Final production versions were the S205AC with 200hp IO-360-A1B6D engine, of which 140 were built for the Aero Club d'Italia, and S208A which is generally similar to the S208.

Siai-Marchetti SF260 / Italy

Photo and data: SF260C

Span: 27ft 4.75in (8.35m)
Length: 23ft 3.5in (7.10m)
Gross weight: 2,430lb (1,102kg)
Max cruising speed: 214mph (345km/h)
Max range: 1,275 miles (2,050km)

The prototype of this all-metal aerobatic light aircraft was the F250 with 250hp Lycoming engine. Designed by Ing Stelio Frati and built by Aviamilano, it flew for the first time on 15 July 1964. Siai-Marchetti acquired production rights and built 100 of the developed three-seat SF260As and SF260Bs with a 260hp Lycoming O-540-E4A5 engine, of which 30-40 were for civil customers. The SF260A was marketed for a time in the USA as the Waco Meteor. Current civil version is the SF260C,

Socata (Gardan) GY-80 Horizon / France

Photo and data: 160hp version

Span: 31ft 10in (9.70m)
Length: 21ft 9.5in (6.64m)
Gross weight: 2,425lb (1,100kg)
Max cruising speed: 145mph (233km/h)
Max range: 590 miles (950km)

Designed as a private venture by Yves Gardan, this four-seat all-metal lightplane was produced under licence by Socata, a subsidiary of Sud-Aviation. The first 75, delivered by March 1965, had alternative 150hp or 160hp Lycoming O-320 engines. A version with 180hp O-360 engine was also produced subsequently, and a total of 260 Horizons of all types was built.

Socata (Aérospatiale) MS880/890 Rallye Series / France

Data: Gaillard

Span: 31ft 11in (9.7m)
Length: 23ft 9in (7.24m)
Gross weight: 2,315lb (1,050kg)
Max cruising speed: 140mph (226km/h)
Max range: 690 miles (1,110km)

The prototype Morane-Saulnier MS880A Rallye-Club, with 90hp Continental engine, flew on 10 June 1959. It went into production, with the MS880B (100hp Continental O-200-A) and the MS885 Super Rallye (145hp Continental O-300-C); all were 3/4-seaters. Many other versions have followed, with various engines and designations. In 1979, the Rallye series was given new 'G' names as follows: Galopin, school 3-seater with 110hp Lycoming O-235L-2A; Garnement, 4-seat trainer/tourer with 155hp Lycoming; Gaillard 4-seat tourer with 180hp Lycoming; Galerien glider-tug with 180hp Lycoming and Gabier 4-seat utility model with 235hp Lycoming O-540-B4B5. More than 3,200 examples of the Rallye family have been built.

Socata Gaucho / France

Span: 31ft 11in (9.74m)
Length: 23ft 9in (7.25m)
Gross weight: 2,865lb (1,300kg)
Cruising speed: 132mph (213km/h)
Range: 560mph (900km)

Spraygear to convert the standard versions of the Rallye into agricultural aircraft has been available for some years. On 16 May 1977, Socata flew the prototype of the Rallye Agricole, intended specifically for this role. Based on the most powerful current version of the aircraft, with a 235hp Lycoming O-540-B4B5 engine, the Agricole, which was renamed Gaucho in 1979, has tailwheel landing gear instead of the normal tricycle type, thicker wing skins and a completely revised cockpit area. Aft of the two side-by-side seats, the rear of the cabin is faired in to accommodate a 110 Imp gal (500litre) chemical tank. A further tank of 17.5 Imp gal (80 litre) capacity can replace the passenger seat. Dispersal is via four Micronair units above the wing trailing-edges, underwing spraybars or a dust spreader.

Socata ST10 Diplomate / France

Span: 31ft 10in (9.70m)
Length: 23ft 9.75in (7.26m)
Gross weight: 2,690lb (1,220kg)
Max cruising speed: 165mph (265km/h)
Max range: 860 miles (1,385km) with full payload

First flown on 7 November 1967, the prototype Diplomate (known initially as the Provence) was evolved by lengthening the fuselage of the GY-80 Horizon and redesigning the cabin. With further changes to the tail unit and a 200hp Lycoming IO-360-C1B engine, the Diplomate was certificated in 1969 and 56 had been delivered by the beginning of 1974. The basic version is a 4-seater, but the 12 bought by Varig of Brazil are used as airline pilot trainers.

Socata TB10 Tobago and TB9 Tampico / France

Photo and data: TB10 Tobago

Span: 32ft 0.25in (9.76m)
Length: 32ft 0.25in (7.64m)
Gross weight: 2,535lb (1,150kg)
Max cruising speed: 146mph (235km/h)
Range: 668 miles (1,075km)

The five-seat TB10 Tobago was developed as the first in a new series of touring aircraft to supplement, rather than replace, the Rallye family of utility/trainers. The protoype TB10 flew for the first time on 23 February 1977, powered by a 160hp Lycoming O-320 engine. Certification was obtained in May 1979, when production deliveries began, the Tobago being powered by a 180hp Lycoming O-320-A1AD.

Second model in the family is the TB9 Tampico, which has the 160hp O-320-D2A and gross weight of 2,327lb (1,060kg); later models may have engines up to 250hp and retractable undercarriages.

Sportavia Avion-Planeur Series / Germany

Photo and data: Sportavia RF5

Span: 45ft 1in (13.74m)
Length: 25ft 7.25in (7.80m)
Gross weight: 1,455lb (660kg)
Cruising speed: 75-118mph (120-190km/h)
Max range: 472 miles (760km)

Designed by Rene Fournier, the Avion-Planeur is fully aerobatic, with a performance that enables it to double as a sporting lightplane and training sailplane. Following production of 95 RF3s by Alpavia in France, production was transferred to Sportavia in Germany, where 160 of the improved RF4D single-seaters, with 40hp Rectimo-converted VW engine, were built in 1966-71. Sportavia continues to manufacture the tandem 2-seat Avionplaneur RF5 (135 built by early 1977) with 68hp Sportavia-Limbach SL1700E Comet engine; the RF5B Sperber,

a high-performance development of the RF5 with 55ft 10in (17.02m) span (more than 80 built); the RF55, differing from the Sperber in having a 60hp Franklin engine; and the SFS31 Milan, which combines the RF4D fuselage, tail unit and power plant with the 49ft 3in (15m) wings of the Scheibe SF-27M sailplane.

Sportavia RS180 Sportsman / Germany

Span: 34ft 5.5in (10.50m)
Length: 23ft 5.5in (7.15m)
Gross weight: 2,425lb (1,100kg)
Cruising speed: 146mph (235km/h)
Max range: 750 miles (1,210km)

The RS180 Sportsman was designed by René Fournier and put into production in Germany by Sportavia-Pützer GmbH. The original prototype, which flew on 1 March 1973, had a 125hp Lycoming O-235-F2A engine. It was followed by a second prototype, representative of the four-seat RF6-180 production version, on 28 April 1976. As well as having a 180hp Lycoming O-360-A3A engine, this introduced a more spacious cabin and an outer skin of glassfibre-reinforced plastics over the plywood covering on the fuselage, wing upper surface and fixed tail surfaces. By early 1977, production had

built up to four RF-6Bs each month, and 25 had been delivered. The designation was changed to RS180 in 1978, when a new raised tailplane position was adopted. The RF-6B Club two-seater is generally similar and is produced in France by Avions Fournier

Stampe SV4 / Belgium/France

Photo: SV4B
Data: SV4C

Span: 27ft 6in (8.38m)
Length: 22ft 10in (6.96m)
Gross weight: 1,716lb (778kg)
Max cruising speed: 109mph (175km/h)

The original SV4B production version of this 2-seat primary trainer was built in Belgium with a 130hp Gipsy Major engine and enclosed cockpits. The open-cockpit SV4C was built by Nord, with a 140hp Renault 4 Pei engine, and large numbers of these continue in service with flying clubs in France and elsewhere. They are highly prized as specialised aerobatic aircraft.

Stearman 75 (Boeing Kaydet) / USA

Photo: Aerobatic Stearman 75

Span: 32ft 2in (9.80m)
Length: 24ft 9in (7.54m)
Gross weight: 2,635lb (1,195kg)
Cruising speed: 106mph (171km/h)
Range: 505 miles (812km)

This tandem 2-seat primary trainer first flew in 1934 and subsequently became standard equipment in the USAAF and US Navy. When declared surplus to military requirements, more than 4,000 were converted for agricultural duties, of which many are still flying, mainly in USA. Some have been improved by fitting special fabric-covered metal high-lift wings, with endplates, produced by the American Airmotive Corp. The standard Stearman 75 has a 220hp Continental R-670 engine. Various other engines are fitted ,including the 225hp Jacobs R-755.

Stinson (Vultee) V-76 Sentinel (and SSVV L-5) / USA

Photo: Sentinel

Span: 34ft 0in (10.36m)
Length: 24ft 1in (7.34m)
Gross weight: 2,050lb (930kg)
Cruising speed: 112mph (180km/h)
Range: 420 miles (676km)

First flown in 1941, the Sentinel was a 2-seat liaison and observation aircraft developed from the Model 105 Voyager (qv). A total of 3,283 was built for the US Army, with L-5 designations, and many of these passed into private ownership, usually with a 185hp Lycoming O-435-1 engine. Since 1972, the SSVV gliding centre in Milan, Italy, has been modifying L-5s into 'Super Stinson' glider tugs, able to tow, fully loaded, a 2,205lb (1,000kg) glider to a height of 3,280ft (1,000m). With a 235hp Lycoming O-540-B1A5 engine, the modified aircraft has a gross weight of 2,250lb (1,020kg) and maximum speed of 130mph (209km/h).

Taylorcraft Plus D (and F-19 Sportsman) / UK/USA

Photo and data: Plus D

Span: 36ft 0in (10.97m)
Length: 22ft 10in (6.96m)
Gross weight: 1,450lb (657kg)
Cruising speed: 102mph (164km/h)
Range: 325 miles (523km)

The prototype Plus D was the 25th aircraft built by Taylorcraft Aeroplanes (England) Ltd before World War II, under licence from the American Taylorcraft company. After delivering eight more, they had to turn their attention to a contract for 100 similar aircraft required for AOP duties with the RAF. The military models were named Auster I and from them evolved the long line of Auster high-wing monoplanes described earlier in this book. After the war, 58 ex-RAF machines were sold as civilian Taylorcraft Plus Ds, supplementing a few survivors of the original eight. A few still fly in the UK and others on the continent. They are 2-seaters, with 90hp Cirrus Minor 1 engine. In current production by Taylorcraft Aviation Corporation of Alliance, Ohio, is the similar Model F-19 Sportsman 100, with 100hp Continental O-200-A engine, gross weight of 1,500lb (680kg) and range of 400 miles (643km) at 115mph (185km/h). More than 100 have been built.

Teal (Schweizer) Model TSC-1A / USA

Photo: TSC-1A1 Teal
Data: TSC-1A2 Teal II

Span: 31ft 11in (9.73m)
Length: 23ft 7in (7.19m)
Gross weight: 2,200lb (998kg)
Cruising speed: 110-116mph (177-187km/h)
Range: 472-748 miles (759-1,203km)

The Teal amphibian was designed by David Thurston for the former Thurston Aircraft Corporation, which set out to develop a simple, economical and easily-handled 2-seater for the general aviation market. The prototype flew in June 1968, and production was eventually taken over by Schweizer Aircraft Corporation. Construction is all-metal and the power plant a 150hp Lycoming O-320-A3B. The first 15 Teals were TSC-1A 2-seaters. Production then switched to the TSC-1A1, with an optional third seat in the baggage compartment, revised fuel tankage and other refinements. Final Schweizer version was the TSC-1A2 Teal II, with slotted flaps; production was continued by the new Teal Aircraft Corp, which also introduced the Teal III with 180hp Lycoming O-360-A1F6D, but only seven had been built when this company ceased operation in mid-1979.

Temco D-16 Riley Twin and Camair Twin Navion / USA

Photo: Camair Twin Navion
Data: Twin Navion D

Span: 34ft 8in (10.57m)
Length: 28ft 0in (8.53m)
Gross weight: 4,500lb (2,041kg)
Max cruising speed: 200mph (322km/h)

In April 1952, Jack Riley of Riley Aeronautics completed a twin-engined conversion of the Navion, substituting two 140hp Lycoming O-290-D2A engines for the original single 205hp Continental. It proved so successful that Temco set up a production line of Riley Twin conversions, stepping up the power to, successively, 150hp Lycoming O-230s and 170hp O-340-A1As. Many are still flying, together with Camair Twin Navions. The latter are more powerful aircraft, the Twin Navion B having 240hp Continentals and the Twin Navion C having 260hp Continental IO-470-Ds. Some Bs and Cs have been converted to Twin Navion Ds, with 300hp Continental IO-520 engines.

Transavia PL-12 and T-320 Airtruk / Australia

Photo and data: PL-12

Span: 39ft 3.5in (11.98m)
Length: 20ft 10in (6.35m)
Gross weight: 4,090lb (1,855kg)
Max cruising speed: 109mph (175km/h)
Range: 531 miles (330km)

This strange-looking aircraft was designed by Luigi Pellarini specifically for agricultural duties. The tail unit is made up of two completely independent assemblies, each carried on its own slim tail-boom; this enables the chemical loader to drive between the booms, right up to the hopper, aft of the single-seat cockpit. The hopper space can be fitted with two seats. Power plant is a 300hp Continental IO-

520-D engine. The prototype Airtruk flew on 22 April 1965, and nearly 100 PL-12s had been delivered to customers in Australia, Denmark, India, Malaysia, New Zealand, Thailand and East and South Africa by January 1977, including some PL-12-U multi-purpose cargo, passenger, ambulance, survey versions, with seats for one person aft of the pilot and four more in a lower-deck cabin. The T-320 version, certificated in January 1976, had a 325hp Continental Tiara 6-320-2B engine. All variants are assembled also in New Zealand by Flight Engineers Ltd.

Trident TR-1 Trigull 320 (and Republic Seabee) / Canada/USA

Photo and data: Trigull-320

Span: 41ft 9in (12.73m)
Length: 28ft 6in (8.69m)
Gross weight: 3,800lb (1,723kg)
Max cruising speed: 154mph (248km/h)
Range: 848 miles (1,364km) at 148mph (239km/h)

Both the Trigull-320 and the Seabee owe their basic concept to veteran US designer P. H. Spencer. After being responsible for the design of a series of amphibians, he was granted a patent for his Air Car configuration in January 1950. In addition to forming the basis of the Trigull-320 and Seabee, the Air Car itself has been built by many amateur constructors from plans supplied by Mr Spencer. A considerable number of the 1,060 RC-3 Seabees built by Republic remain in service, mainly in North and South America; all are four-seaters with a 215hp Franklin engine. Although similar in configuration, the Trigull-320 is larger, with six seats; prototypes built in Canada, with the 285hp Continental Tiara, flew on 5 August 1973, and 2 July 1976. Production Trigulls, from 1980, have the 300hp Lycoming IO-540.

UTVA-60 and UTVA-66 / Yugoslavia

Photo: UTVA-60
Data: UTVA-66

Span: 37ft 5in (11.40m)
Length: 27ft 6in (8.38m)
Gross weight: 4,000lb (1,814kg)
Max cruising speed: 143mph (230km/h)
Normal range: 466 miles (750km)

These aircraft had their origin in the UTVA-56 4-seat utility monoplane which flew for the first time on 22 April 1959. By replacing the 56's 260hp engine with a 270hp Lycoming GO-480-B1A6, and making other improvements, its designers evolved the production UTVA-60. Variants are the U-60-AT1 basic 4-seat utility aircraft, dual-control U-60-AT2, U-60-AG agricultural sprayer/duster, U-60-AM ambulance for two stretcher patients, and U-60H floatplane with 296hp GO-480-G1H6 engine. The UTVA-66, with 270hp GSO-480-B1J6 engine and fixed slots, was added to the range in the mid-1960s in utility, ambulance and floatplane versions.

UTVA-65 Privrednik / Yugoslavia

Photo: Super Privrednik-350
Data: Privrednik-GO

Span: 40ft 1in (12.22m)
Length: 27ft 9in (8.46m)
Gross weight: 4,078lb (1,850kg)
Max speed: 128mph (206km/h)

The prototype of this single-seat agricultural aircraft, completed in the spring of 1965, embodied the basic wings, tail unit and undercarriage of the UTVA-60. It was powered by a 270hp Lycoming engine; but this was replaced by a 295hp Lycoming GO-480-G1A6 on the Privrednik-GO initial production version, which carries a 1,323lb (600kg) payload. In 1967, work began on the Privrednik-IO, with Lycoming IO-540-K1A5 engine, softer landing gear and other changes to make it more attractive in the Western market. Both types were later superseded by the Super Privrednik-350, with a 350hp IGO-540-A1C engine and 1,455lb (660kg) payload.

Varga Kachina Model 2150-A / USA

Span: 30ft 0in (9.14m)
Length: 21ft 3in (6.48m)
Gross weight: 1,817lb (824kg)
Max cruising speed: 135mph (217km/h)
Max range: 525 miles (845km)

This design originated in 1957 as the all-wood Nifty tandem two-seat trainer/sporting aircraft, built by former Douglas Aircraft chief test pilot William J. Morrisey. He formed Morrisey Aviation, which built 10 similar, but all-metal, Model 2150s, with 150hp Lycoming O-320 engine. Production of a slightly modified version, the Model 2150-A, was then taken over by Shinn Engineering, and the current Varga Kachina is generally similar, with an O-320-A2C engine. Deliveries totalled 26 by May 1977.

Wassmer WA-40A Super 4 Sancy (and WA-4/21 and WA-41 Baladou) / France

Photo: Super IV Baladou
Data: WA4/21

Span: 32ft 9.5in (10.00m)
Length: 25ft 7in (7.80m)
Gross weight: 3,108lb (1,410kg)
Max cruising speed: 193mph (310km/h)
Max range: 1,735 miles (2,790km)

The prototype WA-40 flew on 8 June 1959, and was followed by a production series of 52 similar aircraft. The 53rd machine, designated WA-40A, introduced a swept fin and other refinements which became standard on later aircraft. A total of 180 WA-40s was built; all were 4/5-seaters with a 180hp Lycoming O-360-A1A engine. The WA 4/21 is similar but has a 250hp Lycoming IO-540 engine. Also similar is the WA-41 Baladou, except for having a 180hp Lycoming O-360-A2A engine, fixed undercarriage and simplified systems. All of these types have wooden wings and tail unit, and a fabric-covered steel-tube fuselage. They were superseded by the all-plastics WA-51/54 series and the all-metal CERVA CE43 Guépard, prior to the collapse of the Wassmer company in 1977.

Wassmer WA-51 Pacific, WA-52 Europa and WA-54 Atlantic / France

Photo: WA-52 Europa
Data: WA-54 Atlantic

Span: 30ft 10in (9.40m)
Length: 23ft 11.5in (7.30m)
Gross weight: 2,447lb (1,110kg)
Normal cruising speed: 161mph (260km/h)
Max range: 870 miles (1,400km)

In 1962 Wassmer began development of an all-plastics 4-seat light aircraft, with the assistance of the Société du Verre Textile. Major airframe components were moulded in thin layers of glass-fibre, reinforced either by stringers or by double corrugated skin. The resulting prototype WA-50 flew for the first time on 22 March 1966, proving so successful that Wassmer decided to put into production the further refined WA-51 Pacific. This is a 4-seater of generally similar design, with a 150hp Lycoming O-320-E2A engine. First flight of the WA-51 took place on 17 May 1969, and deliveries of production aircraft began in the following year. The WA-52 Europa is similar, but has a 160hp engine and more fuel. The further-refined WA-54 Atlantic, with 180hp Lycoming O-360 engine, entered production in June 1973. About 200 aircraft of the series had been sold when the company ceased operations in September 1979.

Weatherly Model 201 / USA

Data: Model 201C

Span: 39ft 0in (11.89m)
Length: 27ft 2.5in (8.29m)
Gross weight: 4,800lb (2,177kg)
Cruising speed: 115mph (185km/h)

The Weatherly ag-plane has its origins in the Fairchild M-62 Cornell, 19 of which were converted by the Weatherly company in 1961-65 as Model WM-62Cs with Continental W670 or Pratt & Whitney R985 radial engines. The subsequent Model 201, more than 100 of which have been built, is a new-build aircraft of similar design but a little larger. A turboprop version was under development in 1978.

Yakovlev Yak-18 / USSR

Photo: Yak-18PS
Data: Yak-18PM

Span: 34ft 9.5in (10.60m)
Length: 27ft 4.75in (8.35m)
Gross weight: 2,425lb (1,100kg)
Cruising speed: 175mph (282km/h)
Max range: 250 miles (400km)

The Yak-18 was the standard primary trainer of the Soviet Air Force and its allies and friends for more than 20 years. It is still standard equipment of Soviet and East European flying clubs. The original Yak-18 was a tandem 2-seater, with retractable tailwheel undercarriage and a 160hp M-11FR engine. A switch to tricycle undercarriage was made on the Yak-18U. The Yak-18A is a cleaned-up development of the 18U with a 260hp AI-14R and, later, 300hp AI-14RF engine. The Yak-18P is a single-seat version of the 18A for advanced training, including aerobatics. The Yak-18PM is similar, with AI-14RF engine, reduced dihedral and the cockpit farther aft. The Yak-18PS differs from the -18PM only in having a tailwheel undercarriage.

Yakovlev Yak-18T / USSR

Span: 36ft 7.25in (11.16m)
Length: 27ft 4.75in (8.35m)
Gross weight: 3,637lb (1,650kg)
Max cruising speed: 155mph (250km/h)
Range: 560 miles (900km)

The arrival of an unregistered example of this extensively-redesigned cabin version of the Yak-18 was one of the less spectacular surprises of the 1967 Paris Air Show. For several years afterwards there was no further news of the type. Then, in 1974, it was learned that 17 Yak-18Ts were being used to train the complete new intake of 100 pupil pilots at Sasovo Flying School in the Soviet Union. In the meantime, the original 300hp Ivchenko AI-14RF engine had been replaced by a 360hp Vedeneev M-14P, and cabin layout had been improved. During Aeroflot training, the Yak-18T carries a pilot/instructor and up to three pupils, but only an instructor and one pupil on aerobatic flights. As an ambulance the cabin is equipped to carry a stretcher patient and attendant. The passenger seats can be removed for freight carrying. Float- and ski-equipped versions are being developed.

Yakovlev Yak-50 / USSR

Span: 31ft 2in (9.50m)
Length: 25ft 2.25in (7.68m)
Gross weight: 1,984lb (900kg)
Max speed: 186mph (300km/h)
Max range: 310 miles (500km)

The quality of this late development of the 30-year old Yak-18 design was demonstrated at the 1976 World Aerobatic Championships, in which six Yak-50s were entered. They gained first, second, fifth, seventh and ninth places in the men's championships, the team prize, and first five places in the women's championships. The wings dispense with the Yak-18's centre-section and have no dihedral, but retain an asymmetrical section. Construction is all-metal, with a semi-monocoque rear fuselage. A blister canopy ensures an all-round field of view from the single-seat cockpit. The landing gear is retractable. A 360hp Vedeneev M-14P radial engine ensures the desired high power:weight ratio despite the large dimensions of the aircraft. The Yak-52, described below, is a close relative.

Yakovlev Yak-52 / USSR

Span: 31ft 2in (9.50m)
Length: 25ft 2in (7.68m)
Gross weight: 2,840lb (1,290kg)
Max speed: 177mph (285km/h)
Range: 329 miles (530km)

The Yak-52 is the latest in a long line of light training and sporting aircraft developed by the Yakovlev design bureau. First flown in 1977, the Yak-52 was evolved in parallel with the aerobatic Yak-50 (see previous entry) with which it shares many features and it was reported to be entering production in 1978 as a replacement for the elderly Yak-18s in the DOSAAF aeroclubs. It is powered by a 360hp Ivchenko M-14P radial engine and has an unusual 'retractable' undercarriage which remains fully exposed under the wings and fuselage when retracted.

Zlin Trener Series / Czechoslovakia

Photo and data: Z226T Trener-6

Span: 33ft 9in (10.29m)
Length: 25ft 7in (7.80m)
Gross weight: 1,808lb (820kg)
Range: 300 miles (483km) at 121mph (195km/h)

After the war, a new 2-seat primary trainer was needed urgently by the Czechoslovakian air force and flying schools. After evaluation against the Praga E-112, the all-wood Zlin Z26 Trener was put into quantity production, with a 105hp Walter Minor 4-III engine. It was superseded by the all-metal, but otherwise similar, Z126 Trener-2 in 1953, and then by the Z226, with 160hp Minor 6-III engine, which was built in three versions: Z226B Bohatyr glider tug, Z226T Trener-6 trainer and Z226A Akrobat single-seater for specialised aerobatics.

Zlin Trener-Master Series / Czechoslovakia

Photo: Z526
Data: Z726

Span: 32ft 4.75in (9.875m)
Length: 26ft 2in (7.975m)
Gross weight: 2,204lb (1,000kg)
Max cruising speed: 134mph (215km/h)
Max range: 273-490 miles (440-790km) (without/with tip-tanks)

First flown in 1957, the Z326 Trener-Master introduced a retractable undercarriage and other refinements, including a slight increase in span. The Z526 differed in having a constant-speed propeller and the main pilot's seat at the rear instead of in the front of the tandem cockpit. The Z326A Akrobat and Z526A Akrobat were single-seat aerobatic versions. Later production models were the Z526F with 180hp Avia M 137A engine in place of the former Minor 6/III; the Z526 AFS Akrobat with only one seat, double ailerons instead of flaps, shorter fuselage and span of only 29ft (8.84m); and the Z526L with 200hp Lycoming AIO-360-BIB engine but otherwise similar to the Z526F. Only versions still in production in 1977 were the Z726 and Z726K, with 180hp M 137 AZ and supercharged 210hp M 337 AK engine respectively. Both are 2-seaters, differing from the Z526F in having a shorter span than the latter's 34ft 9in (10.60m). More than 1,400 aircraft of the Trener/Trener-Master Series have been delivered; production had ended by 1978.

Zlin 42 and 43 / Czechoslovakia

Photo and data: Zlin 43

Span: 32ft 0.25in (9.76m)
Length: 25ft 5in (7.75m)
Gross weight: 2,976lb (1,350kg)
Cruising speed: 130mph (210km/h)
Max range: 375-714 miles (610-1,150km) (without/with tip-tanks)

These attractive sporting and touring lightplanes are manufactured by the Zlin Aircraft Moravan National Corporation at Otrokovice. The prototype of the 2-seat Zlin 42 flew on 17 October 1967, and more than 140 production aircraft had been completed by early 1979. The current 42M differs from the original 42 in having a constant-speed propeller and tail fin identical to that of the 4-seat Zlin 43. Power plant is a 180hp Avia M137 AZ and the designation is Zlin 42MU when an Avia V503A propeller is fitted. About 80% of the components of the Zlin 43 are identical with those of the 42M, the basic differences being an enlarged cabin, greater span and use of a 210hp Avia M337 A engine. Production of the Zlin 43 ended after about 100 had been built.

Zlin Z50L / Czechoslovakia

Span: 28ft 1.75in (8.58m)
Length: 21ft 8.75in (6.62m)
Gross weight: 1,587lb (720kg)
Range: 397 miles (640km) at 149mph (240km/h)

The Z50L is typical of the current generation of single-seat aerobatic monoplanes in having a fairly powerful engine and symmetrical wing section, with negligible dihedral, so that it handles and performs in much the same way whether it is straight and level or inverted. Except for the fabric-covered tail control surfaces, construction is all-metal, and the Z50L has a 260hp Lycoming AEIO-540-D4B5 engine. The prototype flew for the first time on 18 July 1975. Two more prototypes and seven production models had been completed by March 1976; five of the latter took part in the 1976 World Aerobatic Championships, gaining second place in the team event and third place in the men's individual championship. Ten more Z50Ls were built in 1977.

Part Five

Aérospatiale SA318C Alouette II (and Lama) / France

Photo: SA315B Lama
Data: SA318C Alouette II

Rotor diameter: 33ft 5.5in (10.2m)
Fuselage length: 31ft 11.75in (9.75m)
Gross weight: 3,630lb (1,650kg)
Cruising speed: 112mph (180km/h)
Range: 186-447 miles (300-720km)

The Alouette II (originally as the SE3130 and then the SE313B) with an Artouste engine was the first production variant of the well-known Alouette range originated by the Sud-East company. It was succeeded by the SA318C version with a 530shp Turbomeca Astazou IIA. Production of the SE313B totalled 923 and over 350 of the SA318Cs have been built. The SA315B Lama is similar but has dynamic components of the Alouette III, with an Artouste IIIB. This is also built by HAL in India as the Cheetah. Lama sales totalled 302 by the end of 1979.

Aérospatiale SA316B Alouette III / France

Rotor diameter: 36ft 1.75in (11.02m)
Fuselage length: 32ft 10.75in (10.03m)
Gross weight: 4,850lb (2,200kg)
Cruising speed: 115mph (185km/h)
Range: 298-335 miles (480-540km)

Alouette III is an enlarged and improved version of the Alouette II, the prototype having first flown on 28 February 1959. In its SA316B version the Alouette III is powered by an Artouste IIIB derated to 570shp; a further development is the SA319 which has an 870shp Astazou XIV engine derated to 600shp. The Alouette III is produced under licence in India (as the Chetak), Romania and Switzerland, and over 1,380 have been built in France.

Aérospatiale/Westland SA330 Puma / France/UK

Rotor diameter: 49ft 2.5in (15.00m)
Fuselage length: 46ft 1.5in (14.06m)
Gross weight: 14,770lb (6,700kg)
Cruising speed: 162mph (261km/h)
Range: 385 miles (620km)

The Puma was developed as a medium-lift helicopter for military duties, and is in service in this guise with the French Army, RAF, SAAF and numerous other air forces. Three civil versions have also been certificated — the passenger SA330F with 1,435shp Turboméca Turmo IVA engines, the cargo SA330G with 1,580shp Turmo IVCs, and the SA330J with composite main rotor blades and 16,315lb (7,400kg) gross weight. Under development in 1979, the SA332B Super Puma has Turboméca Malika engines and improved performance.

Aérospatiale/Westland SA341 Gazelle / France/UK

Rotor diameter: 34ft 5.5in (10.50m)
Fuselage length: 39ft 3.25in (11.97m)
Gross weight: 3,970lb (1,800kg)
Cruising speed: 164mph (264km/h)
Range: 223-416 miles (360-670km)

One of the three helicopters in the Anglo-French joint production programme launched in 1967, the Gazelle is of wholly-French origin, and is in production in both military and civil guise. The principal civil version is identified as the SA341G with a 590shp Turboméca Astazou IIIA engine. The civil SA342J has an 870shp Astazou XIVH and 4,190lb (1,900kg) gross weight. Total Gazelle sales, including military, exceed 800.

Aérospatiale AS350/355 Ecureuil / France

Photo and data: AS350

Rotor diameter: 35ft 0.75in (10.69m)
Fuselage length: 35ft 9.5in (10.91m)
Gross weight: 4,190lb (1,900kg)
Cruising speed: 136mph (220km/h)
Range: 570 miles (920km)

The prototype 4/6-seat Ecureuil (Squirrel) flew on 27 June 1974, powered by a 592shp Avco Lycoming LTS 101 turboshaft and, after some refinement, entered production as the AS350C AStar, with first deliveries in the North American market early in 1977. Outside North America, the AS350B has a 641shp Turboméca Arriel; a prototype of this version flew for the first time on 14 February 1975. The AS355 Twin Star is a twin-engined version first flown on 27 September 1979.

Aérospatiale SA360/365 Dauphin / France

Photo: SA365N
Data: SA365 Dauphin 2

Rotor diameter: 38ft 4in (11.68m)
Fuselage length: 36ft 0in (10.98m)
Gross weight: 7,495lb (3,400kg)
Cruising speed: 158mph (255km/h)
Max range: 289 miles (465km)

Designed as a replacement for the Alouette III, the SA360 first flew on 2 June 1970, with a 980shp Astazou XVI engine, and a second example flew on 29 January 1973, with definitive 1,050shp Astazou XVIIIA. Certification of the 10/13-seat Dauphin was obtained at the end of 1975 and deliveries began in 1976. The twin-engined SA365 version, with 650shp Turboméca Arriel turboshafts, first flew on 24 January 1975 and deliveries began in 1978. The SA365N, first flown on 31 March 1979, introduced a retractable undercarriage and other refinements.

Agusta A109A / Italy

Rotor diameter: 36ft 1in (11.00m)
Fuselage length: 35ft 1.75in (10.71m)
Gross weight: 5,400lb (2,450kg)
Cruising speed: 143-165mph (231-266km/h)
Range: 351 miles (565km)

The Agusta company — the main activity of which is the production under licence in Italy of Bell (and Sikorsky) helicopters — launched development of this light twin-engined helicopter in the mid-sixties and the prototype flew on 4 August 1971. Powered by two 420shp Allison 250-C20B turboshafts, the A109A seats up to eight. Deliveries for civil and military use began in 1976 following certification on 1 June 1975. More than 100 had been sold by 1979.

Bell (and Agusta-Bell) Model 47 / USA/Italy

Photo: Model 47G
Data: Model 47G-3B-2A

Rotor diameter: 37ft 1.5in (11.32m)
Fuselage length: 31ft 7in (9.63m)
Gross weight: 2,950lb (1,338kg)
Cruising speed: 84mph (135km/h)
Range: 250 miles (400km)

Originally certificated by Bell on 8 March 1946, the Model 47 remained in continuous production at the parent company until 1974, final production models being the 47G-3B-2A with 280hp Lycoming TVO-435-F1A engine and the 47G-5A with a 265hp VO-435-B1A. Many hundreds are still used world-wide, supplemented by those built under licence by Agusta in Italy. In Japan, Kawasaki built 211 examples of a four-seat version known as the KH-4. Continental Copters Inc produces a series of single-seat agricultural conversions of the Bell 47 under the name El Tomcat.

Bell (and Agusta-Bell) Model 204 and 205 / USA/Italy

Photo: Model 205A-1
Data: Model 205A

Rotor diameter: 48ft 0in (14.63m)
Fuselage length: 41ft 6in (12.65m)
Gross weight: 9,500lb (4,310kg)
Cruising speed: 127mph (204km/h)
Range: 311-344 miles (500-553km)

Although the greater proportion of all Model 204s and 205s built by Bell, by Agusta in Italy, by Fuji in Japan and by the Chinese Nationalist state factory in Taiwan have been military models, substantial numbers are used commercially. The smaller Model 204 was succeeded by the 15-seat Model 205A-1 with 1,400shp Lycoming T5313B engine. The basic design has been evolved into the Bell 212 and 214, described separately.

Bell (and Agusta-Bell) Model 206B JetRanger / USA/Italy

Photo: Model 206L LongRanger
Data: Model 206B JetRanger

Rotor diameter: 33ft 4in (10.16m)
Fuselage length: 31ft 2in (9.50m)
Gross weight: 3,200lb (1,451kg)
Cruising speed: 138mph (222km/h)
Range: 345-388 miles (555-624km)

Like most other Bell helicopters, the JetRanger originated to military requirements, and the commercial model is the counterpart of the OH-58A used by the US Army. Powered by a 317shp Allison 250-C18A, the 206A has been succeeded by the 206B with a 400shp Allison 250-C20 and other improvements. The 206L LongRanger, new in 1973, has a 2ft 1in (0.64m) fuselage stretch and seats up to seven and like the JetRanger III (introduced in 1977), is powered by the 420shp Allison 250-C20B engine. The 206L-1 LongRanger II has a 500shp Allison 250-C28B engine. Nearly 2,500 Model 206s have been built for civil use. The JetRanger is also built in Italy by Agusta.

Bell (and Agusta-Bell) Model 212 (and 412) / USA/Italy

Photo: Model 412

Rotor diameter: 48ft 2.25in (14.69m)
Fuselage length: 42ft 4.75in (12.92m)
Gross weight: 11,200lb (5,080kg)
Max speed: 126mph (203km/h)
Range: 273 miles (439km)

Model 212 is a development of the Model 205, from which it differs primarily in having the 1,800shp Pratt & Whitney PT6T-3 Twin-Pac coupled turboshaft engine. A civil variant of the initial military model was certificated in 1970 as the 15-seat Twin Two-Twelve, and this is now in commercial service in many parts of the world, over 300 having been delivered. The Model 412 differs in having a four-bladed rotor; gross weight is 11,500lb (5,221kg).

Bell Model 214 Big Lifter / USA

Rotor diameter: 50ft 0in (15.24m)
Fuselage length: 45ft 2in (13.77m)
Gross weight: 16,000lb (7,257kg)
Cruising speed: 150mph (241km/h)
Range: 250 miles (400km) at 3,000ft (915m)

Named the BigLifter, the Bell 214B is a commercial version of the Model 214A, originally developed for military duty in Iran from a single Bell 214 Huey Plus prototype. Use of a 2,930shp Lycoming T5508D turboshaft and an uprated transmission, plus other changes, gives the BigLifter major performance advantages over the earlier Bell 204/205 variants. It can accommodate 14 passengers or lift 7,000lb (3,175kg) externally. The Model 214B-I has the gross weight limited to 12,500lb (5,670kg).

Bell Model 214ST / USA

Rotor diameter: 52ft 0in (15.85m)
Fuselage length: 52ft 1in (15.26m)
Gross weight: 16,500lb (7,491kg)
Max cruising speed: 173mph (278km/h)

Despite its designation, the Bell 214ST is virtually a new model rather than a variant of the Bell 214, the ST indicating 'stretched twin'. It differs from the 214 in having a 30-in (76cm) fuselage stretch, increasing accommodation to 18 including two pilots, and switching to a pair of 1,625shp General Electric CT7-2 turboshafts. A twin-engined Bell 214 test-bed first flew in March 1977 and a prototype 214ST with the stretched fuselage on 21 July 1979. Development was linked with Bell's commitments to help Iran establish a helicopter assembly plant but plans for Iran to order 350 Model 214STs (in place of previously-ordered 214As) were abandoned after the Islamic revolution.

Bell Model 222 / USA

Rotor diameter: 39ft (12.12m)
Fuselage length: 36ft 0.25in (10.98m)
Gross weight: 7,650lb (3,470kg)
Cruising speed: 150mph (240km/h)
Range: 400 miles (644km)

The 6/10-seat Bell 222 was launched in 1974 as the first commercial light twin-engined helicopter to be built in the USA. Initially known as the project D306, the Model 222 is powered by two 600shp Avco Lycoming LTS101-650C turboshafts and the first prototype flew on 13 August 1976. Five prototypes were used to obtain certification, and production deliveries began late in 1979, with more than 140 on order.

Boeing Vertol Chinook / USA

Rotor diameter: 60ft 0in (18.29m) each
Fuselage length: 52ft 1in (15.88m)
Gross weight: 47,000lb (21,388kg)
Max cruising speed: 150mph (241km/h)
Range: 713 miles (1,147km) with 39 passengers

British Airways Helicopters' order for three Model 234LR Chinooks, placed in November 1978, served to launch the commercial version after nearly 1,000 CH-47s had been built for military use. The commercial Chinook has a lengthened nose for weather radar, wider fuselage-side fairings for greater fuel capacity, airline-type seats for 44 passengers and civil-rated 4,075shp Avco Lycoming AL5512 turboshafts. Deliveries begin in 1981 and also available is the Model 234 UT heavy cargo-lift version without the fuselage-side fuel tanks. Orders have also been placed by Bristow Helicopters and Columbia Helicopters (234 UT).

Brantly B2 and 305 / USA

Photo: B-2B
Data: B-2E

Rotor diameter: 23ft 9in (7.24m)
Fuselage length: 21ft 9in (6.62m)
Gross weight: 1,670lb (757kg)
Cruising speed: 90mph (145km/h)
Range: 250 miles (400km)

The original B-2 was designed by N. O. Brantly, one of the early postwar pioneers of rotary-wing aircraft in the USA, and was produced by his company prior to its acquisition by Gates Learjet. Manufacturing rights subsequently passed to Brantly Hynes Helicopter Inc, which resumed production of the two-seat B-2B in 1976, with 180hp Lycoming IVO-360-A1A engine. Also in production is the similar five-seat Model 305 with 305hp Lycoming engine.

Enstrom F-28 and 280 Shark, Hawk and Falcon / USA

Photo: Hawk
Data: Model 28C

Rotor diameter: 32ft 0in (9.75m)
Fuselage length: 29ft 6in (8.99m)
Gross weight: 2,200lb (998kg)
Cruising speed: 100mph (161km/h)
Range: 237 miles (381km)

The first Enstrom helicopter flew in 1960, being followed in 1962 by the prototype F-28. A small production batch was built, and about 600 examples of the Enstrom variants have now been built, including the current F-28C and Model 280C three-seat versions with 205hp Lycoming HIO-360-EIAD engine. The F-28F Falcon has the 225hp Lycoming GIAD engine while the F-28L Hawk, first flown on 27 December 1978, has a longer front fuselage and four seats. An F-28A derivative with 420shp Allison 250C-20B is marketed by Spitfire Helicopter Co as the Spitfire Mk I and Spitfire Mk II.

Hughes Model 300 / USA

Photo: Model 300C (269C)
Data: 300C

Rotor diameter: 26ft 10in (8.18m)
Fuselage length: 30ft 11in (9.42m)
Gross weight: 1,900lb (861kg)
Cruising speed: 100mph (161km/h)
Range: 232 miles (373km)

The three-seat Hughes Model 300 (originally certificated as the 269B) is a developed version of the two-seat Model 269 light helicopter. The basic 300 has a 180hp Lycoming HIO-360-A1A, while the later 300C (or 269C) has a 190hp HIO-360-D1A and a bigger rotor diameter, plus other small changes. Several hundred Model 300s have been built. The Model 300CQ has special features that reduce emissions by 25%. A version of the Model 300 is built by BredaNardi in Italy.

Hughes Model 500 / USA

Photo and data: Model 500D

Rotor diameter: 26ft 5in (8.05m)
Length overall: 30ft 6in (9.30m)
Gross weight: 3,000lb (1,360kg)
Normal cruising speed: 150mph (241km/h)
Max range: 335 miles (539km)

The Model 500 is the commercial counterpart of the military OH-6A Cayuse, of which more than 1,400 were delivered to the US Army. Its 317shp Allison 250-C18A turboshaft engine is derated only to 278shp, compared with the military version's 252.5shp. Payload is normally a pilot and four passengers or equivalent freight, but up to seven persons can be carried. The Model 500C differs in having a 400shp Allison 250-C20 engine for hot day/high altitude operations. The Model 500D, with 420shp 250-C20B engine, was certificated late in 1976 and has numerous detail improvements. Model 500 versions are built by BredaNardi in Italy and Kawasaki in Japan.

Kamov Ka-26 / USSR

Rotor diameter: 42ft 8in (13.00m)
Fuselage length: 25ft 5in (7.75m)
Gross weight: 7,165lb (3,250kg)
Cruising speed: 56-93mph (90-150km/h)
Max range: 745 miles (1,200km) with auxiliary tanks

First flown in 1965, the Ka-26 is a standard general-purpose helicopter in the Soviet Union and other East European countries. By podding the two 325hp Vedeneev M-14V-26 radial engines and mounting them on short stub-wings, it has been possible to make the entire rear fuselage detachable, aft of the two-seat flight deck. Standard fuselage pods accommodate six passengers or equivalent freight. Minus pod, the aircraft can be operated as a flying crane; or the space under the rotor can be occupied by a hopper for a ton of agricultural chemicals or a platform for the same weight of cargo. Survey versions are available, with cameras installed in the cabin pod, or with an encircling hoop antenna and towed receiver 'bird' for mineral prospecting. Other potential applications of the Ka-26 include fish-spotting, forest protection, firefighting and ambulance duties.

MBB BO105 / Germany

Photo: BO105S

Rotor diameter: 32ft 2.75in (9.82m)
Length: 28ft 0.5in (8.55m)
Gross weight: 5,070lb (2,300kg)
Max cruising speed: 144mph (232km/h)
Max range: 658 miles (1,060km) with auxiliary tanks

The BO105 flew originally with two Allison 250-C18 turboshaft engines and a conventional rotor. The second and third prototypes followed in 1967, with Allison and MAN Turbo 6022 engines respectively, driving a specially-developed rigid, unarticulated rotor, with feathering hinges only and with folding glassfibre blades. Production BO105Cs can have either 317shp Allison 250-C18 or 400shp 250-C20 engines and seat up to five. The BO105D has special features for the UK market and BO105S is lengthened to seat seven. The BO105L, first flown in May 1979, has 500shp Allison 250-C28C engines and lightened structure for better 'hot and high' performance. About 1,000 BO105s have been sold, including military.

MBB/Kawasaki BK117 / International

Rotor diameter: 36ft 1in (11.0m)
Fuselage length: 42ft 8in (13.0m)
Gross weight: 6,167lb (2,800kg)
Cruising speed: 165mph (264km/h)
Range: 338 miles (545km)

The BK117, first flown on 13 June 1979, in Germany, replaces the earlier MBB BO107 and Kawasaki KH-7 projects on which the two companies were working independently until signature of an agreement on 25 February 1977. Powered by two 600shp Avco Lycoming LTS 101-650B-1 turboshafts, the BK117 is intended for utility duties, carrying up to 10 occupants, stretchers, cargo, etc. Production is shared between the German and Japanese companies, with final assembly lines in each country.

Mil Mi-4 / USSR

Rotor diameter: 68ft 11in (21.00m)
Length: 55ft 1in (16.80m)
Gross weight: 17,200lb (7,800kg)
Economical cruising speed: 99mph (160km/h)
Range: 250 miles (400km) with 8 passengers

Second Soviet helicopter produced in quantity, the Mi-4 is Mil's counterpart to the Sikorsky S-55/S-58 generation. Several thousand were produced for military and civil use, all powered by a 1,700hp Shvetsov ASh-82V piston-engine. Standard Aeroflot version is the 8/11-passenger Mi-4P, which can also carry eight stretchers and an attendant on ambulance duties. The Mi-4S agricultural version has a hopper capable of holding a ton of chemicals in its cabin. The freight-carrying Mi-4 has clamshell rear loading doors. All versions were exported widely.

Mil Mi-6 and Mi-10/-10K / USSR

Photo and data: Mi-10K

Rotor diameter: 114ft 10in (35.00m)
Length: 107ft 9.75in (32.86m)
Gross weight: 83,776lb (38,000kg)
Max cruising speed: 125-155mph (202-250km/h)
Ferry range: 494 miles (795km) with auxiliary fuel

Largest helicopter in the world when it was first revealed in 1957, the Mi-6 was the first turbine-powered helicopter to enter production in Russia. It is powered by two 5,500shp Soloviev D-25V turboshafts and is equipped normally as a rear-loading freighter, with small wings to offload the rotor in flight. These wings are usually removed when the Mi-6 is operated as a flying crane. 65 passengers can be carried. The original Mi-10 flying crane was almost identical with the Mi-6 above the line of the cabin windows; but the depth of the cabin was reduced considerably and the tailboom deepened to give a continuous flat under-surface. The Mi-10K is generally similar except for its shorter undercarriage and provision of an undernose gondola from which a second pilot, facing rearward, can control the aircraft in hovering flight and supervise loading.

Mil Mi-8 / USSR

Rotor diameter: 69ft 10.25in (21.29m)
Fuselage length: 60ft 0.75in (18.31m)
Gross weight: 26,455lb (12,000kg)
Max cruising speed: 112-140mph (180-225km/h)
Range: 264-298 miles (425-480km) with reserves

The original prototype of this 28/32-passenger helicopter had a single 2,700shp Soloviev turboshaft engine. The second Mi-8 switched to two 1,500shp Isotov TV2-117As, with which it flew for the first time on 17 September 1962, and this power plant is standard on production versions. Variants include a VIP version known as the Mi-8 Salon with an eight-place couch, three armchairs and tables; an ambulance for 12 stretchers; and the Mi-8T freighter with 24 tip-up seats along the cabin walls and an optional external cargo sling.

Robinson R22 / USA

Rotor diameter: 25ft 2in (7.67m)
Fuselage length: 20ft 8in (6.30m)
Gross weight: 1,300lb (590kg)
Cruising speed: 108mph (174km/h)
Range: 240miles (386km) (no reserves)

Evolution of the Robinson R22 began in July 1973, the objective being to develop a lightweight two-seat helicopter at a competitive price. A prototype flew on 28 August 1975 with a second following in 1977. Production aircraft switched from a 115hp to 150hp Lycoming O-320, with which certification was obtained in April 1979. Deliveries began in May against a backlog of orders for 550.

Sikorsky S-58 and S-58T and Westland Wessex / USA/UK

Photo and data: S-58T Mk II

Rotor diameter: 56ft 0in (17.07m)
Fuselage length: 47ft 3in (14.40m)
Gross weight: 13,000lb (5,896kg)
Normal cruising speed: 127mph/(204km/h)
Range: 278 miles (447km) with reserves

Sikorsky built a total of 1,821 helicopters of basic S-58 design between 1954 and January 1970. Most were for military customers, but 16/18-passenger commercial S-58s were also used on scheduled services by operators in the USA and elsewhere, each powered by a 1,525hp Wright R-1820-84 piston engine. In the UK, Westland produced both single-engined and twin engined turbine-powered versions under the name Wessex. Some of these also continue in service with commercial operators, notably Bristow, whose Wessex 60s are each powered by two Rolls-Royce Gnome turboshafts, totalling 1,550shp. Sikorsky is currently producing kits for a similasr conversion, known as the S-58T (data above), with an 1,800shp Pratt & Whitney (Canada) PT6T-6 Twin Pac power plant and 10/16 seats. Over 100 S-58Ts have been delivered.

Sikorsky S-61 / USA

Photo and data: S-61N Mark II
Rotor diameter: 62ft 0in (18.90m)
Length: 59ft 4in (18.08m)
Gross weight: 19,000lb (8.620kg)
Normal cruising speed; 138mph (222km/h)
Max range: 518 miles (833km) with reserves

The S-61N is a 30-passenger commercial development of the military Sea King, with a longer fuselage and other changes, but retaining amphibious capability. The S-61L differs in being suitable for land operation only. Both were powered originally by two 1,350shp General Electric CT58-140-110 turboshaft engines, but 1,500shp CT58-140-2s are standard in the current Mark II models. The first S-61L flew on 6 December 1960, and went into service with Los Angeles Airways, which eventually bought seven. S-61Ns have been bought by All Nippon Airways, Ansett-ANA, British Airways Helicopters, Bristow, Elivie, Greenlandair, JAL, KLM and Nitto Airways. More than 100 S-61Ls and S-61Ns have been built for commercial use.

Sikorsky S-64 Skycrane / USA

Rotor diameter: 72ft 0in (21.95m)
Length: 70ft 3in (21.41m)
Gross weight: 42,000lb (19.050kg)
Max cruising speed: 105mph (169km/h)
Max range: 230 miles (370km) with reserves

The S-64 pioneered the concept of a large, turbine-powered flying crane when it flew for the first time on 9 May 1962. Production models served with distinction in Vietnam, under the US Army designation CH-54A. Commercial S-64Es have been supplied to operators such as Rowan Drilling Company, Erickson Air-Crane Company. Tri-Eagle Company and Evergreen Helicopters, for heavy-lift support of oil exploration, logging, power-line, shipping and general construction industries. Powered by two 4,500shp Pratt & Whitney JFTD12-4A turboshaft engines, the S-64E can lift loads of up to 12.5 short tons, suspended from strong points under its slim 'backbone' structure, or in quickly interchangeable containers or pods. A rearward facing compartment in the crew cab enables one of the pilots to control the aircraft from this position during loading and unloading.

Sikorsky S-76 Spirit / USA

Rotor diameter: 44ft 0in (13.41m)
Fuselage length: 44ft 1in (13.44m)
Gross weight: 10,000lb (4,540kg)
Cruising speed: 144-178mph (232-286km/h)
Range: 460-690 miles (742-1,110km)

Sikorsky launched the 8/12 seat S-76 in January 1975, adopting the S-76 designation out of sequence to mark the USA Bicentennial year. Aimed particularly at the off-shore oil support market, the S-76 is powered by two 700shp Allison 250-C30 turboshafts and the second of four prototypes flew on 13 March 1977, while the first was still engaged on ground running. Sales totalled more than 200 when deliveries began in February 1979 and had reached 285 by the end of the year.

Silvercraft SH-4 and SH-200 / Italy

Photo and data: SH-200

Rotor diameter: 29ft 7.5in (9.03m)
Max length: 34ft 4.25in (10.47m)
Gross weight: 1,900lb (862kg)
Cruising speed: 49-62mph(78-100km/h)
Max range: 220 miles (354km)

Silvercraft SpA flew its original Model XY prototype light multi-purpose helicopter in October 1963. With the help of SIAI-Marchetti, this was evolved into the three-seat SH-4, which flew for the first time in March 1965 and was followed by five pre-production examples by the end of 1967. A demonstration model of the SH-4A agricultural version followed, with 32ft 9.5in (10m) spray-bars and tanks for 441lb (200kg) of chemicals. Over 50 SH-4s had been built up to the end of 1976, with 235hp (derated to 170hp) Franklin 6A-350-D1B engines, and a 205hp (170hp) Lycoming LHIO-360-C1A was offered as an alternative in 1976. First flown on 12 April 1977, the SH-200 is a two-seater with 205hp Lycoming LHIO-360-C1A engine for light utility duties.

Westland WG30 / UK

Rotor diameter: 43ft 8in (13.31m)
Overall length: 52ft 2in (15.90m)
Gross weight: 11,750lb (5,330kg)
Max speed: 127mph (204km/h)
Range: 380 miles (612km) with eight passengers

The WG30 is a development of the Westland/Aérospatiale Lynx military helicopter, with both commercial and military rôles. Powered by two 1,060shp Rolls-Royce Gem 41-1 turboshafts, the WG30 has the same basic transmission and dynamic components as the Lynx, with a new, larger fuselage that provides adequate space for executive layouts and a wide range of arrangements for various other duties.

The first of two prototypes of the WG30 flew on 10 April 1979 and certification was expected during 1981.

WSK-Swidnik Mi-2 / Poland

Data: Mi-2M

Rotor diameter: 47ft 6.75in (14.50m)
Length: 37ft 4.75in (11.40m)
Gross weight: 8,157lb (3,700kg)
Cruising speed: 118-124mph (190-200km/h)
Range: 242 miles (390km) with max fuel and reserves

The Mi-2 was designed in the Soviet Union by Mikhail Mil's bureau, as a turbine-engined replacement for the Mi-1, with the same overall dimensions. By switching to the lightweight power of two Isotov GTD-350 turboshaft engines, mounted above the cabin, it was possible to provide accommodation for up to eight passengers and their baggage, or 1,543lb (700kg) of freight in the basic versions. Development and production were taken over by the WSK-Swidnik organisation in Poland, to follow its earlier

manufacture of the Mi-1/SM-1. Over 2,000 have been delivered, for both military and civil use, with 400shp and later 450shp GTD-350P engines. The Mi-2M, first flown on 1 July 1974, has a wider, 10-seat cabin and retractable nosewheel.

Index